ENGLISH ENTERPRISE IN NEWFOUNDLAND 1577-1660

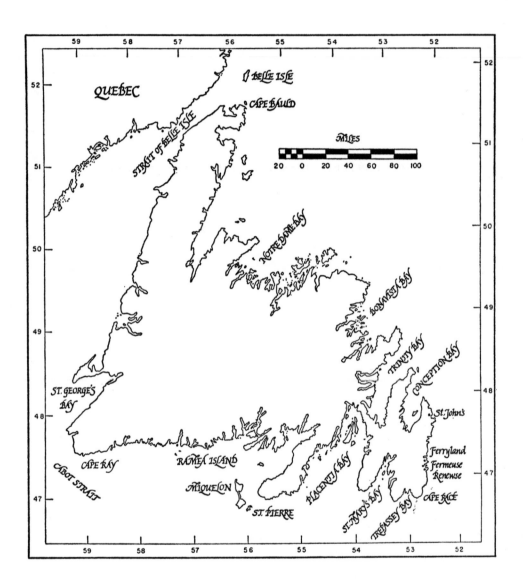

GILLIAN T. CELL

English Enterprise
in Newfoundland
1577-1660

UNIVERSITY OF TORONTO PRESS

© University of Toronto Press 1969
Printed in Canada
by University of Toronto Press
Toronto and Buffalo

ISBN 0-8020-5232-0

Contents

ACKNOWLEDGMENTS vii

ABBREVIATIONS viii

INTRODUCTION ix

I/The Organization of the Newfoundland Trade 3

II/The Fishery: A Time of Expansion 1577-1604 22

III/An Island Becomes Known 34

IV/The First Colony 1610-31 53

V/Further Experiments in Settlement 1616-37 81

VI/Prosperity and Crisis 1604-30 97

VII/The Beginnings of Government Intervention 1630-60 108

VIII/Conclusion 126

APPENDICES 129

BIBLIOGRAPHY 155

INDEX 169

Acknowledgments

URING THE PREPARATION of this book I have incurred many obligations which I am now delighted to be able to recognize. In England the staffs of the Public Record Office, of the British Museum, of the city record offices of Bristol, Exeter, Plymouth, and Southampton, and of the libraries of Liverpool, Nottingham, and London universities were unfailingly helpful. In the United States I am grateful to the staffs of the Duke University library and of the library of the University of North Carolina at Chapel Hill. Mr. R. A. Skelton, until recently keeper of the map room in the British Museum, Mr. David Bracchi of the University of Hull, Mr. R. S. Smith, librarian of the University of Nottingham, Dr. Patrick McGrath of the University of Bristol, and M. Maurice Carmona all gave me the benefit of their expert knowledge on some aspect of my study. Mrs. Helen King first made me aware of the existence of Sir Percival Willoughby's Papers and most generously put at my disposal her late husband's transcripts. I am deeply grateful to Professor Gerald S. Graham for his advice and kindness while I was a member of his seminar at the Institute of Historical Research. At various stages of its existence the entire manuscript has been read and commented upon by Professor Robert Moody of Boston University, Dr. Theodore K. Rabb of Princeton University, and my colleague at the University of North Carolina, Dr. Stephen B. Baxter. More recently the staff of the University of Toronto Press have been both patient and helpful; and I remember with much gratitude the interest of the late Professor George W. Brown of the University of Toronto and the *Dictionary of Canadian Biography* who first suggested that I submit my manuscript to that press. The University of North Carolina provided me with a grant to cover the cost of preparation of the manuscript and the Publications Fund of the University of Toronto Press made a grant to assist publication.

There remain two very particular debts which it gives me the greatest pleasure to acknowledge. The first is to Professor David B. Quinn of the University of Liverpool, who began it all by putting me to work on Newfoundland as an undergraduate, and who has been most generous with his knowledge, his encouragement, and his friendship ever since. The second is to my husband, fellow-historian, and critic, John W. Cell of Duke University; how much I owe to him I can acknowledge but never express.

GILLIAN TOWNSEND CELL
University of North Carolina
at Chapel Hill

ABBREVIATIONS USED IN THE FOOTNOTES

APC	*Acts of the Privy Council*
APC Col.	*Acts of the Privy Council, Colonial*
BM	British Museum
CSP Col.	*Calendar of State Papers, Colonial*
CSP Dom.	*Calendar of State Papers, Domestic*
CSP For.	*Calendar of State Papers, Foreign*
CSP Sp.	*Calendar of State Papers, Spain*
CSP Ven.	*Calendar of State Papers, Venetian*
CO	Colonial Office
DNB	*Dictionary of National Biography*
HCA	High Court of Admiralty
HMC	Historical Manuscripts Commission
KR	King's Remembrancer
NU	Nottingham University
PC	Privy Council
PRO	Public Records Office
SP	State Papers
SRO	Southampton Record Office

In all quotations from primary sources the original spelling
has been retained, but contractions have been expanded.

Introduction

BEFORE 1577 the island of Newfoundland was the preserve of the fishermen of the Atlantic coasts of Europe who had of their own initiative built up a pattern of annual fishing voyages there. From the beginning Englishmen had participated in the cod fishery and yet, almost a century after its discovery, the English industry was not large, its value to the national economy not yet fully recognized. Nor is this so surprising when one realizes that interest in the New World, and in its northern latitudes particularly, was still largely confined to a but slowly expanding circle of geographers and courtiers. The gradual transformation of Newfoundland from relative obscurity into the centre of a booming and valued industry, into the site of one of England's first colonies, and into a place of such strategic importance that no English government could afford to ignore it – all these developments took place within the period 1577 to 1660.

The themes of fishery and settlement are of course closely interwoven but, for the present purpose, it has been necessary to separate them in somewhat arbitrary fashion. Not an ideal arrangement, the separation nevertheless seemed the only way to present both an analytical study of the fluctuations of the fishing industry and the more detailed account of the early settlements which the discovery of new materials makes possible.

The most significant new documentation is that relating to the London and Bristol Company for the colonization of Newfoundland, established in 1610, and its settlement at Cupids Cove in Conception Bay. Hitherto this has been perhaps the most obscure part of the oft-told story of England's early overseas expansion. It can now be told in some detail from the substantial collection of papers of Sir Percival Willoughby, an investor in the company for some twenty years or so. These papers, belonging to Lord Middleton and now deposited at the University of Nottingham, were briefly and inadequately calendared in the Historical Manuscripts Commission's report on the Middleton manuscripts prepared in 1911. Thereafter they were ignored, except by the late Professor H. King of the University of Hull who had, before his death, done little more than transcribe them. They include nineteen letters and a journal all written in Newfoundland between 1610 and 1631, correspondence between Willoughby and the company's treasurer and mainstay John Slany, a few business documents, as well as some copies of the company's official records.[1] The Willoughby Papers rank, therefore, as some of the most valuable

1 NU, Middleton MSS Mi x 1/1-66.

records we have to illuminate the involvement of individual subscribers in the affairs of a seventeenth-century colonizing company. And they, together with other smaller collections of papers previously overlooked, reveal the Newfoundland Company and the independent settlements which were its offshoots as much more serious and long-lived enterprises than they have so far appeared, and as an important episode in the colonial experiments and experiences of the seventeenth century.

More complex are the problems involved in an analysis of the fishing industry, although its importance has long been recognized. Not only was it England's first regular trade with the New World, but economically it was of very real value to the nation: in return for a few provisions, fishermen could get a cargo at Newfoundland and exchange it for Mediterranean and Levantine luxuries. The Newfoundland voyage, then, brought money into the kingdom, but what one commentator dubbed "Greate Britaines Indies" caused none of the little-understood economic problems that followed from Spain's more glamorous empire. The industry was centred in the southwest of England – "the stay of the West Countries," Sir Walter Raleigh called it – and it grew rapidly in the late sixteenth and early seventeenth centuries. A contemporary reported that no more than four or five ships made the voyage annually in the early 1570s, yet in 1615 it was estimated that the Newfoundland fleet numbered 250.

But, once these well-known facts have been repeated, a number of questions remain. How accurate are these contemporary figures which were put forward after all by propagandists? Just how dependent upon the Newfoundland trade were the west-country ports; what proportion of their shipping was involved in going to Newfoundland and in carrying fish abroad? How did the vogage fit into their general pattern of trade, and which ports were most deeply involved? When one of the periodic slumps to which English commerce was liable occurred, how was the fishing industry affected? What proportion of the fish caught at Newfoundland was absorbed by the English market; how much was re-exported; how much went directly from the island to European markets via the triangular trade?

On the whole the answers to these questions must be tentative because of the deficiencies of the evidence. Any assessment of the size of the trade must be based on the port books, kept in the Public Record Office. The dangers of using these customs' records to gather trade statistics, a use for which they were never intended, have been so often stressed that they need not be repeated here. But the valid point remains: if we do not use these records, what do we use? Certainly the broken nature of the series makes it difficult to trace the fortunes of any trade. For a study of the Newfoundland fishery, however, the port books have particular disadvantages. Since they record only the departures of ships with customable cargoes, the majority of vessels leaving for Newfoundland were not recorded, for most of them went out in ballast or carrying only salt which was duty-free. Ships returning from the island were entered in the port books if they carried train oil, a customable commodity which most of them did import, but usually not if they carried only fish. Ships making the triangular voyage from England to Newfoundland to Europe can be traced only if their departure was recorded in the spring, and if they can be identified returning from the continent the following winter. Otherwise the practice of noting only the final port of call makes it impossible to tell whether the incoming vessels had visited Newfoundland before Europe.

An examination of the port records of France, Spain, Portugal, and Italy – the most popular markets for dried fish – would undoubtedly supply further information on the triangular trade, but to collect it would be the work of a lifetime. Using notaries' ledgers and customs records, M. de la Morandière has made a two-volume study of the French–Newfoundland industry before 1789, but even he has not attempted to cover all the French ports.[2] And, even where customs records have survived, the work of MM. Braudel, Romano, and Carmona on the *portate* of Leghorn suggests that the results as far as the English triangular trade is concerned might be disappointing.[3]

The port books are supplemented by the records of the High Court of Admiralty, also preserved in the Public Record Office. These records relate to breaches of contract, piracy, or any other matter connected with the sea and ships which gave rise to legal action. Most of the information they supply on the fishery is incidental rather than primary, but it does include something on the character of the fishery, the conduct of voyages, practices in marketing fish abroad, and the organization and financing of both fishing and trading voyages. This last is an aspect of the English fishery which has been almost ignored. The late Professor Innis gave some detail on the French system but little on the English, while Dr. Lounsbury's work concentrated on administrative history to the neglect of economics.[4] And reason good: in England notaries' records have not survived as they have in France, and so the network of detailed agreements relating to every aspect of the financing of the trade has been lost. All that remains is an occasional, usually abbreviated, copy of a charter-part such as may be found in the archives of some of the west-country ports.

The sources then have their limitations, as indeed have those for almost all trades in this period. A precise, statistical analysis may not be possible, but some attempt can and should be made to chart the development of England's first trade to North America.

2 C. de la Morandière, *Histoire de la pêche française de la morue dans l'Amérique septentrionale des origines à 1789* (2 vols., Paris, 1962).
3 F. Braudel and R. Romano, *Navires et marchandises à l'entrée du port de Livourne, 1547-1611* (Paris, 1951). M. Maurice Carmona is continuing this study and has kindly sent me details of English ships entering Leghorn with Newfoundland fish after 1611.
4 H. A. Innis, *The Cod Fisheries* (rev. ed., Toronto, 1954); R. G. Lounsbury, *The British Fishery at Newfoundland, 1634-1763* (New Haven, 1934).

ENGLISH ENTERPRISE IN NEWFOUNDLAND 1577-1660

I

The Organization of
the Newfoundland Trade

ETWEEN 1480 AND 1494 Bristol merchants may have discovered the island of Newfoundland.[1] If so, the wealth of its fishing grounds must have been known in Bristol and perhaps throughout the west-country even before John Cabot's voyages. Already the west-countrymen were experienced fishermen: in home waters, off the Irish and Scottish coasts, even as far afield as Iceland their ships could be found. By the end of the fifteenth century, however, Danish restrictions and Hanse competition threatened the Iceland trade, England's main source of dried codfish. The fishing merchants must have heard with relief of the "new found isle" which could supply "so many fish that the kingdom would have no further need of Iceland."[2] Under this stimulus the Newfoundland voyage did not long remain an adventure. After Cabot, the Anglo-Portuguese expeditions set out from Bristol in the first decade of the sixteenth century. Then, cautiously at first, ships from neighbouring ports must have begun to dare the Atlantic. Soon Bristol's early predominance faded as ports from the Severn to Southampton absorbed the voyage into the pattern of their trade, helped by their geographical position, their experience in fishing, and their established links with those ready markets for fish, France and Spain.

To participate in the new industry raised few problems for the average west-country merchant. Special ships and therefore increased expenditure were not necessary: any vessel capable of crossing the Atlantic, whether 20 tons or 300 tons, might go to Newfoundland in the summer months and be back in time to trade to Europe during the winter. But the ideal ship, according to such contemporary experts as Robert Hitchcock and Captain Richard Whitbourne, was between 70 and 100 tons. At the beginning of the period a ship of 70 tons cost £200 to build and equip; it could be handled by a master and crew of twenty-four, only half of whom needed to be experienced seamen. At Newfoundland, Hitchcock reckoned, such a crew could make 200 quintals of wet fish and 100 quintals of dry fish;[3] in fact a crew

1 See D. B. Quinn, "The Argument for the English Discovery of America between 1480 and 1494," *Geographical Journal*, CXII (1961), 277-85, and J. A. Williamson, ed., *The Cabot Voyages and Bristol Discovery under Henry VII* (Hakluyt Society, 1962), pp. 19-32. The word "discovered" is used here in the sense of effective discovery and disregards the probable discovery of Newfoundland by the Vikings.

2 Williamson, *The Cabots and Bristol Discovery*, p. 210.

3 Robert Hitchcock, *A Pollitique Platt for the Honour of the Prince* (J. Kingston, 1580), sigs. A 2, 4.

of this size could make, and a vessel of 70 tons could carry, far more fish than that and it would have been extremely unusual to find an English ship making more wet than dry fish. Writing some forty years later and from deep personal experience, Richard Whitbourne recommended a ship of 100 tons, with a crew of forty. Fishing from eight small boats, each manned by three men, this crew could make 2000 quintals of medium-sized dry fish and perhaps some 100 quintals of wet fish. In a good season, which might continue as late as mid-October, an extra 800 quintals of dried cod over and above what the fishing ship itself could carry might be made and sold at Newfoundland.[4]

Fishing ships usually left England between January and April, taking advantage of the prevailing easterlies to go north after clearing Ireland. Near the American coast the Arctic current would carry the ships south to Newfoundland, which the fishermen would plan to reach before May when the codfish usually arrive offshore. An alternative route, and the one taken by Sir Humphrey Gilbert in 1583, was to sail west by southwest to about the fortieth parallel, and then north towards Cape Race.[5] But such a course is more likely to have been followed by vessels sailing in the early summer, as did Gilbert's, than by the majority of the fishing fleet.

Once at Newfoundland and the chosen harbour, the ship would be unrigged for the season and her crew would go ashore to cut timber and to build stages, flakes, cookrooms, and shacks. The stages were begun on shore and extended into the sea, so that the cod could be thrown up from the small boats in which the fishing was done. These fishing boats, usually of three to five tons, could hold between 1000 and 1200 fish and were handled by as many as five men. The skilled work of cleaning and preparing the fish was done on the stage, the waste being thrown into the sea and the livers saved to make train oil. An expert "splitter" could bone some 480 fish in thirty minutes. It passed next to the salter who applied salt with a brush; this too was skilled work for too much salt "burned" the fish, causing it to become wet and break, while too little made it turn red when dry. The elaborate drying process now began. The cod was first stacked in piles three feet high where it stayed for three to ten days depending on the weather. Next it was washed and laid in a second pile, skin side up, "on a platt of stones, which they call a horse." A day or so later the men placed it on flakes, erections of branches laid over a frame, where it dried in the air and sun. By night or in wet weather, the fish was made up into "faggots," four or five fish with the skin side up and a broad fish on top. When it was well dried it was put into a "press pile," where the salt sweated out leaving the fish looking white. After one more day of drying on the ground, it was finally stacked into a "dry pile" and there it remained until the ship was ready to sail, when the cod was weighed and carried on board.[6] The hold of the ship had to be completely waterproof and, once the fish was put down, the hatches were sealed and could not be opened again until the vessel reached its destination.[7]

4 Richard Whitbourne, *A Discovrse Containing a Loving Invitation* ... (F. Kyngston, 1622), sigs. E 2^v-3^v.
5 R. Hakluyt, *The Principal Navigations ... of the English Nation* (12 vols., Glasgow, 1903-5), VIII, 42, 45.
6 This account of the technique of the English fishery is based on observations made by a ship's surgeon, James Yonge, in 1663; see *The Journal of James Yonge, 1647-1721, Plymouth Surgeon*, ed. F. N. L. Poynter (London, 1963), pp. 56-8.
7 PRO, HCA Examinations, Instance and Prize, HCA 13/35: June 1601, William King.

This arduous and lengthy drying process – it could take as long as three months – was imposed upon the English fishermen because of their shortage of salt. Virtually all the salt used at Newfoundland had to be purchased in Europe or bought at the island from the Portuguese and French. Cod dried mainly by the air required much less salt to preserve it than did wet or green fish, which was made by the easier and quicker process of fishing directly from the ship and then simply putting the cleaned fish in the hold and covering it with thick layers of salt. This was the usual technique of many European fishermen who had access to large supplies of cheap salt;[8] the English, on the other hand, made wet fish only towards the end of the season when they had no time for the drying process. The tedious business of the dry fishery naturally gave the English industry a sedentary character. Whereas foreigners, French and Spanish Basques particularly, ranged freely in the St. Lawrence area and developed other interests such as whaling and sealing, the English returned year after year to the most accessible part of the island, the coast between Cape Race and Trinity Bay. There they left their equipment and stores, hoping to use them and their stages and buildings in another season. So, over a period of years, the English became entrenched in the Avalon peninsula; the same merchants set out fishing voyages year after year; and many fishermen probably spent as much of their lives in Newfoundland as in England.

With their cargoes stowed aboard, the fishing fleet began to leave the island in August. If the prevailing westerlies were kind, England could be as little as seventeen days away,[9] but the average crossing probably took nearer four weeks. The port books show that the first-comers might begin to trickle into port in late August and that the Newfoundlanders became a steady stream throughout September and October. During those two months the fishing fleet virtually took over the ports of Plymouth and Dartmouth; in September 1620, for example, a total of 70 ships entered Plymouth, 50 of which came from Newfoundland.[10] To these ports and to Exeter, Southampton, Bristol, Barnstaple, Weymouth, and Poole came not only their own ships but also those of the smaller neighbouring creeks and subports. For in the larger harbours waited foreign buyers and the victuallers of merchant vessels, of the army and the navy.

To the west-country also came London ships. Although the Newfoundland fishery was primarily a west-country concern, it was never exclusively so. John Cabot's expedition of 1498 had been financed by a partnership of London and Bristol merchants, while the abortive voyage of the *Barbara* and the *Mary Barking* in 1517 was planned by Londoners, seemingly with the dual purposes of fishing and colonization.[11] London shipping continued to participate regularly in the fishery, albeit on a small scale, and may well have pioneered the triangular trading voyage between England, Newfoundland, and the continent. The first instance of such a voyage which I have found concerns a London ship which in 1584 sailed to Newfoundland

8 Innis, *The Cod Fisheries*, p. 48.
9 In 1627 the *Fisher* of Southampton left Cape Broyle on 23 August and was off Plymouth by 8 September, R. C. Anderson, ed., *The Book of Examinations and Depositions, 1622-1644* (4 vols., Southampton Record Society, 1920-36), II, I.
10 PRO, Exchequer KR, E 190/1029/19.
11 See J. A. Williamson, ed., *The Voyages of the Cabots and the English Discovery of North America* (London, 1929), pp. 245-8; J. Parker, *Books to Build an Empire* (Amsterdam, 1965), p. 24.

and on to Cadiz.[12] When London vessels returned directly to England they sold their fish in the ports of the southwest, especially perhaps in Southampton which had served as the capital's outport since the fifteenth century.[13] What Newfoundland fish reached the capital came around by the coasting trade; but the majority of fish entering the port of London came from Iceland and the North Sea via the ports of the east coast.[14] London merchants too may have popularized the use of the sack ship in the Newfoundland trade. The sacks – so called because they were originally employed in the wine trade – left England in ballast about May or June, stayed in Newfoundland long enough to receive their cargo of fish, and then sailed for English or continental markets. Although the west-countrymen did employ sack ships themselves, they resented the London vessels which often had advantages of size and speed.

But despite this London interest in the industry, the Newfoundland fishery was primarily the preserve of the west-countrymen. They felt it to be so, and their pre-eminence was usually accepted by the government. It was they who set the pattern of the trade in its infancy; they who established its customs: the absolute freedom of fishing which forbade the reservation of beach space from year to year, and the right of the first-comer in each harbour to take first choice of drying space and to be admiral of that harbour for the season. From the start they moulded the character of the fishery to suit their own circumstances as seasonal visitors to the island. This seasonal character of the industry and the well-entrenched domination of the west-countrymen help to explain the struggle between fishermen and colonists that would develop during the seventeenth century.

THE FINANCIAL ORGANIZATION OF THE NEWFOUNDLAND TRADE

To describe the financing of the Newfoundland trade, to sort out the tangle of people involved, is no easy task; there were so many ways in which the business might be managed, so many roles – financier, shipowner, victualler, master – which many individuals or one individual might play. Nor are the problems simplified by the fact that in England notaries' records have not been preserved. The few surviving contracts are in such summarized form as to obscure further the roles of the parties involved. It is clear, however, that the way in which the English shipping industry as a whole was organized was peculiarly suited to a trade, such as the Newfoundland fishery, run by men of limited capital.[15] Of course the essential characteristics of that industry had evolved during the Middle Ages when few merchants

---

12 PRO, HCA 13/25: 21 Jan. 1584/5, Anthony Bowen; 26 Jan., John Hayes; 19 Oct. 1585, Samuel Lucke.
13 A. A. Ruddock, *Italian Merchants and Shipping in Southampton, 1270-1600* (Southampton, 1951), p. 263.
14 See A. M. Millard's exceptionally useful "The Import Trade of London, 1600-1640" (PHD thesis, University of London, 1956).
15 In describing the organization of the English shipping industry, I am very much indebted to the works of Dr. Ralph Davis, "The Organization and Finance of the English Shipping Industry in the Late Seventeenth Century" (PHD thesis, University of London, 1955), and *The Rise of the English Shipping Industry in the Seventeenth and Eighteenth Centuries* (London, 1962). The majority of my references will be to his thesis which contains the greater wealth of detail on the period closer to my own.

enjoyed extensive reserves of capital. Although this situation had changed, certainly in London by the late sixteenth century, the small man still retained his importance, particularly in some locally dominated trades which were not overly expensive to set out. The way in which Newfoundland voyages were managed meant that backer, owner, victualler, ship's master, and even the crew might share the risk: a wise precaution for "ships are but boards, sailors but men: there be land-rats and water-rats, water-thieves and land-thieves, I mean pirates; and then there is the peril of waters, winds and rocks" (*Merchant of Venice*, I, iii). And the habits of the codfish too are unreliable.

As no initial expenditure on an outward cargo was required, it was not costly to equip a Newfoundland fishing ship. In the west-country could be found merchant-families, specializing in the trade and sending out ships year after year, as well as merchants whose interests embraced many branches of trade, and men perhaps not primarily involved in overseas trading but who invested in the occasional voyage. The essentials were a ship, victuals which could be obtained locally, fishing gear, and salt. A suitable ship was relatively cheap; being of moderate tonnage it could be built of English timber. In 1580 Robert Hitchcock estimated that a fishing ship of 70 tons would cost £200, a price which seems to have been fairly standard for, early in the next century, it was reckoned that a Flemish-built vessel of 200 tons would cost £400 in the west-country.[16] Buying rather than hiring was suggested by Richard Whitbourne as being more efficient and in the long run less expensive.[17] And even here costs could be cut by owning in partnership. For the first division of financial responsibility, in the Newfoundland trade as throughout the shipping industry, was in the ownership of vessels; not because of the cost of buying the average merchant ship, but as a means of cutting the owners' loss in case of accident. To own an interest in a number of vessels was a primitive form of insurance at a time when organized marine insurance had not yet become a popular device. Most commonly a ship would be divided into thirty-two parts, any number of which might be owned by the same merchant, but on occasion there might be as many as sixty-four.[18] In 1638, for example, the *Charity* of Southampton belonged to five merchants, one of whom owned half the ship, two others jointly held three-eighths, and the remaining two one-eighth.[19] Sack ships, being generally larger, tended to belong to more partners: the *Alethia* and the *Diamond*, both of London, had eleven and twelve owners respectively.[20] While a division into multiples of four was most usual, it was not invariable; a Newfoundland ship, the *Providence* of Barnstaple, belonged to four merchants, two of whom owned one-third each and the other two one-sixth each.[21]

Voyages in which the owners set out their own ships to Newfoundland need little comment; as no outsiders were involved, each partner received a share of the profits

16 Hitchcock, *A Pollitique Platt*, sig. A 2, and see appendix c.
17 Whitbourne, *A Discovrse and Discovery of Newfoundland* (F. Kingston, 1622), sigs. 1ᵛ-2.
18 V. Barbour, "Marine Risks and Insurance in the Seventeenth Century," *Journal of Economics and Business History*, I (1928-9), 561-96; Davis, *Rise of the English Shipping Industry*, p. 82.
19 Anderson, *Examinations and Depositions*, II, 73-5.
20 Davis, "Organization of the English Shipping Industry," p. 142; PRO, HCA 13/51, ff 2ᵛ-5; HCA Miscellaneous, HCA 30/635, f 86.
21 PRO, HCA 13/59, ff 757-8ᵛ.

in proportion to his share in the ship itself. The chartering of ships under contract, however, remained an integral part of the industry and also had the effect of splitting the risk. There were three forms of agreement: which was chosen depended mainly on the type of voyage. The lump-sum charter specified a fixed payment to be made in return for the use of the ship on a clearly defined voyage. The tonnage charter calculated payment according to the cargo capacity of the ship, which was guaranteed to within five tons by the owner; the charterer agreed to load the ship to its full capacity and, even if he failed to do so, was still obliged to pay the full price for the wasted space or "dead freight." The time charter fixed payment at a monthly rate. All three types of charter-party represented a compromise between the interests of the two sides, the owner being concerned with the length of time that his ship would be unavailable to him, the charterer with the cost of carriage in relation to the price he would receive for his goods. The time charter was therefore best adapted to long voyages – to the east or across the Atlantic or when trading at a number of ports was involved. The lump-sum and tonnage agreements were commonly used when the length of the voyage could be estimated with some certainty, and when the bulk of a cargo was high in proportion to its value.

All charter-parties, of course, contained the essentials of the contract: the voyage, the time limitations, and the cost of hiring the ship; otherwise they varied widely in precision. The port of return in England was usually specified; the port of departure, those places to be visited, and the cargo might be stipulated, or might be left open to the discretion of the master or of the merchant's factor. Time charters especially tended to leave such details open, but they did state a maximum and minimum duration for the voyage and full freight had to be paid even if the ship returned in less than the minimum agreed time. Neither lump-sum nor tonnage charters mentioned time, except to specify the number of days allowed for loading and unloading. If these were exceeded it could prove expensive to the charterer who had to pay demurrage at a rate agreed in the original contract. But even the number of days for which he might pay this penalty was limited, and when it ran out the master was within his rights to sail before the cargo was completed.

Payment for hire of the ship was usually made in two parts: half immediately the ship discharged its cargo at the port of return, and the balance twenty to forty days later. In the case of a time charter, however, a part of the charge was usually payable when the minimum time expired. This arrangement ensured the owner of some recompense for, if the ship were lost before reaching its port of discharge, the charterer paid nothing. The majority of contracts concluded with a penalty clause binding both parties to pay a fixed amount – usually double the freight – should there be an unjustified breach of contract by either side.[22]

All three types of charter-party were employed in the Newfoundland trade.[23] The lump-sum charter was perhaps most suited to the direct voyage between Eng-

22 All the above information on the use of charter-parties is based on Davis, "Organization of the English Shipping Industry," pp. 222-36.
23 Dr. Davis analyzed 49 charter-parties, dating from the latter part of the seventeenth century; they included 9 relating to triangular voyages from Newfoundland to the Mediterranean, of which only 1 was a lump-sum charter, 6 were tonnage charters, and 2 were time charters, "Organization of the English Shipping Industry," p. 224. In the earlier period I did not find that any one type clearly predominated.

land and Newfoundland, or to voyages involving ports of discharge not too distant from England, such as the Atlantic ports of France. Such contracts can be found throughout the period. In the closing years of the sixteenth century an undated summary of a lump-sum agreement shows that the charterer was to pay £62 10s. within forty days of the return of the *Judith* from Newfoundland to Stonehouse. If the ship were prevented by accident from reaching the fishery, the charterer undertook to pay £20 within twenty days of her return; nothing was payable should the vessel be lost.[24] Towards the end of the period, in 1641, the cost of hiring a ship of 90 tons for a Newfoundland voyage was only £25 8s., to be paid within thirty days of her return to Barnstaple or whatever her port of discharge should be.[25] Tonnage charters were employed in very similar circumstances – on limited voyages when the time likely to be taken could be reckoned fairly closely. Such was the voyage to be made by the *Clemence* of Cherbourg, 70 tons, which was hired in 1605 by Richard Cornellis of Southampton at 18 crowns the ton, to go from Southampton to Newfoundland, Malaga, and back again to Southampton, or whichever English port Cornellis should decide upon.[26] Although Malaga is fairly distant from England, it was the only continental port to be visited, so that sailing and lading times could be reckoned with some accuracy. As was usual in such tonnage charters, the harbours to be visited in Newfoundland were prescribed – St. John's, Old Perlican, and "Soano" – and the full agreement doubtless stipulated the precise amount of time that might be spent at the island. It appears that payment was to be made at the termination of this particular voyage, but the owners of the *Owners' Adventure* and the *Friends' Adventure* later in the century stipulated in a tonnage charter that they receive, in the first case, half the total freight and, in the second, 500 *milreis* when the fish was sold in the Mediterranean.[27]

As might be expected time charters were mainly used for ships making long Mediterranean voyages after visiting Newfoundland. Here the duration of the voyage would be uncertain, especially when it included visits to a number of ports. Such voyages were most often made by the larger London sack ships, whose owners could probably afford to wait for their profits. However, the owners of the *Little Lewis*, whose ship left London in June 1655 to collect a cargo of fish at Newfoundland but which then went on a trading voyage to Cadiz, Genoa, Leghorn, Smyrna, Constantinople, Alexandria, Marseilles, Lisbon, Madeira, Angola, and finally Brazil, must have been more than a little anxious before their vessel returned some five or six years later.[28] One trusts that the charterers of the *Little Lewis* managed to pick up some profitable cargoes on their wanderings, for the costs of hiring under a time charter were high. In 1636, for example, the *Mary and John* of London was hired by a group of merchants at £220 a month, to collect fish worth £2500 at Newfoundland and proceed directly to the Straits.[29] The voyage would have taken at least six

24 Agreement between George Moiles and N. S., nd, Plymouth City Archives, Serjeant Hele's Precedent Book, 1593-1601, f 46ᵛ.
25 Agreement between George Shurte and Robert Lane, 15 April 1641, North Devon Athenaeum, MS 4116.
26 Agreement between Clement Bason and Richard Cornellis, 8 June 1603, SRO, Second Book of Instruments, 1597-1689.
27 Davis, "Organization of the English Shipping Industry," p. 234.
28 PRO, HCA 13/74: 15 April 1662, Henry Buckler.
29 PRO, Colonial Office Registers, CO 1/9, no 13.

months, and she must have been expected to sell her fish well and to pick up valuable cargo in the Mediterranean to cover the freight charge. The high rate suggests that she was a large ship, suggests too perhaps that the crew's wages were being paid by the owners rather than by the freighters, as was sometimes the arrangement under a time charter. Cheaper to freight were the *Adventure* which in 1650 sailed to the Canaries, Newfoundland, and St. Lucar at a cost of £110 a month, the total freight amounting to £740, and the *Matthew and John* which, in the same year, was chartered by five merchants to go to Newfoundland, Bilbao, and the Canaries at £138 a month.[30] On such voyages it would be in the charterers' interests to ensure that the ship's master and factor acted as quickly as possible in selling the fish and securing a new cargo. The *Matthew and John* seems to have been managed very efficiently: the ship arrived at the fishery on 29 July 1650, reached Bilbao three months later, and the Canaries in January of the following year. In all these instances it appears that payment was due only when the vessel returned to England.

The contrast between the expense of hiring one of these large sacks for a lengthy Mediterranean voyage and a smaller, west-country fishing ship for a less ambitious enterprise is striking. In 1622 Richard Whitbourne wrote that a fishing ship of 100 tons might be chartered for a nine months' voyage to Newfoundland and Marseilles at £40 a month or less.[31] Even cheaper was the *Speedwell* of Barnstaple, tonnage unknown, which Anthony Dennes hired in 1641 to go to the fishery and on to Bilbao and La Rochelle for only £16 15s. a month, he being obliged to keep the ship for at least six months. But Dennes was an old hand in the Newfoundland trade and doubtless knew where to get a bargain.[32] Although the charter-party system had grave disadvantages and its use in the Newfoundland trade was severely criticized by such an expert as Whitbourne, the practice of hiring ships did mean that, in case of accident, a double loss was avoided; for the owner lost only his ship and the charterer only his cargo.

Both owners and freighters protected themselves further by making use of the loan on "bottomry" to finance their voyages. The system of bottomry was one of the oldest and most popular forms of loan; it had the virtues of simplicity while the agreed premium avoided any accusation of usury at a time when the church still frowned upon the taking of interest. Because the risk to the lender was high – should the ship be lost he received no recompense – loans tended to be small. Robert Hitchcock supplies a description of the way in which the system worked in the Newfoundland industry at the end of the sixteenth century:

In the West countrey ... the fishermen conferres [sic] with the money man, who furnisheth them with money to prouide victualls, salte, & all other needefull thinges to be paied twentie fiue pounde at the shippes returne, vpon the hundreth pound in money lent. And some of the same money men doth borowe money vpon ten pounde in the hundreth pounde, and [put] it forthe in this order to the fishermen. And for to be assured of the money venturered, they will haue it assured, geuying sixe pounde for the

30 PRO, HCA 13/65: 16 July 1651, George Hearsnip; 17 May 1652, Edward Arlibeer.
31 Whitbourne, *Discovrse Containing a Loving Invitation* (1622), sig. E 4ᵛ.
32 Agreement between Anthony Dennes and the owners of the *Speedwell*, 13 June 1641, North Devon Athenaeum, MS 3987, vol. 17; PRO, E 190/951/5, 952/4.

assuring of euery hundreth pounde to hym that abides the venture of the Shippes returne.[33]

Such an arrangement as this was concluded when John Jeffrey, a Southampton merchant, lent £20 to the joint-owners of half the ship the *George* of that city. Jeffrey was to receive £25 within fourteen days of the ship's arrival at Bordeaux or La Rochelle from Newfoundland, or within a month of her return to England if she did not go to France. The half-owners, George Lyde and George Balin of Swanage, agreed that their half of the vessel was to be enjoyed by Jeffrey as his own property, and gave bonds of £50 as security.[34]

Whether the rate of interest was a standard 25 per cent, as Hitchcock says and as was agreed by Lyde and Balin, is impossible to verify because the other shortened contracts which I have found give either the sum borrowed or that to be repaid, but never both. Probably Hitchcock describes a common but not invariable arrangement. Other details certainly varied from case to case and, during the sixteenth century at least, repayment might be in fish rather than in cash. So, for example, the owner of the *Sweet Rose* of Salcombe promised to deliver to William Putt, who had presumably lent him money, 4400 dry fish within forty days of the ship's return, or £15 if the ship failed to reach Newfoundland.[35] The practice of payment in kind, however, seems to have been most usual during the early part of the sixteenth century. The "money man" was usually described as a merchant; the status of the borrower, at least in the abbreviated surviving documents, was rarely noted, but he might be the owner or part-owner, the master who frequently held a share in the vessel himself, or the victualler. Thus William Goodman, who was both master and part-owner of the *Hopeful Luke*, borrowed £130 on bottomry in 1650 to outfit his share of the ship; in 1581 Robert Gellet borrowed £185 on bottomry to enable him to act as victualler of a Southampton ship of 55 tons, the loan was to be repaid within eight days of the vessel's return, and both parties were bound in the sum of £220 to fulfil their contract.[36] In bottomry agreements, as in charter-parties, sailing dates and lading times were fixed, and either a specific port of discharge was named or a limited choice given. In the case of the *George* of Southampton, described above, the choices listed were Bordeaux, La Rochelle, Poole, or Southampton.

Loans on bottomry mortgaged the ship to the backer but gave him no compensation if the ship were lost. Consequently the practice of marine insurance gained slowly in acceptance as providing yet a further measure of security. Marine insurance had been known in England since the later Middle Ages, when contact with Hanseatic and Italian merchants was at its peak, and, by the second half of the sixteenth century, it had become an accepted part of the English shipping industry. In

33 Hitchcock, *A. Pollitique Platt*, sigs. F 1-1ᵛ.
34 Agreement between George Lyde, George Balin, and John Jeffrey, 27 Feb. 1600/1, SRO, Second Book of Instruments, 1597-1689.
35 Agreement between G. B. and William Putt, nd, Plymouth City Archives, Serjeant Hele's Precedent Book, 1593-1601, f 57.
36 PRO, HCA 13/64: 25 Feb. 1650/1, William Appleton; HCA 13/68: 12 Dec. 1653, John Taylor; and see Davis, "Organization of the English Shipping Industry," p. 150.

1574 the Queen granted the monopoly of making and registering policies to Richard Candeler, but this proved no more popular than most other monopolies. Although an Office of Insurance was established within the Royal Exchange, it proved impossible to limit the business to one agent.[37] By 1589 a book of advice for the apprentice merchant included the form of a typical insurance policy in its collection of business documents with which the young man should be familiar.[38] Not until 1601, however, did marine insurance find recognition in the statute book, when it was described in that convenient but noncommittal formula as a custom established "tyme out of mynde," whereby losses on perilous voyages fell lightly upon many rather than ruinously upon a few (45 Eliz. i, c. 12). The statute created the London Chamber of Assurance together with a special court to hear cases arising from disputed policies; but the court never became popular and most suits seem to have continued to go before the Admiralty Court.[39] During the sixteenth and seventeenth centuries it remained customary to insure only a part of the value of the ship or its goods; to insure fully was regarded as a preliminary to fraud. Generally speaking the holder of the policy, who might be either the owner or the freighter, would bear 10 per cent of the risk, including the premium, for "with most merchants insurance was rather a means of mitigating than of covering risks."[40]

Hitchcock makes it clear that the insurance policy had become an established instrument in the financial organization of the Newfoundland industry by 1580. In fact, the earliest known copy of an insurance policy relates to a Newfoundland voyage made by the *Hopewell* of London in 1604. The freighter, A. J. of London, insured the ship's cargo of fish from the day of its lading into the ship at Newfoundland until it should be discharged at Toulon or Marseilles. The risks covered were:

... of the Seas men of warre, Fier, Enemies, Pirates, Robers, Theeves, Jettesons, Letters
of Mark and counter Mark, Arrestes, Restraintes, and detaynements of kinges and princes
and of all other persons, barratrye of the Master and Marriners of all other perilles,
Losses and misfortunes whatsoeuer they be, or howsoeuer the same at any time before
the date hereof haue chaunce or hereafter shall happen or come to the hurte detriment
or damage of the said Fishe or any parte or parcell thereof.

Neither the sum for which the cargo was insured nor the names of the insurers are given, but A. J. paid £7 for every £100 worth of goods covered.[41]

The terms of insurance policies, then, were as precise and as detailed as all the other types of contract employed in the shipping industry; they enumerated just what was insured, which ports the ship might visit, the exact period for which the policy was valid, and the risks covered. A policy might be taken out on the ship or

37 Barbour, "Marine Risks," pp. 572-3.
38 I. B[rowne], *The Marchants Avizo*, ed. P. V. McGrath (Cambridge, Mass., 1957), pp. 52-3.
39 F. Martin, *A History of Lloyds and of Marine Insurance in Great Britain* (London, 1876),
   p. 34.
40 Barbour, "Marine Risks," p. 590.
41 Printed in D. W. Prowse, *A History of Newfoundland* (London, 1895), pp. 84-5. This
   policy antedates by ten years that cited by Martin as the first known policy, *History of
   Lloyds*, p. 46.

on its cargo but not necessarily on both and, when the ship was let to freight, it seems on the whole to have been the owner rather than the charterer who insured it. Thus, in 1635, Samuel Hawkings hired the *Grace* of Dartmouth for a voyage to Newfoundland and Nantes, but the vessel was insured for £150 by its owners, Peter Therrye and Clement Parker.[42] The joint-owners of the cargo of the *Peter* of Milbrook insured their fish for £120 from the time it left the fishery for Alicante, Denia, and Jávea, but not the ship itself.[43] Philip Ley and Luke Dottin who, in 1619, insured both the *Comfort* of Topsham and its goods from its departure from England for Newfoundland, Marseilles, and Toulon were probably both owners and freighters of the ship.[44] In all these instances, as in the case of the *Hopewell* of London, the risk was borne by a number of insurers; the chances of loss were thus divided yet again.

The seventeenth-century practice of underinsuring is seen quite clearly in several cases relating to Newfoundland voyages, although merchants at least claim to have borne considerably more of the risk than the 10 per cent which Miss Barbour suggested was standard.[45] If the ship foundered, the merchant stood to suffer a very considerable loss, as two Southampton men discovered in 1627. They had taken the precaution of insuring the ship and their share of its cargo for £300, but when the vessel was captured by the French they estimated that they lost a total of £635, which figure did not include the value of the quarter share of the catch belonging to the crew.[46] A similar loss was borne by the owner of the *Seth* of Poole who, in 1629, insured his ship for only £100; later in the Admiralty Court the value of the ship alone was assessed as £180 and of the fish as £173.[47] More serious still were the losses suffered by the owners and crew of the *Olive* of Dartmouth which was seized in 1650 on its way from Newfoundland to Bilbao. The ship had been insured for £300, but the owner assessed his personal loss as £2000 and that of his crew as £700.[48] No merchant, of course, was going to minimize his losses in court. One case in which a Newfoundland cargo was highly insured proved to be an attempted fraud, and William Stanley, a prominent citizen of Southampton, was accused of insuring fish for £400 when it was actually worth less than £100.[49]

Hitchcock, writing in 1580, implies that the rate at which ships were insured was a fixed 6 per cent; in fact the rate seems to have varied widely. In 1604 the *Hopewell*, as we have seen, was insured at 7 per cent. In 1634 the *Pleasure* of Dartmouth was insured for £500 at 3 per cent on the outward voyage from Dartmouth to Newfoundland; six months later she was reinsured for the same sum but at 2½ per cent to cover her homeward voyage.[50] Twenty years later, in 1654, the *Naples Merchant* was insured for £100 at 4 per cent for a voyage from the fishery to Naples.[51] In

42 PRO, HCA 13/52, ff 171, 171ᵛ.
43 PRO, HCA 13/43: 4 July 1620, Simon Cowell.
44 *Ibid.*, 26 [June 1620], Philip Ley.
45 "Marine Risks," p. 590.
46 Anderson, *Examinations and Depositions*, II, 18-19.
47 PRO, HCA 13/49: 28 May 1631, John Melmouth.
48 PRO, HCA 13/64: 7 Feb. 1650/1, Gifford Bale; 8 Feb., James Saunders.
49 Deposition of William Stanley, 15 Jan. 1649/50, SRO, Book of Examinations, 1648-63, ff 26ᵛ-7.
50 PRO, HCA 13/53, ff 171, 171ᵛ.
51 Prowse, *History of Newfoundland*, p. 85.

1676 it was said that the rate might be anything between ". . . 5 and 20 per Cent. according as the Times are";[52] certainly it would rise appreciably in times of war, and the evidence suggests that the taking out of policies increased in popularity at such times.

Although insurance had become an accepted expedient throughout the shipping industry, it was both costly and open to fraudulent practice so that merchants taking out policies remained in a minority.[53] And in the Newfoundland trade, at least, a more traditional method of sharing the risk was available, namely the practice of setting out a ship in shares and paying the crew with one of these shares. The custom had been established in the English fishing industry long before the days of transatlantic voyages, and, being peculiarly suited to such an uncertain trade as fishing, it had been retained in the new industry. The contract involved three parties: the shipowner, the victualler, and the master and crew, each of whom received roughly a third:

The Master and Company have a third part thereof, allowing some small matter from the same, towards the victualling; and there is another third part likewise to be allowed towards the Ships travell and charge, deducting some thing likewise towards the Master of the Ship, for taking charge, and for some other of the better sort of men, which they usually have over and above their share of the former third: and the other third remaines unto the Victuallers forth of the Ship.[54]

On occasion the owner and victualler would be one and the same person: so for example, in 1638, the owners of the *Exchange* of Southampton, about 250 tons, victualled and manned their vessel for Newfoundland at a total cost of £700.[55] But very often the owner preferred to limit his expense to fitting out the ship and to have a partner who would provide the victuals, fishing equipment, and salt. In 1622 Richard Whitbourne reckoned that to victual a ship of 100 tons, with a crew of 40, for a voyage to Newfoundland and Marseilles would cost £420 1s. 4d., which included £104 for 130 quarters of salt. Part of this outlay went on tools and on other gear which could presumably be used from year to year. He also estimated the total profit from a successful trip at £2250, of which £750 would fall to the victualler, giving him, according to Whitbourne's somewhat erratic calculations, a net gain of £331 11s., or approximately 79 per cent.[56] The costs of victualling, like all other expenditure, might be divided; thus Christopher Daniel, in 1635, was both half-victualler and half-freighter of the *Blessing* of Southampton.[57] Nor is it at all unusual to find the victualler borrowing money at bottomry to help finance his share in the enterprise, as did Robert Gellet in 1581.[58]

52 Barbour, "Marine Risks," p. 592.
53 *Ibid.*, pp. 582-5, 586-9.
54 Whitbourne, *Discovrse Containing a Loving Invitation* (1622), sig. E 4.
55 PRO, State Papers Domestic, Charles I, SP 16/381, no 32; the ship's size is taken from PRO, E 190/825/2, 6.
56 See appendix D.
57 Anderson, *Examinations and Depositions*, III, 30.
58 Agreement between Thomas Dumareske and Robert Gellet, 23 March 1580/1, SRO, Second Book of Instruments, 1597-1689.

Naturally, the profits from a Newfoundland voyage varied enormously according to the scope of the venture. A simple fishing voyage by a small west-country ship which returned directly to England was not an expensive undertaking and, as the outlay could be so minutely subdivided, participation would be open to many men of very small capital. More ambitious voyages, while demanding a larger initial expenditure, could also prove extremely profitable. In 1635 Nicholas Pescod of Southampton claimed to have laid out £2500 on victualling and rigging two ships of 500 tons and 70 tons for Newfoundland fishing voyages; undoubtedly the larger vessel at least was intended to go on to the Mediterranean.[59] Certainly, expeditions such as those of the *Alethia*, which in 1633 exchanged 2721⅓ quintals of Newfoundland fish at Lisbon for a full lading of sugar and spices, or of the *Jonas*, 240 tons, which in return for its fish collected 344 butts and 1 hogshead of wine, 309 barrels of raisins, 100 barrels of figs, and 80 chests of oranges and lemons from St. Lucar in 1648, must have earned a most satisfactory profit for their freighters.[60] Indeed it was this aspect of the voyage – the exchange of Newfoundland fish for costly Mediterranean commodities with no draining away of bullion from England – that made the trade so valuable to the nation, and so prized by the contemporary economist.

On a voyage which included fishing, when the crew was usually paid by shares, the men's remuneration was in proportion to the profit made by the owners and victuallers. The advantages of such a system were two-fold. In the first place, it meant that employer and employee alike bore the risk of a bad season or a glutted market, and profited alike when catch and prices were good; this could not happen in an industry based simply on a fixed wage system. Secondly, it reduced the amount of ready capital required to finance a voyage.

In the wet fishery the usual practice was for the master and crew to receive only a quarter of the proceeds, as it had to be split among fewer men who had made a reasonably short and easy voyage.[61] But in the dry fishery the most common arrangement was a division into thirds, such as Whitbourne described. How such voyages might work out for the crew is well illustrated by a dispute which came before the Court of the Star Chamber.[62] On 16 March 1611 a contract had been drawn up between Thomas Eliot, a Southampton merchant, and a mariner, William Wilkins, concerning a Newfoundland voyage to be made by Eliot's two ships, the *Thomas* of Southampton and the *Evangelist* of Gosport. The *Thomas* was to sail first and to take part in the fishing; the *Evangelist* would join the larger vessel at Newfoundland and collect a cargo of fish for England, while the *Thomas* continued on a trading voyage to the Mediterranean.

It was agreed that Wilkins would serve as master of the *Thomas* and would have command of both ships when they were in consort. His responsibilities included hiring a company of thirty-two men and boys to serve for both vessels, it being quite usual for the size of the crew to be fixed in such contracts as it affected the

59 PRO, SP 16/283, no 95.
60 PRO, HCA 13/58, ff 683ᵛ-4ᵛ; HCA 13/61: 12 March 1648/9, Peter Vittrey; 14 March, Henry Pearne.
61 Innis, *Cod Fisheries*, p. 21.
62 Copies of all the relevant documents are in the Southampton Record Office, SC Misc., *Eliot* v *Bedford*, 1617.

amount of each man's pay. All the fish and oil made were to be divided into three equal shares of which Eliot, as both owner and victualler, would receive two, and Wilkins and his men one. Over and above this, the master and crew were to allow Eliot 200 fish out of each man's share – the "small matter" which Whitbourne said was regularly deducted from the crew's part. It was further arranged that all the crew's fish and oil would be sold to Eliot at the agreed price of 7s. the 100 for dry fish, 14s. the 100 for wet fish, and £8 the tun for train oil. Again this was a customary arrangement; although in the English fishery it seems to have been a matter of agreement rather than of right, whereas in the French industry the shipowner was entitled to first option on his crew's fish.[63] Dissension arose when it was found that Wilkins had hired only thirty men, so that Eliot received 400 dry fish less than he had expected. The unscrupulous master had also tried to cheat his crew by dividing its shares into thirty-five parts and keep the extra five as a perquisite for himself. The letter of lading sent home from the fishery revealed that the total catch had been 103,000 dry fish, 4200 wet fish, and 5¾ tuns of train oil. The crew's third therefore amounted to 28,342 dry fish, 1400 wet fish, and 7½ hogsheads of oil, worth in all £124 6s. od., which Eliot agreed to pay in full even though the terms of the contract had been broken. Each member of the crew therefore received £3 17s. 9d. as payment for the voyage, together with a small supplementary wage according to his rank: one member of the crew deposed that he had been promised 30s., another £3, and the carpenter £5. Wilkins' duties had also included fixing these wages with the men, and in consideration of his extra responsibilities he received an allowance of £32 over and above his share, while the master of the *Evangelist* was paid £12. Whitbourne's statement that it was customary for ships' masters to receive such a bonus is further confirmed by the case of Richard Strowe who, in 1606, was given an extra £18 for having hired a crew of twenty for the Newfoundland ship of which he was master.[64]

The crew's share was not invariably divided into equal parts; on occasion it would be split into many more parts than there were men, and varying numbers would be awarded to each crew member according to his rank aboard ship and his skill as a fisherman. Thus, in 1650, such a division of profits from the voyage of the fishing ship, the *Hopegood*, gave the carpenter shares worth £14 4s., the mate £6 15s., and various mariners between £5 and £3. Supplementary wages brought the carpenter's total pay up to £32 6s., the mate's to £28 5s., and some of the crew's to £22 12s., £18 18s., £17, and £9.[65]

The division of the catch into thirds remained a recognized feature of the fishing industry throughout the period under consideration, although it was dying out in other branches of the shipping industry from the sixteenth century onwards.[66] Attempts were even made to collect tithes on the fishermen's shares during Archbishop Laud's campaign to increase tithe payments. A petition, forwarded to the

---

63 PRO, HCA 13/35: June 1601, Andrew Casley; Innis, *Cod Fisheries*, p. 21.

64 Agreement between Richard Strowe and Peter and John Pryaulx, 2 July 1606, SRO Second Book of Instruments, 1597-1689.

65 PRO, HCA 13/71: 17 Aug. 1654, John Heyward.

66 The only other exception was the privateering industry where it was also difficult to reckon profits in advance, Davis, "Organization of the English Shipping Industry," p. 263. On the payment of privateering crews, see K. R. Andrews, *Elizabethan Privateering, 1585-1603* (Cambridge, 1964), pp. 39-40, 44, 135.

Privy Council in 1635 and bearing more than 800 signatures of residents in the Devonshire parishes of St. Marychurch, Tormoham, Paignton, Brixham, Churston, and Stoke Gabriel, complained that Newfoundland fishermen were being thus taxed, even though they got only a third of the profits in return for their long voyage, while the owners and victuallers paid no tithes on their two-thirds.[67] The traditional mode of payment might have yet another advantage, or so wrote Richard Breton in a letter to Secretary Windebank in 1640, for it would make it easy to ascertain how much fish each ship had made and so to levy an impost on it.[68]

The share system, however, proved not altogether adequate as the industry developed and as prices and wages rose, and so during the seventeenth century at least a wage system evolved alongside it. Payment by a small lump-sum wage as well as by share seems to have become customary on longer voyages which combined fishing with trading to the continent, as the cases of the *Thomas* and the *Hopegood* suggest. On such trips the crew might be away from home for nine months or more, and a simple share of the catch had probably ceased to be a sufficient reward. From the voyage of the *Blessing* in 1647 to Newfoundland, Alicante, Cartagena, Venice, Cadiz, Zante, and other Mediterranean ports, the crew were to collect both a quarter of the fish and monthly wages paid from the time the ship left the fishery. As wages the second mate received 50s. a month, the carpenter 40s., the bosun 38s., and the merchant's apprentice 27s. In all, thirty-nine men were hired, and most of them served for almost two years, although their original contracts had stipulated a voyage of between fourteen and sixteen months.[69] The crews of sack ships invariably received wages, for they could expect no share of the fish; Table III gives some examples of the rates of pay for such voyages. The total wage amassed could be quite substantial, for seamen's wages were generally higher than landsmen's;[70] and on an exceptionally long voyage, such as that described above as made by the *Little Lewis* and lasting between five and six years, the carpenter must have earned the best part of £200, and the bosun's mate better than £100.

Who paid these wages varied according to the type of voyage. Customarily the shipowner engaged both master and crew, and paid their wages; if he then let his ship out under charter, he had to make sure that the freight charge would be sufficient to cover these expenses as well as to contribute to the upkeep of his vessel. On a long voyage made under time charter, however, victualling costs and wages were likely to be exceptionally high and so were usually the responsibility of the charterer. When the owner hired out his ship and retained no interest in the voyage, he would pay the men either by wage at a fixed monthly rate, or for short voyages by an agreed lump-sum.[71] When the crew was paid by the freighter, there were three possible methods of payment: the share and wages systems already described, and portage.[72]

Portage was an arrangement whereby a seaman was allotted a certain amount of

67 PRO, SP 16/307, no 47.
68 PRO, CO 1/10, no 79.
69 PRO, HCA 13/60: 7 March 1649/50, Richard Suttebye; HCA 13/62: 22 Feb. 1649/50, John Wakeham; 4 March, John Gore; 28 March 1650, George Horsfall; 11 April, Edward Wormewood; HCA 13/63: 17 June 1650, John Gore.
70 Davis, *Rise of the English Shipping Industry*, pp. 151-2.
71 Davis, "Organization of the English Shipping Industry," pp. 233, 262.
72 H. D. Burwash, *English Merchant Shipping, 1460-1540* (Toronto, 1947), 42-3, 44.

cargo space which it then became his responsibility to fill, or which alternatively was filled by the merchant with the seaman receiving the freight charge. The practice had virtually died out by the sixteenth century except in the fishing industry,[73] and even here it was probably used mainly as a supplement. The Admiralty Court records provide instances of this system at work. For example, the master and company of the *John* of London laded 4800 fish at Newfoundland and exchanged it for about two tons of wine, oil, and figs in the Mediterranean.[74] In yet another case the crew, finding that there was no room in the hold for their fish but determined not to be cheated out of their rights, sailed all the way to Italy with the fish stowed in their cabins.[75] In Italy, one trusts, they exchanged it for a more sweet-smelling cargo; certainly they had earned whatever profit they might have made. But the practice of portage led to frequent disputes as to whether the freighter's interests had been neglected by a crew who laded too much fish for themselves, or who kept the best fish for themselves. So the master of a Newfoundland ship who, in 1634, sold his own fish at St. Sebastian in Spain for the very good price of 40 *réals* a quintal, was accused of securing better quality for himself than for the freighter. Evidently he had felt the need to distinguish carefully between the two lots, for it was said in evidence that the master's fish had been put down "with the fishy side vppermost all the rest of the fishe being laden with the skinny side vppermost."[76] Again a master and company were alleged to have put their own 30,000 fish in the hold first, so that there was not sufficient space for all the freighter's cargo.[77] When a freighter had hired a ship under tonnage charter he was particularly likely to object to the custom of portage; and a crew found guilty of abusing the privilege might find the full freight cost of their goods deducted from their wages.[78]

THE ORGANIZATION OF THE TRADE IN FISH

As the financing of the Newfoundland and other trades was regulated through the use of charter-parties, so the business of buying and selling fish, whether at Newfoundland or elsewhere, was managed through equally detailed contracts. During the days of slow and uncertain communications, the charter-party gave the merchant at home strict control over his investment under terms fixed by himself before the ship left England. Consequently a master's freedom to manage his ship as he thought fit or as circumstance might suggest could be and usually was very limited; sailing dates and cargoes alike could be prearranged for the whole voyage. Unless a master were known to have considerable experience of foreign trade, and the necessary familiarity with weights and measures, currency values, forms of agreement, letters of credit, bills of exchange, and all the other paraphernalia of the commercial world,[79] he would probably collect a cargo of fish at Newfoundland which the

73 *Ibid.,* 47-8.
74 PRO, HCA 13/51, ff 523^v-4, 525^v.
75 PRO, HCA 13/45: 18 July 1626, John Haies.
76 PRO, HCA 13/51, ff 233^v-5, 250-1.
77 PRO, HCA 13/50, f 436^v.
78 PRO, HCA 13/45: 13 July 1626, Lambert Pitcher; H. E. Nott, ed., *The Deposition Books of Bristol, 1643-1647* (Bristol Record Society, 1935), p. 218.
79 Davis, *Rise of the English Shipping Industry*, pp. 168-70; see also B[rowne], *Marchants*

merchant had already purchased, and either bring it straight back to England or exchange it in the Mediterranean for another prearranged cargo.

But when a voyage did involve trading at foreign ports, a freighter would very often choose to send along a supracargo or factor – often an apprentice – to supervise that aspect of the voyage.[80] In such cases the circumstances of the voyage might be less closely regulated. Thus the merchant of a sack ship might rely upon his factor to buy fish at Newfoundland, supplying him with letters of credit for the purpose; under such an arrangement James Dewey, factor of the *William and John* of London, purchased 248,000 dry fish and 16,000 codfish for John de la Barre in 1633.[81] Such flexible arrangements, however, did have their disadvantages. A factor would not necessarily be able to get a full cargo of fish and so, for example, the *John and Ambrose* was forced to sail for Lisbon with twenty-seven tons of dead freight, even though her factor had conscientiously tried to buy fish in St. John's, Bay Bulls, Fermeuse, and Trinity Bay.[82] Such experiences as these, expensive as they would be especially to the freighter under a tonnage charter, would drive the merchant back to prearranged voyages even when he employed a factor.

How such a voyage might work out in practice is revealed by a case in Chancery arising from a broken contract. In February 1617 Thomas Gourney of Dartmouth, owner of two fishing vessels, undertook to supply the factor of four London ships with 6000 quintals of fish, at an agreed price of 9s. a quintal, on or before 10 August 1617. Knowing that his own ships could supply only 2500 quintals, Gourney published the contract in Dartmouth and attracted two partners, Richard Lane of Dittisham and Robert Philpott of Dartmouth, who were to make up the difference. In payment Lane and Philpott were each to receive at Newfoundland three bills of exchange: one to be met immediately, a second – for half the balance – after thirty days, and the third within four months.[83] This method of payment seems to have been standard; in 1618 the same arrangement was made by the owner of a west-country fishing ship with the freighters of the *Syon* of London.[84]

Both types of voyages – those made under contract and those managed by the factor or master – had their advantages and disadvantages. With a contract, sacks were certain of finding a lading and fishing ships of selling their surplus catch which they could not carry to market themselves. The possible disadvantages lay in the system's rigidity which could make no allowance for unforeseen circumstances. A price fixed months in advance in England could obviously cause serious financial loss to either side, given the inevitable fluctuations in the market. More damaging still were possible delays, to either type of vessel, in crossing the Atlantic or in preparing the fish; breaches of contract attributable to "perils of the sea" voided the agreement but this saving clause did not include bad weather. Should the cod not be ready for collection, the outfitters of a sack ship stood to lose heavily on freight

Avizo, and particularly L. Roberts, *The Merchants Mappe of Commerce* (R. Oulton for R. Mabb, 1638).

80 On the role of the supracargo see T. S. Willan, "The Factor or Agent in Foreign Trade," in his *Studies in Elizabethan Foreign Trade* (Manchester, 1959), pp. 1-33.

81 PRO, HCA 13/50, f 436ᵛ.

82 PRO, HCA 13/61: 8 May 1648, Daniel Bradley.

83 PRO, Chancery, c 2 Jas 1, G 7/52, G 11/56.

84 PRO, C 2 Jas 1, D 5/10.

costs and on profits from the sale of their fish; nor could they necessarily make good the deficit by suing the suppliers. So the freighters of the *Syon* of London claimed that they had lost £100 in freight charges because their cargo was not ready, and a further £400 because the price of fish at Marseilles had dropped from 16s. to 10s. a quintal by the time their ship arrived. Another £300 was lost because they were given short measure at the fishery, and the fraud, being committed overseas, was difficult to prove.[85] Similarly the master of a fishing vessel might find himself with fish left on his hands should the sack ship not arrive; yet it was risky for him to go ahead and sell the fish before the final delivery date had passed. John Fletcher, master of the *Exchange* of Southampton, took this chance and regretted it. For a month he had watched the sacks arriving at Newfoundland, but not the *Frances and Thomas* of London for which he was waiting. Finally on 15 August, convinced that the sack ship must have been captured – for the year was 1630 and the seas were full of pirates – he sold his fish. Just two days later the factor of the *Frances and Thomas* appeared, demanding the 120,000 fish guaranteed by contract, and the embarrassed Fletcher could supply only a fraction of that amount.[86]

Similar disadvantages were apparent in the next stage of the trade: the sale of the fish in the Mediterranean. A master was obliged to leave Newfoundland by a certain date, whether his cargo was complete or not, to sail for a specified port of discharge. It was this aspect of the system that Whitbourne so particularly disliked, perhaps because he had suffered under it during his long career as master of fishing vessels:

... although the place where they arriue, be neuer so much ouerlaid with the like commodity that they bring; yet there must they discharge and also relade, according to the conditions in the Charter partie; though such Commodities, which they are to relade, bee there much dearer then at some other place not farre from it; which hath beene a great losse to many Marchantes; yea, diuers cauills haue risen thereby ... [87]

The master who disregarded his instructions in favour of his own initiative was liable to find himself the centre of a lawsuit when he got home, as did the master of the *Hector* in 1637. He had been directed to sell his fish at Cartagena but, aware that a fleet of Newfoundlanders had put into that port two days ahead of him and that the arrival of his ship of 300 tons fully laden would inevitably force down the price, he elected to go straight to Italy which should have been his second port of call. His fish sold well at Genoa and Leghorn, and he picked up a new cargo of aniseed and oil. Naturally the freighters of the *Hector* produced witnesses to swear that prices stayed high at Cartagena, and that a better return cargo could have been obtained there.[88]

As at Newfoundland so in Europe the conduct of a ship with a factor aboard, or one consigned to overseas agents, was likely to be less rigidly supervised by charter-party. Particular advantages did attach to the use of resident merchants in foreign ports, and cases in the Admiralty Court show freighters of Newfoundland ships

85 *Ibid.*
86 Anderson, *Examinations and Depositions*, II, 77-8.
87 Whitbourne, *Discovrse and Discovery* (1622), sigs. I 1ᵛ-2.
88 PRO, HCA 13/54, ff 214-16, 216-17, 232ᵛ-3, 245.

employing agents in the major ports of Spain, Portugal, and Italy. A resident agent had more contacts and could arrange in advance for the sale of the fish and the provision of a new cargo. William Marston, for example, acted as agent in Seville and other Spanish ports during the 1630s. In August 1632 he was warned to expect the arrival at Cadiz of a Newfoundland ship, and he arranged for the English consul in that city to sell the fish and to purchase a return cargo of sherry. His preparations were disrupted by the ship's master taking her to St. Lucar, a diversion which cost the freighter some £300.[89] The consul at Cadiz was employed the following year by two Barnstaple merchants and, in return for their fish, he bought sack, Alicante wine, figs, and raisins.[90] But the strict limitation of lading times abroad could weigh heavily on these agents too, and shipping could be delayed by their inability to sell the fish or to provide a cargo quickly enough.

Disadvantages or no, the charter-party continued to be a convenient and indispensable instrument in the conduct of overseas trade. The occasional loss of profit was accepted in return for the certainties which the use of these legally enforceable contracts provided. In no other way could a merchant, far removed from his ship, have supervised his investment. In no other way could the responsibility of each party have been so precisely defined and compensation or immunity guaranteed.

The charter-party, then, was the cornerstone of an elaborate edifice of safeguards – partnership, marine insurance, loans – erected by the shipping industry to insure the investor of the maximum control and the minimum possible financial risk. But in the west-country fishery the process was taken one step further, as we have seen, by the retention of the otherwise dying practice of payment by shares; a system not needed in the sack ship trade where the carriers might compensate for a poor fishing season or low prices by astute bargaining in continental ports. Here, throughout the history of the Newfoundland trade in our period, is revealed the difference between the financial resources of the two classes of participants – fishermen and carriers. A Newfoundland voyage could be set out as economically or as ambitiously as the merchants' resources dictated. In the west-country a small fishing ship could be hired for as little as £16 a month; a London sack might cost as much as £220 a month. The first might be freighted by a small merchant who needed to see a modest return on his investment within six months; the second by a speculator who could afford to wait a year or two for his very substantial profits. In the fear of the west-country fishermen that capital, supported by monopoly, could drive them out of the fishery, lay the seeds of the bitter conflict which was to dominate, to bedevil, the early history of Newfoundland.

89 PRO, HCA 13/51: 7 Aug. 1634, William Marston.
90 PRO, HCA 13/50, ff 604-5ᵛ.

II

The Fishery: A Time of Expansion
1577-1604

THE GROWTH OF THE FISHING FLEET

LTHOUGH ENGLISHMEN had been perhaps the first to visit the Newfoundland fishery, they seem to have been strangely slow to exploit their discovery. By 1519 John Rastell was lamenting that his fellow-countrymen were outnumbered by a fleet of more than 100 foreign vessels.[1] Legislation of the 1540s might class the transatlantic trade with such old-established and popular fisheries as Iceland, Shetland, and Ireland, but port book evidence suggests that only a handful of vessels went annually to Newfoundland during the greater part of the sixteenth century and that the trade did not yet have a significant part in the commerce of the west-country. A Bristol man, Anthony Parkhurst who had considerable personal experience of the fishery, reported that in the early 1570s the English fleet consisted of only four "small barkes."[2] While this figure may well be something of an underestimate in support of Parkhurst's special pleading for greater English involvement in the whole St. Lawrence area, the fact remains that no Newfoundlanders are recorded as entering Plymouth in 1568-9 or in 1570-1, and that only three came into Dartmouth in 1574 and none in 1575-6.[3] The returns to Exeter are no more impressive.[4] Yet within a few years these three ports would become the most important centres of the Newfoundland fishing industry, and the trade in fish would have become indispensable to their prosperity.

That the industry grew steadily from the 1570s onwards seems indisputable. Parkhurst himself put the fleet at 40 or 50 by 1578, "whereof the one halfe ar worthy shippes, so that I dare be bolde to affirme to brynge home as mutche fysshe in some one of these as all the navy did before."[5] By 1604 perhaps some 150 English ships made the voyage annually. Such a growth would always be remarkable. It is the more so considering that England was at war, in fact or in effect, for most of this time and that a serious economic depression resulted from the dislocation of her valuable Iberian and French markets. Nevertheless conditions now, more than ever before, favoured the expansion of the Newfoundland industry.

1 The relevant extract from John Rastell's *Interlude of the Four Elements* (J. Rastell, 1525?) is printed in Williamson, *Voyages of the Cabots*, pp. 88-93.
2 E. G. R. Taylor, ed., *The Original Writings and Correspondence of the Two Richard Hakluyts* (2 vols., Hakluyt Society, 1935), I, 123.
3 PRO, E 190/1011/12; 1011/23; 928/9.
4 See W. J. Harte, "Some Evidence of the Trade Between Exeter and Newfoundland up to 1600," *Trans. Devon Association*, LXIV (1932), 475-84.
5 Hakluyt, *Principal Navigations*, VIII, 10; Taylor, *Hakluyts*, I, 123, 128.

War on land in northern and western Europe, war at sea, piratical and privateering activity, as well as the unprecedented volume of intercontinental commerce, all created a greater demand for a portable, durable protein food such as dried cod. At home the increasing probability of war with Spain brought the strongest governmental encouragement yet for the fisheries, as a source of shipping and trained seamen in time of national emergency. It was a policy especially dear to the Queen's influential secretary, William Cecil. "Remedyes must be sought," he had written as early at 1563, "to increase marrynors by fishyng as a cause most naturall, easy and perpetuall to brede and mayntene marynors."[6] In an attempt to arrest the decay of navigation, Cecil pushed through the Commons a bill increasing the number of fish days from one to two a week and permitting the custom-free export of fish in English bottoms (5 Eliz. 1, c. 5).[7] The first provision he intended to stimulate home demand, as he saw little prospect of increasing English exports of fish; the second was to give control of the carrying trade to native merchants, so encouraging the construction of merchant shipping. Both provisions were frequently reinforced by proclamation until the end of the century.

While Cecil was undoubtedly right in thinking that the trade to the Baltic could not be wrested from the Dutch, Scandinavians, and Scots, he was wrong to dismiss the Mediterranean market. For it was not at home but in Catholic Europe, especially in the Iberian peninsula, that the English would find their chief outlet for Newfoundland fish – would find, in fact, an expanding market which encouraged the industry as never before. In Spain and Portugal the fishermen could take advantage of the generally flourishing state of trade during the 1570s, and of the decline in the supply of fish from Iceland. English-made stockfish had long found a market in both countries, but a drift away from the Iceland fishery had begun when Denmark had regained that island. It would be hastened when, in 1580, the Danish king began to exact systematically the payment of licence fees; by 1586 a petition from the east coast ports referred to the time "when the Iceland voyage was most frequented."[8] Coincidentally as the Iceland supply failed, so the Iberian demand for fish soared to unprecedented levels, for a Spanish army was engaged in the Netherlands and her fleets, and those of Portugal, ranged the seas as never before. Dried cod from Newfoundland was the perfect replacement for Icelandic stockfish, for its keeping properties were equally good. By a further fortunate coincidence English trade through the Straits, virtually abandoned earlier in the century because of the ravages of Turkish pirates, now revived. The years after Lepanto found English traders returning, not only with their staple export of cloth, but with tin, lead, and dried fish.

By 1577, then, the combination of official protection at home and changing commercial conditions abroad favoured the expansion of the Newfoundland fishery. Some 50 or 60 ships were said to visit the island annually by 1580 and, three years later, Sir Humphrey Gilbert found about 16 at St. John's harbour alone.[9] In 1585

6 R. H. Tawney and E. E. Power, eds., *Tudor Economic Documents* (3 vols., London, 1924), II, 107-8.
7 For Cecil's efforts to get this bill passed, see Conyers Read, *Mr. Secretary Cecil and Queen Elizabeth* (New York, 1955), pp. 271-4.
8 Prowse, *History of Newfoundland*, p. 28.
9 Taylor, *Hakluyts*, I, 166; Hakluyt, *Principal Navigations*, VIII, 51, 82.

the fleet was large enough for the government to despatch Bernard Drake to the island to warn the fishermen not to take their catch to Spain, lest their ships be seized under the recently imposed embargo.[10] While the port book records of ships returning directly to England in the eighties do not entirely reflect the extent of this growth, they do show that, despite stays of shipping, impressment of crews, and seas made hazardous by Spanish vessels, the trade did continue to increase throughout the decade. In 1589 the number of vessels entering the ports of Exeter and Dartmouth was the largest yet known in any single year (see Table IV).

Having survived the difficulties caused by the outbreak of war in the 1580s, during the following decade the fishermen really began to prosper. They escaped some of the worst effects of the deepening depression because the ever-protective government either relaxed embargoes on trade and shipping in their favour or turned a blind eye to their infringements of its restrictions. Such latitude was a practical and evidently highly successful way of encouraging the growth of the merchant marine, in case it should be needed again for national defence as it had been in 1588. The war with Spain itself stimulated the industry by increasing demand and opening up new markets. Under wartime conditions the chartered trading companies could no longer hope to impose their monopolies. The Spanish and Levant companies in particular seem to have suffered at the hands of enterprising interlopers, although it is not really clear how effective their monopolies had ever been. Of even greater importance to the prosperity of the English fishing industry was the inability of the Spanish and Portuguese fishermen to satisfy their countries' own needs, let alone any foreign market.[11]

English harassment of Iberian fishermen at Newfoundland had begun in 1582 with an apparently private raid on Portuguese shipping by vessels belonging to Henry Oughtred, a Southampton merchant, and Sir John Perrot.[12] Three years later came the government-sponsored expedition of Bernard Drake, who not only warned English fishermen against going to Spain, but who proceeded to seize 16 Portuguese ships. One motive behind Drake's onslaught must have been to reduce the supplies of dried fish available to victual the Spanish navy. Certainly the attack must have deterred those Spaniards who financed Newfoundland voyages. The following year the Spanish government decreed that no ships were to sail for the island; by the time that order was relaxed in June 1586 it would have been too late to participate in the fishery.[13] In 1589 Sir Francis Walsingham was informed that 70 Spanish Basque ships had been barred from going to Newfoundland.[14] Five years later over 60 Basque ships were fishing in Placentia Bay, but only 8 of these were Spanish.[15] All during the war, then, the Spanish government crippled the industry by its constant demands on the ships and seamen of the Basque provinces, first for projected invasions of England and then for the long-delayed Irish campaign of 1601-2. The Spanish export trade in fish was lost as mercantile regulations forbade

10 See below, pp. 47-8.
11 See H. A. Innis, "The Rise and Fall of the Spanish Fishery at Newfoundland," *Trans. Royal Society of Canada*, 3rd ser., xxv (1931), sect. 2, 51-70.
12 See below, p. 48.
13 *CSP Dom., 1581-90*, p. 302; *CSP For., 1585-86*, p. 644; Innis, "Spanish Fishery," p. 58.
14 *CSP For., Jan.-July 1589*, p. 151.
15 Hakluyt, *Principal Navigations*, viii, 165.

alien participation in the carrying trade, while the high cost of timber and naval stores prevented the replacement of wartime shipping losses.[16] Frequent attacks made by the English upon Basque shipping returning from Newfoundland deprived the Spaniards of a considerable quantity of fish and of valuable ships. By 1597 Spain was forced to rely upon the French Basques for fish,[17] but they too suffered from English aggressiveness. When the war ended, a Spanish seaman described the state of the merchant marine thus:

Within the last twenty-five years there were in Spain more than 1,000 sea-going ships belonging to private owners. Biscay alone had more than 200, which navigated to New-foundland for cod and whale and to Flanders with wool. And now there is not one ... In Portugal they always had more than 400 sea-going ships, and more than 1,500 caravels ... [engaged in] the ordinary trade to India, St. Thomas, Brazil, Cape Verde, Newfoundland and other parts ... Now there is hardly a single ship belonging to private owners in the whole kingdom.[18]

The statement was doubtless an exaggeration for English consumption, but certainly the destruction of competition did encourage English fishermen to flock to New-foundland as never before. Throughout the 1590s the government diverted convoys to guard the fleet, a precaution never again taken with any regularity until the period of the Interregnum. In 1594 a ban on shipping was lifted to allow 36 ships to leave for the island, 22 English vessels were observed fishing at Ferryland alone, and Sir Walter Raleigh estimated that, as over 100 ships had visited the fishery that year, their loss "would be the greatest blow ever given to England."[19] The following year it was reported from Plymouth that 50 Newfoundlanders had reached that port alone within a fortnight, and that some 2,000,000 fish were available.[20] There was some justification, then, for Raleigh's statements to the Commons that the trade was "the stay of the West Countries."[21]

The port books for the nineties reflect the industry's expansion more adequately than do those of the previous decade, and it now becomes apparent which of the west-country ports were most deeply involved. The books for Exeter, Dartmouth, Barnstaple, and Bristol in particular show a consistently higher level of returns than do those for the 1580s (see Table IV). The lack of "inwards" port books for Ply-mouth for the majority of the years between 1590 and 1604 is unfortunate. How-ever, there are indications, such as the report of the entry of 50 Newfoundland ships in 1595, and the statement made in 1603 that the town's well-being was entirely dependent upon its fishermen,[22] that Plymouth was at least as important a centre

16 Innis, "Spanish Fishery," pp. 54-8.
17 Charles Leigh, "A briefe platforme For a voyadge with three ships unto the Iland of Ramea," 4 Oct. 1597, BM, Add. MS 12505, ff 477-77ᵛ.
18 M. Oppenheim, ed., *The Naval Tracts of Sir William Monson* (5 vols., Navy Records Society, 1902), I, 33.
19 *CSP Dom.*, *1591-94*, p. 451; Hakluyt, *Principal Navigations*, VIII, 165; HMC *Hatfield*, IV, 566.
20 HMC, *Hatfield*, V, 387, 418.
21 L. F. Stock, ed., *Proceedings and Debates of British Parliaments Respecting North America, 1542-1688* (5 vols., Washington, 1924), I, 7.
22 HMC, *Hatfield*, V, 387; XV, 151.

of the industry as nearby Dartmouth. Yet, an unusually complete run of Southampton books contains, interestingly and surprisingly enough, no record of Newfoundlanders coming into that port. Southampton in fact never held that place in the trade for which Sir Humphrey Gilbert had destined it. Later figures suggest that its smaller neighbours, Weymouth and Poole, may have already outstripped it. Nevertheless Southampton did continue to participate in the fishery and many of its ships, being rather bigger in tonnage than the average fishing ship (see Table 1), may well have preferred the direct voyage to continental markets. Of course, the existence of this triangular trade means that estimates of the size of the Newfoundland fleet can never be based upon the port books alone.

THE DOMESTIC MARKET

Once in the home port the fish might be distributed within England, it might stay in the port to be sold as provision to merchant shipping or to the victuallers of the army and navy, or it might be re-exported abroad. In fact William Cecil was mistaken in thinking that he could materially increase the consumption of fish in England by legislation. The Reformation had removed the moral compunction to eat fish, and governmental measures to enforce the observance of Lent and other fish days for the good of the nation did not carry the weight of church commandments for the good of the soul. Moreover a rise in the standard of living had brought the price of meat within the pockets of an increasing number of people. Despite the legislation, the Fishmongers' Company frequently complained that the Lenten abstinence was broken, and by 1597 it was estimated that only one fish day a week was kept although 153 a year were officially listed.[23]

Had the fish days been observed, it is difficult to see how the demand could have been supplied. For the fact is that, small as the home market was, the industry failed to satisfy it. Complaints were heard that too much fish was shipped abroad, either directly or by re-export, where it found a surer market and probably a higher price. What did remain did not find its way to other parts of the country. Newfoundland fish coming into the southwestern ports was distributed within a limited area bounded by London on the east coast and Chester on the west. "[In other partes] of the Realme fish was much desyred but cowld not [be had]," wrote Edward Hayes in a proposition for the establishment of a corporation to manage the Newfoundland trade. He suggested that centres of distribution be set up in at least five major ports – London, Southampton, Bristol, Plymouth, Chester, Newcastle, and Harwich were all possibilities.[24]

The coastal port books show that Hayes was right in diagnosing the problem as one of distribution. Much of the west-country ports' coasting trade was carried on among themselves and its volume – with the exception of that from Southampton and Bristol – was small. A typical example of the rather strange pattern of trade

23 CSP Dom., 1547-80, p. 411; ibid., 1595-97, p. 540.
24 "A proposal for a corporation of the Newfoundland trade," 1585[-6], BM, Lansdowne MS 100, ff 83-94. The proposal was addressed to Burghley (see Hayes to Burghley, Lansdowne MS 37, ff 166-7), but despite the latter's concern for the welfare of the fishing industry, the scheme was never developed.

which resulted may be taken from the records of Southampton for 1587.[25] In that year more than 47,000 Newfoundland fish left the port by water for London (4 ships), Poole (2), Weymouth, Rye, and Newhaven (1 each), while 91,000 fish entered from Weymouth, Exeter, and Dartmouth. From time to time all the fishing ports received shipments from their neighbours, and during the 1590s both Southampton and Bristol regularly received more than they shipped. Of course some fish was sent further afield than the west-country. Bristol and Barnstaple regularly despatched small quantities to Gloucester, Wales, and Chester, while the ports on the south coast supplied Sussex, Kent, and London. Plymouth and Dartmouth appear to have been most active in this coasting trade, as befitted their predominant position in the industry as a whole, and London was their main market.

The amounts of fish exported from any one port rarely exceeded 50,000 in a year. Often the quantity was but a few quintals. In part the size of shipments was restricted by the nature of the coasting trade itself. Managed by a multitude of small merchants and ships' masters – often the same people – who dealt in mixed cargoes and with a number of ports, its main advantage was cheapness. Road transport was perhaps twenty times as expensive, or so a contemporary estimated,[26] and it would be particularly impractical for a commodity so high in bulk in relation to its value. What Newfoundland fish did reach parts of England not engaged in the fishery would mostly have been carried by sea, but the quantity was so inconsiderable that Newfoundland fish is never mentioned in Professor Willan's detailed analysis of the commodities in which the west-country dealt.[27]

The quantity used in the ports themselves cannot be calculated as ships were not required to list their provisions for customs' purposes. In a time of increased seagoing and of war, however, demand must have soared. "The State was at this time [1586] coming into the food market on a bigger scale than ever before, buying for the armed forces" in the Netherlands, Ireland, the Channel Islands as well as for the fleet. Every seaman's rations included a quarter of stockfish three days a week.[28] To make sure that these needs could be met, a ban placed on the export of fish in 1594 was relaxed only when merchants agreed to reserve a quarter of the catch for home consumption. Two years later and again in 1597 Robert Cecil was advised on the amounts of fish available in the west-country for the Queen's service.[29]

THE RE-EXPORT TRADE

Both the small quantities moved by the coasting trade and especially the small re-exports of the early 1580s are understandable in the light of the heavy demand in the ports. For the years from 1577 to the outbreak of war very few port books recording exports have survived (only about three for each of the major ports), and many of these do not record any exports of Newfoundland commodities. Many of the

---

25 PRO, E 190/930/26; 934/7.
26 T. S. Willan, *The English Coasting Trade, 1600-1750* (Manchester, 1938), p. xii.
27 *Ibid.*, chapters IX, X.
28 B. Pearce, "Elizabethan Food Policy and the Armed Forces," *Economic History Review*, XII (1942), 39-46; PRO, State Papers Domestic, Elizabeth, SP 12/191, no 28, i, ii.
29 HMC, *Hatfield*, V, 418; VI, 337; VII, 385.

books kept during this period cover only half a year, from Michaelmas to Easter or from Easter to Michaelmas. The most likely time to find fish being exported is immediately after Michaelmas when the Newfoundlanders were coming home; by Easter the previous season's catch would already have been sold. As the exports in the years before 1585 were so small, they can be summarized briefly without the use of tables.

Bristol exported no Newfoundland fish between Easter and Michaelmas 1577, but between Michaelmas 1579 and Easter of the following year 4 ships, 2 going to St. Sebastian and 1 each to Marseilles and La Rochelle, included small amounts of fish in their cargoes.[30] This distribution reflects the general pattern of Bristol's trade which was directed mainly towards the south Atlantic coast of France and to the Iberian peninsula. During the same period in 1579-80 a total of 31 ships left Bristol, of which 11 went to the French ports of La Rochelle, Bordeaux, and Marseilles, 15 to Spain and Portugal, and only 6 to other destinations. No fish left the port during the year Michaelmas 1582 to Michaelmas 1583.[31] There are records of Southampton's exports for four years: Michaelmas to Michaelmas 1578-81 and 1583-4, but none of them shows any shipment of Newfoundland fish or oil.[32] Fish is known to have been available during this time (see Table IV), and the absence of exports is the more surprising in the light of Edward Hayes's statement, made about 1585, that "as vnto a famous [ma]rt the Marchauntes from the most partes of Christendome doe yearly repayre thither with [gre]ate store of shipping only for the benefitt of Fish."[33] The evidence for the Devon ports is no more satisfactory. Dartmouth's books for the years from Michaelmas to Michaelmas 1576-7, 1581-2, and 1583-4 contain no references to the export of Newfoundland fish. The book running from Michaelmas 1582 to Michaelmas 1583 shows a single French ship sailing to Fécamp with 2200 Newfoundland fish and 24 barrels of herring.[34] Of the three surviving books for Exeter – Michaelmas 1581 to Easter 1582, and Michaelmas to Michaelmas 1583-4, 1584-5 – only the first has entries referring to Newfoundland fish.[35] In the months of January and February 1582, 4 ships left Exeter, all of them for Normandy, with a total of 8000 fish valued for customs' purposes at £35. The absence of any re-export trade from Barnstaple is not surprising,[36] for at this date the total export trade of that port was still very small and mainly directed towards the Spanish Atlantic seaboard which before 1585 could supply its own needs. These figures suggest that even before the outbreak of war most of the Newfoundland fish available in England was used in the port through which it entered.

After 1585 a decline in the volume of re-exports is only to be expected as the government banned all trade to the Iberian countries in retaliation against Philip's embargo on English shipping. Hard following came the disruption of Anglo-French commerce as contact with Brittany and all ports held by the Holy League was forbidden. These two blows destroyed the established pattern of west-country commerce.

30 PRO, E 190/1130/1; 1130/3.
31 PRO, E 190/1130/4.
32 PRO, E 190/815/7; 815/6; 815/9; 816/4.
33 BM, Lansdowne MS 100, f 83ᵛ. On the decline of Southampton trade in the late sixteenth century, see Ruddock, *Italian Merchants*, pp. 262-72.
34 PRO, E 190/930/14; 933/3; 934/16; 934/5.
35 PRO, E 190/933/3; 934/3; 935/5.
36 PRO, E 190/931/12; 932/5; 934/3.

None of the ports had any sizeable trade to northern Europe where they were excluded from the cloth market by the Merchant Adventurers' monopoly. The trade to the Mediterranean remained, could one manage to slip past the watchful Spaniards hovering off the Straits of Gibraltar.

In the face of these difficulties almost no Newfoundland fish left the southwest between 1585 and 1590; at least no exports are recorded in the surviving port books for these years. Possibly some was smuggled out, for west-country fishing merchants never believed that the domestic market could absorb all their catch. In 1585 Devon traders asked permission to send fish to France and Italy despite the restrictions on shipping, and the following year a Dartmouth ship was reported selling Newfoundland fish at Le Havre where it was reshipped to Spain.[37] Three years later, in 1589, the Devon ports again petitioned, on grounds of hardship, to be allowed to export the fish that remained unsold. The government agreed, but required that licences be first obtained and that merchants enter into bonds not to transport their fish to Spain, Portugal, or those French ports not in obedience to Henry IV.[38]

Very gradually commercial conditions improved during the 1590s. The trade with France particularly shows signs of having revived even before the coronation of Henry IV in 1594, when all French ports were officially open again to English shipping. In 1591, for example, ships from Dartmouth, Plymouth, and Bristol visited ports on the Atlantic coast of France from Normandy to Bayonne, and one Bristol vessel braved the Straits to reach Marseilles.[39] In the customs' year 1593-4 a total of 46 ships cleared Southampton for France; Exeter's French trade began, after 1594, to reapproach the level of the early 1580s, and occasional west-country ships reached Leghorn and Venice from 1591 onwards.[40] Naturally enough trade with the Iberian peninsula, which had disappeared completely from the customs records after 1585, was slowest to revive. It did, however, reappear before the conclusion of peace, and west-country vessels were entering Spanish ports from 1599.[41] Trades such as that with Ireland, which had become unusually important in the attempt to compensate for the loss of more valuable European markets, now fell off sharply. By 1600 the pattern of west-country trade showed signs of returning to normal.

Nevertheless the 1590s had been a period of serious economic depression during which, or so it was reported from the west-country, the Newfoundland trade had been "the only voyage that maketh both owner and mariner flourish."[42] Although the government still felt the need to keep a watchful eye upon the amounts of fish leaving the country, it was prepared to relax its restrictions. In 1594, for example, a ban on fish leaving the west-country was lifted when Sir Robert Cecil was advised of the hardship to fishermen which its imposition involved; he did insist, however, that a quarter of the catch be reserved for home needs.[43] The following year exports were again forbidden, but later were allowed to all places "in league and

37 *CSP Dom.*, *1581-90*, p. 276; *CSP For.*, *1585-86*, p. 301.
38 *APC 1589-90*, pp. 179-80.
39 PRO, E 190/935/7; 1017/7; 1131/3.
40 PRO, E 190/818/1; 818/6; 935/7; 1017/7; 1131/10; 1132/8.
41 PRO, E 190/937/6; 937/8.
42 HMC, *Hatfield*, IV, 479.
43 *Ibid.*, V, 418.

amytie with her Majestie."[44] By 1598 the mayor of Southampton could complain
that so much fish reached Spain from the west-country by way of France that there
would be none left in England with which to keep Lent.[45] Despite his complaint
restraints continued to be withdrawn. In 1599 a licence was issued for the shipment
of 60,000 Newfoundland fish to any destination, whilst a request for permission
to send fish to Spain and Portugal in 1600 seems to have been made because of
restrictions on the export of fish rather than on places of trade.[46]

The port books confirm that a sizeable trade in fish to France had been conducted
ever since 1591, with Italy the next most popular destination (see Tables v-x). The
Italian trade, though employing less shipping, tended to be more valuable, at least
as far as the port of Dartmouth was concerned (see Table v). On the basis of the
port books Dartmouth emerges as the biggest re-exporter of Newfoundland fish,
although too few Plymouth books survive to show whether that port might have
rivaled its neighbour. The figures for 1591 and 1593-4 do indicate the existence of a
considerable re-export trade (see Table vi), the existence of which is confirmed by
reports from Plymouth itself. Every fall an international group of merchants
seems to have been in the town awaiting the return of the fishing fleet. In 1595 there
were Dutch and French traders, in 1597 Irish too. They bought so much fish that,
in 1596 and 1597, Cecil was warned to secure what was needed for the Queen's
service before foreign demand forced the price up.[47]

None of the other west-country ports exported much fish. Bristol's and Southampton's exports, for example, were regular but of insignificant quantity (see
Tables viii and ix). When, in 1601, the known figure of fishing ships returning to
Bristol reached its highest total (10), the value of the Newfoundland commodities
re-exported was only £50. Yet the overall picture of the town's trade was healthy,
with ships clearing for France, Italy, the Netherlands, the Baltic, Ireland, and the
Channel Islands. France was the sole destination for fish leaving Southampton, and
traffic to France did indeed dominate that port's commerce. Usually at least half
the shipping from Southampton was bound for France, mostly for Normandy and
the Atlantic coast. The greater part of the Italian trade was directed to Venice, not
a port to which much fish was shipped, and the only other regular destinations for
Southampton ships were the Netherlands, which could supply its own needs, and
the Channel Islands.

Southampton, unlike Plymouth, was not an entrepôt for the Newfoundland
trade and only French merchants came to the port to buy fish. Even though the
participation of alien merchants and shipping in the carrying trade was not yet the
cause of bitter dispute between London and the outports, as it would become in the
next century, their role was considerable in the years before 1604. Surprisingly
enough, however, Dutch merchants were outnumbered by the French (see Figs I
and II). Only in the Italian trade did the Dutch predominate, carrying larger and
more valuable cargoes than the French. The Anglo-Spanish war does not appear,

44 APC 1595-96, p. 33.
45 HMC, Hatfield, VIII, 415.
46 CSP Dom., 1598-1601, pp. 323, 389.
47 HMC, Hatfield, v, 387; VI, 337; VII, 385.

then, to have given the Dutch the advantage in the carrying trade from the west-country that it did give them from London.[48]

THE TRIANGULAR TRADE

Not even in the period 1590-1604, and certainly not before that, do the port book figures of fishing ships returning directly to England or those for the re-export trade really reflect the reported growth of the fishing fleet. Even in 1599, when the number of Newfoundlanders known to have entered the west-country ports reached 51 and, given more complete evidence, might have totalled 75 or more (see Table IV), there would still be 50 to 100 fishing ships to account for, if we accept the reports of responsible contemporaries. This apparent discrepancy must in large part be explained by the triangular trade which, in all probability, had existed from the earliest days of the Newfoundland fishery. Bristol merchants, at least, had long been used to send their vessels on the voyage from Iceland to Portugal to sell stock-fish. Nor would a triangular voyage necessarily require an unusually large ship. According to Whitbourne the average fishing ship was about 60 tons, but smaller ships than this could make a triangular voyage.[49] In 1601, for example, a vessel of 40 tons went straight from Newfoundland to the Atlantic coast of France.[50] Those ships planning an extended voyage could easily obtain extra supplies through the well-established barter trade at the fishery. The larger sack ships, coming mainly from London and Southampton, probably made the longer voyage more safely and more profitably, but even a fishing ship could reach the Levant as did the *Sunne* in 1600.[51]

Careful combing of the High Court of Admiralty records for the earlier part of the sixteenth century might well reveal that triangular voyages were being made then. As it is, the first known instance of such a voyage is not until 1584 when the *White Hinde* of London, belonging to a Thames-side shipbuilder Peter Hill, sailed "to Newefoundeland on fisshing fare, and from thence to Cales [Cadiz] in Spain, and soe to this porte of London."[52] The ship reached Spain in November so that the whole voyage need have lasted no more than nine months. And other evidence proves that the triangular trade was quite common by the mid-1580s, otherwise why should the Queen have thought it necessary in 1585 to send Bernard Drake to New-foundland to warn English fishermen not to go directly to Spain? Even if this were a blind to cover his aggressive intentions, it could hardly have been convincing had the trade not been considerable. About the same time too the promoter, Edward Hayes, maintained that

by reason of the late accidentes between vs and [the Spanyards] the Newland Voyage wilbe altogither vnprofittabell, for so [greate a store] of fish and Trayne Oyles will

48 Millard, "Import Trade of London," p. 107.
49 Whitbourne, *Discovrse and Discovery* (1622), sig. H 4.
50 Agreement between George Lyde, George Balin, and John Jeffrey, 27 Feb. 1600/1, SRO, Second Book of Instruments, 1597-1689.
51 PRO, HCA 13/35: 18 June 1601, Andrew Casley, Thomas Pynchet.
52 PRO, HCA 13/25: 21 Jan. 1584/5, Anthony Bowen; 26 Jan., John Hayes; 19 Oct. 1585, Samuel Lucke.

not be found good now [that no waye] into Spayne and the Strayghtes is left. Whither for th[e moste parte] our Merchantes were accustomed to carry theyr Commoditie.[53]

The previous examination of the volume of re-exported fish in the early 1580s suggests that Hayes cannot have been referring to that trade. He must surely have been speaking of the direct voyage and, when he was in Newfoundland with Sir Humphrey Gilbert in 1583, he may have observed ships being repaired and revictualled for trading voyages.

The problems of assessing the size of the triangular trade have already been discussed. The records of the Admiralty Court for the last quarter of the sixteenth century provide only rare instances of such voyages, but the Southampton Book of Instruments which contains summaries of legal documents, affords a tantalizing glimpse of what might have been had the notaries' original records survived. The book for 1597-1689 mentions four triangular voyages made from Southampton by ships of from 40 to 240 tons in the years between 1600 and 1604: one to the Straits, another to Bordeaux or La Rochelle, a third to Malaga in 1603, and the last to Marseilles. And one may suspect that the triangular voyage would be even more popular from the major Newfoundland ports of Dartmouth and Plymouth. London ships too were involved; the *White Hinde* was from London, as were the *Solomon* which went to Toulon in 1592, the *Sunne* which reached the Levant in 1600, and the *Hopewell* which traded to the Mediterranean coast of France four years later.[54]

The popularity of the triangular trade may have resulted at least in part, from the higher prices obtained abroad, although wartime demand in England did raise the price from the standard ten shillings a quintal for small, dry fish and twenty shillings for medium-sized dry or wet fish. According to Edward Baeshe, general surveyor for the navy, prices of all foodstuffs had risen by 1586 because of the need for provisions for the forces; stockfish, which in this context probably included Newfoundland-made fish as well as Icelandic cod, brought between £9 and £20 a 1000.[55] In 1590 English fish fetched 14 shillings in the Basque ports and 16 to 18 shillings four years later. The *Sunne*'s cargo sold for 5 to 16 shillings at Marseilles in 1600, and a case concerning sale came before the Admiralty Court because this price was considered so poor.[56] The second cargo which a ship on a triangular voyage picked up in Europe – and the *Sunne*, for example, came home with 130 tons of eastern Mediterranean goods – would ensure a higher profit than a mere fishing voyage, despite the greater cost involved in setting out a more ambitious voyage. Profit may have emboldened merchants to dare seas made hazardous by war, especially when a direct return to England – where they might find their ships and crews impressed, their cargoes forcibly purchased or their export forbidden – provided an alternative that was none too attractive.

53 BM, Lansdowne MS 100, f 89.
54 PRO, HCA 13/96: 21 Aug. 1591, R. Pitt; Prowse, *History of Newfoundland*, p. 84.
55 PRO, SP 12/191, no 28, i, ii.
56 PRO, HCA 13/29: 27 April 1591, John Maien; HCA 13/32: 17 Jan. 1595/96, Stephen de Harembilett; HCA 13/35: 18 June 1601, Andrew Casley.

War, in fact, created the ideal situation for the expansion of the English fishery at Newfoundland. A consistent policy of governmental protection, personally supervised by the two Cecils, enabled the fishermen to take advantage of trading conditions which hardly seemed ideal. The war boosted prices at home and abroad and, even more fortuitously, crippled Spanish and Portuguese competition. Without a doubt the Spanish fishing industry was hit harder than the English, which was not only able to survive the war but which used the circumstances it created to grow at an unprecedented rate.

III

An Island Becomes Known

THE GROWTH OF KNOWLEDGE

WARTIME CONDITIONS had favoured the expansion of the fishery; so too they helped to focus attention on the island of Newfoundland iself, as a factor in that war. But this was not the only reason why Newfoundland became of interest to the English in the late sixteenth century. Nor, chronologically, was it the first. From the middle of the century economic and social problems, fear and envy of Spain, all combined to force Englishmen to look outwards towards that New World to which thus far they had been strangely indifferent. Naturally enough they thought to find their new markets especially for cloth, their sources of raw materials, their colonies for surplus population, their counter-balance to Spain's glittering empire in the more obviously attractive southern regions of the continent. South and central America and the West Indies, if not themselves Cathay, might yet produce the riches of Cathay. Less, it was generally agreed, could be expected of northern latitudes.

These interests and prejudices found accurate reflection in the geographical literature which appeared in such abundance in continental Europe, although not at first in England. Before the 1580s the English had to rely on translations, mainly of Spanish works, for most of their knowledge of the New World. Consequently much of their information was out of date by the time it became available. Not until 1541, for example, did Roger Barlow of Bristol and Seville produce the first description in English of the American continent; and then he based it upon a Spanish world geography of 1519.[1] Apparently ignorant of Jacques Cartier's recent discoveries, Barlow believed Newfoundland to be a part of the mainland and placed it far to the north of its true latitude. Of the region's value he was contemptuous:

What comoditie is within this lande as yet it is not knowen for it hath not been labored, but it is to be presupposed that there is no riches of gold, spyces nor preciose stones, for it stondeth farre aparted from the equinoctiall whereas the influens of the sonne doth norishe and bryng fourth gold, spices, stones and perles. But whereas oᵣ englishe marchantes of brystowe dyd enterpryse to discover and discovered that parte of the land, if at that season thei had folowed toward the equinoctiall, no dowt but thei shuld have founde grete riches of gold and perle as other nations hathe done since that tyme.[2]

1 Martin Fernández de Enciso, *A Briefe Summe of Geographie*, ed. E. G. R. Taylor (Hakluyt Society, 1932).
2 *Ibid., pp.* 179-80.

In 1555 Richard Eden published his translation of Peter Martyr's *De Orbe Novo Decades* which, more than any other single book, stimulated English curiosity about America.[3] But again the focus was the West Indies; Newfoundland was dismissed in a sentence as being remarkable only for fish and ice. The sixties brought English versions of French works on Florida and of André Thevet's book on Brazil, as well as Sir John Hawkins' account of his voyage to the West Indies, but still nothing on the north. Finally in 1580 the really important discoveries about Newfoundland and the St. Lawrence area made by Jacques Cartier in the 1530s, which had been available in Italian since 1556, were translated into English.[4]

For by 1580 the old English indifference to America was vanishing completely. Sir Humphrey Gilbert had already launched one ill-fated expedition across the Atlantic and was planning a second. Within the next five years Sir Walter Raleigh would establish the first English settlement in the New World. And the indefatigable Richard Hakluyt had begun his long career as publicist for the new lands. It was Hakluyt who financed John Florio's translation of the Cartier voyages[5] and who included it in the second edition of his own *Principal Navigations*; Hakluyt who collected and preserved almost all the information we have on Newfoundland. Letters, propaganda, accounts of voyages, experience, and knowledge which might otherwise never have been written down, let alone printed – he welcomed anything that might inflame the sluggish interest of his fellow-Englishmen.

But the nature of the voyages made to Newfoundland and the lack of settlement there seriously limited the nature of the information available during the sixteenth century. The west-country fishermen's deep personal knowledge of the island, built up from years of experience, they jealously kept to themselves. Hakluyt generally had to rely upon the impressions of men who had visited the island once or twice, and briefly during the summer months. Perhaps only once before 1610 was a more detailed and systematic survey made and, if so, its results have been lost. During his visit in 1583, Sir Humphrey Gilbert appointed men to explore the island, to search out its resources, and to learn what they could from those with long experience. A little of this material survives in Edward Hayes's narrative of the voyage, but the original instructions called for the making of maps, topographical drawings, and natural history sketches, and for the keeping of a journal of the surveyor's observations.[6] Some maps certainly were made but they were lost in the wreck of the *Delight* on the homeward voyage. Of course the work that could have been

3 Richard Eden, *The Decades of the Newe World or West India* (G. Powell, 1555); reprinted by E. Arber, ed., *The First Three English Books on America* (Birmingham, 1895).
4 G. B. Ramusio, *Delle Navigationi et Viaggi* (3 vols., 2nd ed., Venice, 1554-9), III, 435-53ᵛ; Jacques Cartier, *A Shorte and Briefe Narration of the Two Nauigations ... to Newe Fraunce*, translated by John Florio (H. Bynneman, 1580). For a complete list of the geographical works available in England, in manuscript and in print, see E. G. R. Taylor, *Tudor Geography* (London, 1930), and the same author's *Late Tudor and Early Stuart Geography* (London, 1934).
5 F. A. Yates, *John Florio* (Cambridge, 1934), p. 58. For the best account of Hakluyt's career, see G. B. Parks, *Richard Hakluyt and the English Voyages* (2nd ed., New York, 1961).
6 Hayes's narrative was printed by Hakluyt, *Principal Navigations*, VIII, 34-77. The instructions prepared for Gilbert's expedition are in BM Add. MS 38823, ff 1-8; for comment on them, see D. B. Quinn, ed., *Roanoke Voyages* (2 vols., Hakluyt Society, 1955), I, 51-4, and E. G. R. Taylor, "Instructions to a Colonial Surveyor in 1582," *Mariner's Mirror*, XXXVII (1951), 46-62.

done in the three weeks that Gilbert spent at Newfoundland must have been limited, but Hayes's account does include information of a kind not found elsewhere in this early period. His knowledge of the winter climate and of the Banks, for example, suggests consultation with European fishermen. In the case of this Gilbert expedition we have the instructions but not the results; for the Roanoke colony we have Thomas Hariot's and John White's invaluable work, but not the instructions under which they proceeded. In all probability the two sets of instructions were very similar; and it is the more tantalizing to think that a collection of material conceived, if not executed, on the scale of the Roanoke surveys has been lost.

Rather than any systematic and detailed collection of knowledge on Newfoundland, then, we have before 1610 the gradual accumulation of bits and pieces of information. And nothing perhaps better reflects this process than the history of the island's cartography. For the greater part of the sixteenth century the English had to depend upon continental cartographers for their maps of the New World, just as they relied on continental authorities for their written sources. And there were many popular and increasingly fine European maps available in England. Perhaps the most influential in the later part of the century were Gerard Mercator's world chart of 1569, and Ortelius' "Typus orbis terrarum" of the following year.[7] The representation of Newfoundland was similar on both these works: both showed a grouping of four islands. This fragmentation of Newfoundland had been a characteristic of maps made since the 1540s. Before then Newfoundland had generally been shown as part of the mainland, with straits to north and south occasionally suggested.[8] But reports of the earliest explorers, of Sebastian Cabot and the Cortereals for example, had stressed the broken nature of the coastline; and Cartier's account of his 1534 voyage had confirmed this impression. In many of the maps of the mid-century Newfoundland was shown as consisting of as many as ten widely separated islands, almost completely blocking the mouth of the St. Lawrence.

Mercator's representation, apparently derived from Portuguese sources, was an improvement on these; although, compared with other parts of the map, the outline of Newfoundland is somewhat disappointing. Each of his four islands is clearly identifiable as a particular part of Newfoundland: one represents the northern peninsula, two the Avalon peninsula, and the fourth and largest the central land mass with a much exaggerated Placentia Bay on its southern coast. Both the Mercator and Ortelius maps were available in England from the time they were printed, although there was no English printing of Ortelius' atlas until 1602. In 1589 Richard Hakluyt reproduced Ortelius' "America sive novi orbis" in the first edition of his *Principal Navigations*, for there was still no English map to compare with it.

So far only one known map had ever shown Newfoundland as a single triangular-shaped island, and that was a manuscript map made in 1563 by a Norman, Nicholas Desliens.[9] Not until the 1590s was such a form reproduced again and then apparently by cartographers ignorant of Desliens' work. The first to do so was the

7 See A. E. Nordenskjöld, *Facsimile Atlas to the Early History of Cartography* (Stockholm, 1889), plates 46, 47.

8 See, for example, the map designated Kunstmann, no IV, reproduced in H. Harrisse, *Découverte et évolution cartographique de Terre-Neuve* (Paris, 1900), plate 8.

9 *Ibid.*, fig. 91.

Dutch cartographer, Jodocus Hondius, who published a map of North America in England about the year 1590.[10] Although the shape of the island was somewhat compressed from east to west and elongated from north to south, nevertheless it was the best representation yet found in any printed map. Apparently Hondius compiled it from new information, for it differs markedly from the Portuguese models used by another Dutchman, Petrus Plancius. A beautifully engraved map of "Nova Francia," even more accurate than Hondius', is now generally ascribed to Plancius and to the year 1592; but it was probably not available in England. Plancius evidently derived his information from a collection of maps made by the Portuguese Bartholomew Lasso, which he acquired about 1592 but which he did not presumably have when he compiled his world map which was printed in London in 1592.[11] This world map is carelessly and crudely engraved; its representations of Newfoundland derives in part from Mercator and in part from earlier Portuguese works.

But, despite the availability of so many fine and increasingly accurate continental models, English maps tended to be strangely old-fashioned. Many of them indeed were made not by professional cartographers but by interested, though not necessarily skilled, laymen. Those dating from the early 1580s seem to have been closely connected with the projects of Sir Humphrey Gilbert. In 1580, for example, one of Gilbert's associates, John Dee, presented the Queen with a map intended to support her right to the St. Lawrence region. The map is a curious blend of the 1569 Mercator world chart with earlier Portuguese works. The large north island of Newfoundland is copied very closely from Mercator; the rest, including the failure to draw the west coast at all, is taken from a map of 1554 compiled by Lopo Homem, a Portuguese whose work was well known in England.[12] Again in a copy of the pilot Simon Fernandez' map, made for Dee in 1580 shortly after Fernandez returned from his reconnaissance voyage for Gilbert, the influence is Mercator.[13] Michael Lok, yet another of Gilbert's circle, compiled an even more inaccurate and out-of-date map which, strangely enough, Hakluyt chose to reproduce in his *Divers Voyages* (1582). It shows a crude, poly-insular Newfoundland, such as can be found in maps made soon after Cartier's return from his first voyage.

When in 1587 Richard Hakluyt needed a map to illustrate his edition of Peter Martyr's *De Orbe Novo*, he used not an English cartographer but probably Francisco Gualle, the Spanish navigator. In the preface to the 1589 edition of the *Principal Navigations*, Hakluyt referred to the "comming out of a very large and most exact terrestriall Globe, collected and reformed according to the newest, secretest and latest discoueries ... composed by M. Emmeric Mollineux of Lambeth, a rare gentleman in his profession." By 1592 Mollineux had finished his beautiful globe,

10 Reproduced in R. A. Skelton, *Explorers' Maps* (London, 1958), fig. 59.

11 The map was identified by F. C. Wieder, *Monumenta cartographica* (2 vols., The Hague, 1927), II, 27-46. See also *Portugaliae monumenta cartographica* (6 vols., Lisbon, 1960), III, 88-9, plates 370, 378, 381. The world map of 1592 is reproduced in Wieder, *Monumenta cartographica*, II, plate 26.

12 See W. F. Ganong, *Crucial Maps in the Early Cartography and Place-Nomenclature of the Atlantic Coast of Canada* (Toronto, 1964), fig. 116.

13 Harrisse, *Découverte et évolution cartographique*, fig. 89.

but all the information derived from the "latest discoueries" did not make the drawing of Newfoundland any the more accurate.[14] A few years later Mollineux engraved a new world map which had been compiled by Edward Wright. Apparently prepared for the second edition of the *Principal Navigations*, this was the first world map composed by an Englishman, and is unquestionably the finest English map of America made before 1610.[15] Here Newfoundland is drawn as a single, triangular island. The outline is much freer and less stylized than in the Plancius "Nova Francia," and this, together with the lack of place names, recalls the Hondius map of 1590 which may have been Wright's model. It is also entirely possible that Wright had new and direct lines of information both from English explorers of the Gulf and perhaps from the French successors to Cartier, Jacques Noel and Pont-Gravé, with whom Hakluyt was in communication.

"NORTHERNE MEN"

Both the maps, then, and most of the written information on Newfoundland current in sixteenth-century England were connected with Hakluyt and with that more elusive figure, Sir Humphrey Gilbert, whose career provided another great stimulus to English interest in the New World. As early as 1566 Gilbert had proposed the establishment of a colony in North America, as a means of relieving poverty at home.[16] He thus became the first Englishman to recommend such a colony since John Rastell had done so in his *Interlude of the Four Elements* almost fifty years before. By the time that Gilbert's manuscript was published in 1576, he had behind him some four years' experience as a soldier and colonist in Ireland, and had lately become associated with the Cathay Company which financed Martin Frobisher's expeditions.[17] By 1577, too, Gilbert was becoming personally involved in plans for a transatlantic voyage.

For by now the international situation was extremely tense. The breathing space provided by the Anglo-Spanish agreement of 1575 was over, and Spain was fomenting rebellion in Munster. Many of the most influential men at court, among them Walsingham and Leicester, had come to regard war with Spain as inevitable. In 1577 Francis Drake's projected voyage of exploration to *Terra australis incognita* had been rerouted to allow an attack on Spanish America, his new mission being a well-kept secret so that the Queen might profit while ostensibly disapproving. In "A discourse how hir Majestie may annoy the King of Spayne," Gilbert hoped to attract the devious Elizabeth by offering her the same protection from accusations of complicity.[18] Letters patent for discovery and colonization should be granted, he proposed, with "speciall proviso for their safetyes whome pollisy requyreth to have most annoyed." Under this cover, ships could be sent to Newfoundland where "your highnes may at the first distres both the FRENCH, SPANYSHE, and PORTINGALL

---

14 Ganong, *Crucial Maps*, fig. 119.
15 Nordenskjöld, *Facsimile Atlas*, plate 50.
16 *A Discourse of a Discoverie for a New Passage to Cataia* (H. Middleton for R. Jhones, 1576); reprinted by D. B. Quinn, ed., *The Voyages and Colonizing Enterprises of Sir Humphrey Gilbert* (2 vols., Hackluyt Society, 1940), I, 129-64.
17 Quinn, *Gilbert*, I, 31.
18 *Ibid.*, 170-5.

yet there needeth none to be towched but the SPANIARDES, and PORTINGALL, or the SPANIARDES alone." The raid on Newfoundland, recommended Gilbert, should be followed up by a stronger one on the West Indies, in an attempt to wrest Spain's empire from her. Elizabeth's reaction is not recorded, but probably her enthusiasm for the two projects – Drake's and Gilbert's – varied in direct proportion to the profit she might expect from each. And with investments already made in the Drake and Frobisher expeditions, she would be disinclined to venture further. But Gilbert's ideas were not forgotten; Walsingham himself would revive them, with official approval, at a time critical in the struggle with Spain. For, as men like Gilbert and Walsingham realized, there was good reason, mere curiosity apart, to be interested in Newfoundland. In time of war the island had great strategic value, both offensively and defensively. The Spanish fishing fleet, an essential part of that nation's naval reserve and a victualler of both army and navy, could be destroyed there; and the island itself could be used as a base from which to harass Spain's empire. An English colony would prevent the island from coming under foreign domination, would stimulate the fishing industry so providing more ships and men for England's own naval reserve, and might with profit tax the foreign fishermen.

In the following year, 1578, Gilbert received his letters patent for an overseas expedition, the implication being that he would within the next six years establish a colony somewhere. An exact location was not specified; the Spaniards might work that out for themselves, if they could. It seems clear, from the date of his departure among other things, that his destination in 1578 was not Newfoundland, but somewhere south of the 45th parallel.[19] And before he left, Gilbert's circle busied themselves collecting information for him. The elder Richard Hakluyt prepared a pamphlet of good advice on the problems of colonization.[20] Probably connected too with Gilbert's plans were two letters written by Anthony Parkhurst of Bristol, a man who had already made four voyages to Newfoundland and who had far-sighted ambitions for English domination not only of that island but of the whole St. Lawrence area.[21] In 1577 or 1578 he wrote to an unknown acquaintance setting forth his ideas, and the letter came into Burghley's hands, as Parkhurst had perhaps always intended that it should.[22] Obviously familiar with Burghley's long-standing concern for the prosperity of the English fishing industry, Parkhurst devoted himself to proving that the presence of colonists would make the fishery "twyse, ye[a] thryse, as good as yet yt ys." Settlers could fish, make salt, and prepare equipment, so enabling the visiting fishermen to give all their time to their trade. The resultant increase in the fishery must enlarge the marine and benefit the economy generally:

19 Gilbert's patent was published by Hakluyt, *Principal Navigations*, VIII, 17-23. For a discussion of his intentions, see Quinn, *Gilbert*, I, 35-46.
20 "Notes framed ... heretofore to bee giuen to one that prepared for a discouerie, and went not," in R. Hakluyt, *Divers Voyages Touching the Discovery of America*, ed. J. W. Jones (Hakluyt Society, 1850), pp. 132-8.
21 For a biography of Parkhurst, see *Dictionary of Canadian Biography* (Toronto, 1966), I, 530-1.
22 BM, Lansdowne MS 100, no 10; printed in Taylor, *Hakluyts*, I, 123-7. Professor Taylor suggests that the recipient was Edward Dyer, who was then acting as an intermediary between John Dee and the Privy Council in connection with overseas expansion, *ibid.*, 123, n. 1. Dyer was also associated with Gilbert, see Quinn, *Gilbert*, I, 31, 33, 167.

... howe mutche this voyage ys to be preferred before a spanysshe viage or other cuntryes. In primis, they cary forthe nether ware nor mony, nether spend they abrode halfe the vyttels that at home they woulde, and yet brynge they home greate store of fysshe, suffycyent to serve our realme and others from whence with yt we brynge home rytche commodyte.

For the rest Parkhurst applied the standard propagandist arguments to the particular conditions of Newfoundland. Was it necessary to prove that a colony would help to make the mother-country economically self-sufficient? Parkhurst could advertise Newfoundland as a source of those naval stores so essential to England's defence and to her merchant fleet, a pertinent consideration when supplies from Germany and the Baltic were jeopardized by retaliation against the cancellation of some of the Hanse merchants' privileges, as well as by the Danish imposition of heavy dues on shipping entering the Sound. The mining and smelting of iron on the island were again timely possibilities, for iron smelting came under severe restrictions in England because of the fear of deforestation. The production of cheap food too was promised by the ever-hopeful Parkhurst. Iron there certainly was in Newfoundland, but its exploitation had to await the technical advances of the nineteenth century. As for the fertility of the soil, Parkhurst was misled by a dangerous combination of limited experience and unlimited optimism.

A second and if possible even more enthusiastic letter, addressed to the elder Richard Hakluyt in 1578, aimed "to certifie you of the fertilitie and goodnesse of the countrey" and dealt at length with the island's terrain, fauna, resources, and climate.[23] Tests he had made of the soil had convinced Parkhurst of its suitability for most English crops; summer visitors were often so deceived for they did not stay late enough to see the early frosts destroy their crops. His concern to correct fishermen's tales about the severity of the weather led him into his own exaggerations about the mildness of the climate, but he did recognize that the cold was not the result of the latitude but of ice carried down from the Arctic. If it is in the nature of promotion literature that it should exaggerate, then Parkhurst's letters are no exception. But as the earliest detailed reports of Newfoundland, written by an Englishman from first-hand experience, they had considerable value. Eighty years or more of voyages had produced nothing better.

In this second letter Parkhurst did not develop further his earlier arguments in favour of colonization, perhaps because Hayluyt was already acquainted with them. He did, however, introduce one new and significant thesis: were Newfoundland, he claimed, to be "peopled and well fortified ... wee shall bee lordes of the whole fishing in small time, if it doe so please the Queenes Majestie." The fishery, according to Parkhurst, was then frequented annually by more than 100 Spanish, about 50 Portuguese, and over 150 French ships. It must have been pleasant to dream of England's controlling these fleets – perhaps exacting dues as did the Danish king at Iceland, perhaps excluding a rival altogether. Pleasant, but scarcely realistic. Yet the idea appealed in the light of the tension between England and Spain, and would soon be taken up by yet another of Humphrey Gilbert's associates, Edward Hayes, who

23 Hakluyt, *Principal Navigations*, VIII, 9-16.

would in the 1580s take on Parkhurst's role as principal advocate of Newfoundland.

Late in 1578 Gilbert's expedition of seven ships set sail from Plymouth; only one of them got further than Ireland before being forced to return home. Because of the piratical activities of some of his captains, the Privy Council forbade him to leave again in 1579. Four years would elapse before his next voyage. Meanwhile, Gilbert disposed of large tracts of land in the St. Lawrence area to those more interested in the north than he.[24] Such a one was John Dee, astrologer, alchemist, dabbler in the occult, whose spirit voices do not seem to have given him much help with the practical problems of setting out a colonizing expedition.

Not until 1583 was Gilbert able to organize a second voyage, and again his destination lay south of Newfoundland. But circumstances dictated otherwise. Short of provision when he left England, Gilbert knew that only at the fishery could he hope to replenish his supplies. Moreover as he set sail later in the year than was advisable, it would be easier for his ships to take the northern route across the Atlantic and then to follow the coast southward, searching for a place to winter. Had all gone as originally planned, and few of Gilbert's projects ever did, the visit to Newfoundland would have been nothing more than an incident on the way south.[25]

With Gilbert went Edward Hayes as captain of the *Golden Hind*, the only ship of the five to complete the whole voyage safely. Hayes's account of the expedition, printed by Hakluyt, contains a detailed picture of events and his first reflections on the problems of colonizing Newfoundland.[26] His story of Gilbert's arrival in St. John's and of the ceremonial taking possession of the island for the crown is so well known as to need no retelling. Gilbert's motive is the vital thing. Evidently he considered that his action automatically gave him control of an area of 200 leagues in any direction from St. John's. It would perhaps be wise for him to make sure of a foothold somewhere in North America, even in the despised northern latitudes, as his grant expired the following year. His interpretation of the patent is dubious; in fact it allowed Gilbert to expel anyone who, without his permission, tried to settle "within the space of two hundreth leagues neere to the place or places ... , where the said sir Humfrey, his heires or assignes ... , shall within six yeeres next ensuing, *make their dwellings and abidings*,"[27] a condition which the ceremony scarcely fulfilled. Also in his mind may have been a desire to strengthen England's position at the fishery, for he had already shown himself to be very conscious of the island's significance in the conflict with Spain. It is, however, very doubtful that his action gave England any legal right to the island. It is even more unlikely that, on the basis of the ceremony, Gilbert himself could have exercised any real authority there. The three laws which he promulgated: that public worship be according to the Anglican rite, that any act prejudicial to the crown's possession of the island be deemed high treason and so punishable by death, and that anyone speaking disrespectfully of the

24 For an account of the 1578 expedition and of Gilbert's subsequent activities, see Quinn, *Gilbert*, I, 40-9, 96-100; II, 482-9.

25 Hakluyt, *Principal Navigations*, VIII, 40-3.

26 *Ibid.*, 34-77. For Hayes's career, see D. B. Quinn, "Edward Hayes, Liverpool Colonial Pioneer," *Trans. Historical Society of Lancashire and Cheshire*, CXI (1959), 25-45.

27 Hakluyt, *Principal Navigations*, VIII, 19 (my italics).

Queen be liable to lose both his ears and his ship, could never have been enforced on the scattered, international community without an armed force far beyond Gilbert's power to organize and pay.

As his visit continued, however, Gilbert's interest in Newfoundland itself grew until he abandoned thoughts of settlement to the south, refused to make any further grants of land to the fishing merchants at St. John's, and having become "a Northerne man altogether," resolved to return to the island the following spring. Much of this sudden interest sprang from his conviction that the island held rich deposits of silver. Hayes's account of Gilbert's conversion, together with this promise of silver and of "Iron very common, lead, and somewhere copper," must have made the island appear a more attractive and potentially valuable place than ever before. Hayes also included a brief descriptive section on the "new found lande and the commodities thereof" on lines similar to Parkhurst's letters, stressing the possibilities of naval stores, furs, hides, and corn.

One of the most valuable aspects of Hayes's narrative was the addition which it made to existing geographical knowledge, for most of his information was remarkably accurate. The latitudes he supplies, 46° 20' to 52°, err by only a few seconds; his estimate of the island's length from north to south, 300 to 400 miles, is very fair considering the broken nature of the coastline. Furthermore he supplied the fullest description yet of the position of the Banks, their extent and their latitudes, at a time when these fishing grounds were not marked on any known English map – knowledge which he presumably gained in conversation with French Bank fishermen who came ashore at the end of every season for provisions, wood, and water.

Hayes's story, simply but vividly told, was in fact much more effective propaganda than the elaborate promotion document written by another of Gilbert's circle, Sir George Peckham. The latter's *A True Reporte of the Late Discoveries ... of the Newfound Landes*[28] included a summary of events drawn from Hayes; the rest was propaganda designed to attract subscribers to his own projected expedition of 1584.[29] Lengthy and tedious, over-embellished with biblical, classical, and historical allusions, the book lacked the direct impact so necessary in this type of literature. With its repetition of the familiar, stock inducements, it can surely have attracted few investors. Peckham, like Richard Hakluyt in his "Discourse of the Western Planting" of 1584,[30] was more concerned with a colony to the south of Newfoundland; but his contention that a fishing colony in North America would increase England's merchant marine, the country's "greatest Jewell ... , and the cheefest strength and force of the same, for defence or offence," was in fact best applicable to the already established Newfoundland trade. At least his book did focus attention on the possibility of combining fishing and settlement.

Hakluyt in his "Discourse" devoted little space and less enthusiasm to the island. An area that could offer only naval stores could hardly compete with other regions of North America which, according to him, promised minerals, gems, spices, and furs. His sole concession was to omit the most derogatory parts of a letter which he had received from an intimate friend, Stephen Parmenius, who had lost his life on

28 Published by J. C[harlwood] for J. Hinde, 1583, and in a shortened version by Hakluyt, *Principal Navigations*, VIII, 89-131; reprinted in full in Quinn, *Gilbert*, II, 435-80.
29 See Quinn, *Gilbert*, I, 90-3.
30 Taylor, *Hakluyts*, II, 211-326.

Gilbert's expedition.[31] For Parmenius had written of a "wildernesse," impassable because of tangled undergrowth and fallen trees, of the heat of the summer and of the "greate heapes, and mountaines of yce" that betrayed the cold of winter, and of "ayre upon land indifferent cleare, but at Sea ... perpetuall mists, and ... about the Banke ... no day without raine." And so Hakluyt creates the impression that, while not wishing to discourage an English settlement anywhere, he personally had very few hopes for Newfoundland. Appreciating as he did the strategic importance of the St. Lawrence, he preferred to recommend a colony at Cape Breton from which

... partly by the strengthe of our fortification and partly by the aide of our navye of Fishermen which are already commaunders of others there, ... wee shalbe able upon every soodden to cease [seize] upon one or twoo hundreth Spanishe and Portingale shippes, which for tenne weekes or three monthes are there on fisshing every yere.

This vulnerability of his fishing fleets would, Hakluyt believed, deter Philip II from seizing English shipping within his own domains.

Perhaps Parmenius' letter, written as it was by an impartial observer and a close friend, had convinced Hakluyt that the climate was an insuperable barrier to the settlement of the island. Otherwise his attitude is somewhat surprising. For Hakluyt as a practical man must have realized that Newfoundland did possess one great advantage over other, milder regions; it had a guaranteed staple product, cod, which found a ready market in Europe. But, as a realist, wishing above all to enlist Elizabeth's financial support for Raleigh's Virginia, he knew that a prosaic commodity such as codfish would appeal little to a Queen eager for more spectacular profits and more glittering spoils. Moreover, the recent Frobisher fiasco had probably made prospective investors, including the Queen, more sceptical about reports of mineral wealth in the northern parts of America; and all Gilbert's samples of ore had perished with the *Delight*.

Although some others might not share his enthusiasm, Edward Hayes was not discouraged. Clearly he had intended his account of the 1583 voyage to sustain that interest which the expedition and Gilbert's dramatic death had evoked, and perhaps to incite Sir John Gilbert to continue his brother's work. If so, he failed. Sir John did send two ships to the island in 1584, but it was later claimed that their only purpose was to attempt to recoup the losses suffered when the *Delight* was wrecked.[32] If he also received reports on Newfoundland's resources and on the possibilities of enforcing his brother's charter, they cannot have been encouraging for, as far as we know, he took no further interest in the island. With the expiration of Humphrey Gilbert's patent and the award of Raleigh's Virginia patent, both in 1584, the focus of English attention swung to the south. Hayes would eventually follow the trend, but now he was hard at work on an elaborate plan for a Newfoundland colony to be financed by a commercial company, having a monopoly of the fishery and control of the distribution of fish at home. By such an organization, although it lacked the extensive powers which Hayes envisaged, was the first Newfoundland colony to be established. But that was still almost thirty years away.

31 Hakluyt later published the letter in full, *Principal Navigations*, VIII, 81-4.
32 Quinn, *Gilbert*, II, 428.

In May 1585 Hayes sent a summary of his ideas, now lost, to Lord Burghley.[33] Burghley acted as Hayes's patron in a number of speculative schemes, and Hayes could expect this latest project to appeal particularly strongly, for it embraced so many of the Lord Treasurer's favourite causes: the encouragement of the fishing industry, the discovery of new sources of raw materials (especially naval stores), and the plantation of North America without provoking such violent reaction as the choice of a site nearer to Spanish possessions might do.

Unlike his earlier narrative, the finished scheme of 1586 was pure propaganda for the development of Newfoundland.[34] It added nothing to current geographic knowledge. New, however, was his direct appeal to the Queen to give her support to the colony: not her financial support, for not even Hayes was sanguine enough to hope for that, but simply her positive approval of an undertaking represented as richly beneficial to her kingdom. After repeating the orthodox arguments – that the voyage was short and safe, that colonization would be easy and profitable, and that the island belonged to England through priority of discovery – he reached his main point of appeal to Elizabeth, and one which places the document firmly in the setting of mounting Anglo-Spanish hostility. The initiative then held by the French and Spanish kings because of their ability to seize English shipping with their dominions might be balanced, according to Hayes, if England controlled Newfoundland. In fact the events of 1585 had already made plain to the Spaniards the vulnerability of their fishing fleets; the effects of Bernard Drake's raid can only have strengthened Hayes's case.

Hayes's inducements to subscribers offered the same blend of old and new. His idea of a trading corporation had not been applied to Newfoundland before, but such an organization was necessary in his opinion because no one man could bear the full expense of a settlement. At its head he envisaged someone, perhaps Sir John Gilbert, with sufficient prestige and influence to hold the enterprise together. To this "General" and the other investors, who would be merchants and shipowners holding £25 shares, Hayes promised immediate profit from the imposition of a 10 per cent tax on the 400 fishing ships visiting Newfoundland annually. Hayes reckoned, probably over-optimistically, that the ships' cargoes grossed £200,000, so that the levy would provide the company with an annual income of £20,000, apart from the profits on the sale of their own fish and oil. The foreign fishermen, he asserted, had already agreed to accept English domination in return for protection against pirates and assurance of their regular fishing stations. Such an agreement, if indeed it existed, can only have been concluded by Sir Humphrey Gilbert in 1583. But would the fishermen really have traded their freedom, plus 10 per cent of their catch, for a vague promise of protection when, by moving south to Cape Breton and New England, they could fish unrestricted? It seems improbable. And how from all the many, scattered fishing harbours could such a tax be collected? It would require an enormous fleet. The weaknesses of the scheme, then, were obvious; but Hayes, like Sir David Kirke who did later try to impose such a tax,[35] correctly

33 Referred to in a letter from Hayes to Burghley, 10 May 1585, BM, Lansdowne MS 37, ff 166-7, damaged. On Hayes's connections with Burghley, see Quinn, "Edward Hayes," 27-8, 30, 33.
34 BM, Lansdowne MS 100, ff 83-94.
35 See below chapter VII.

realized the importance of some immediate source of revenue to cover the large initial cost which any colony must incur.

His other inducements echoed those which both he and Parkhurst had advanced earlier: that Newfoundland would be a source of raw materials and cheap food, both of which would attract foreign shipping. But again he struck a new note with his warning that, if the English delayed further, they would likely find themselves forestalled by the French who had only been prevented from colonizing Newfoundland that year by the likelihood of civil war at home. He probably had in mind here the plans of the Marquis de la Roche to establish a North American settlement in 1584, in which year Hayes may well have been at work on his project. Since then the Holy League had allied with Spain and French activity in the St. Lawrence had become doubly alarming; especially as the French must now have replaced the Spaniards and the Portuguese as the chief competitor in the European fish market.

To the prospective colonist, Hayes boldly offered a life free from the hardship and poverty endured by so many in England. Their transportation would be free as the subscribers would be liable to carry so many settlers and their supplies each year, instead of letting their ships sail out in ballast. A market for the settlers' fish was assured, and the merchants who came to buy would willingly bring further provisions in exchange. In the sixteenth and seventeenth centuries, however, adventurers preferred to risk their purses rather than their persons. Even those prospective colonists who might accept Hayes's efforts to play down the severity of the climate would have been deterred by the absence of any provision of land for them. The average Elizabethan who was prepared to risk his life in some overseas venture did so because of his hunger for land, as government schemes in Ireland and the successful reorganization of Raleigh's Virginia colony show; he was not interested in remaining simply the paid servant of a commercial company.

But to Hayes it was most vital to attract investors; the settlers would then follow. Throughout he stressed the revenues that could be expected from the fishery, unrealistically claiming that the company would need only enough capital to set out fishing ships each year; the profits from these ships would more than cover the expenses of the colony. Undoubtedly Hayes was right to emphasize Newfoundland's one advantage in having a staple product, for failure to find a staple could mean failure for a whole enterprise. His more sophisticated readers, however, may have doubted that fishing could alone support a settlement: and justly so, as the London and Bristol Company later discovered. They may have questioned too the likelihood of an amicable alliance, such as Hayes took for granted, of London, the west-country, and outports not yet engaged in the fishery. For, to ensure distribution throughout the country, Hayes believed that merchants in at least five ports should subscribe to the company; and he named London, Southampton, Bristol, Plymouth, Chester, Newcastle, and Harwich as possibilities. But the outports and London had conflicting trading interests; and the west-countrymen who, because of their more limited reserves of capital, would not have controlled such a company, would not lightly surrender their traditional dominance in the fishery.

Hayes certainly anticipated objections to a "co[u]rse to draw so comen a trade vnto a Societie." Even before he outlined the financial organization of his company, he took pains to prove that a monopoly would not be injurious to any interest. To win Burghley's support, Hayes knew that he must prove conclusively that the fishermen would not suffer in any way, but that they and therefore England's merchant marine would flourish as never before. He maintained that more shipping would be attracted to Newfoundland once merchants could earn freight on both their outward and homeward voyages, and that this growing volume of shipping would more than offset any reduction in the size of crews which might follow from the colonists' production of dried fish. Hayes may have been aware that antagonism to a Newfoundland colony had already been triggered by Gilbert's arbitrary action in granting land to some fishermen but not to others. Gilbert's behaviour had clearly threatened the long-established tradition of the right of the first-comer each season to take the best place in the harbour of his choice, for the fishermen would now find their stations permanently occupied by a settler or a favoured merchant. Objections to Gilbert's actions may have been one reason why Newfoundland was specifically excluded from Sir Walter Raleigh's grant of 1584.[36]

Despite all Hayes's arguments and his connection with Burghley, no attempt was made to implement his plan. It is doubtful whether he had succeeded in persuading any of those to whom he appealed that their interest in Newfoundland could best be served by its settlement. The fishery could be exploited, the merchant marine encouraged, the Spaniard threatened, all without a colony. Men such as Sir Walter Raleigh and Sir John Gilbert were distracted by other projects dearer to their hearts, or busy with local preparations against a possible Spanish invasion. As for the government, it was not yet prepared to give active support to any overseas plantation, with the exception of Ireland which was regarded as a matter of national security. Above all, Hayes needed the support and the capital of the merchant class. He had to convince them that a monopoly of the fishery was possible, and that such a monopoly would secure them control of the carrying trade in fish to Europe. His idea would have been difficult enough to sell at any time, and it was impossible now that privateering offered rewards such as no colony could match. The settlement of Newfoundland, indeed a successful English settlement anywhere in America, had to await the end of the war when the capital of London merchants became available again.

His failure to kindle support for his project apparently dampened Hayes's enthusiasm for Newfoundland. The star of his patron, Burghley, was waning and Hayes himself needed a fresh approach. Taking advantage of the burgeoning interest in New England, he produced a new treatise in which he abandoned the idea of a Newfoundland colony in favour of the newer fishery.[37] For the first time Hayes admitted the severity of the climate as an obstacle to the settlement of the island. Perhaps the failure of the Roanoke experiment had forced him to realize that plantation overseas could never be the uncomplicated, inexpensive business that he had described. Perhaps, too, he recognized the stubborn west-country opposition to any interference with the status quo in Newfoundland. The New England fishery did not have a century-old tradition of absolute freedom for colonial promoters to overcome.

36 See Quinn, *Roanoke Voyages*, I, 85n.
37 "A discourse conserning a voyage intended for the planting of the chrystyan religion and people in ye Northwest region of America," [1592?], Cambridge University Library, MS Dd.3.85, no 4. For a fuller discussion of this document, see Quinn, "Edward Hayes," 37-9, where the date 1592 is suggested.

THE ENGLISH BECOME AGGRESSIVE

While Hayes had been dreaming of dominating the fishery through settlement, more practical measures had been taken to exclude the Spaniards. Since Gilbert had presented his "Discourse how hir Majestie may annoy the king of Spayne" in 1577 the international situation had deteriorated sharply. The union of Spain and Portugal in 1580 had signalled a recovery in Spanish fortunes: the victory of Terceira, an advance in the Netherlands, and an alliance with the Guise party to foment trouble for Elizabeth in Scotland. When, in the autumn of 1584, the Queen finally steeled herself to intervene in the Netherlands, the war which Sir Francis Walsingham and his party had long foreseen was not far off.

Ever since Francis Drake's return from his voyage of circumnavigation, Walsingham had been fretting to use him in an offensive against Spain in the New World. A plan for a three-pronged attack had been submitted to the Privy Council in October 1584 but, with the Queen irresolute, preparations had apparently been abandoned early in 1585.[38] The main objective in this plan had been the West Indies, with support coming from an English settlement which could serve as a base for sorties against the Spanish treasure fleet and as a refuge for English privateers, and from a raid on the Spanish fishing fleet at Newfoundland. This then was one, though not the only, reason for the establishment of the colony at Roanoke Island in 1585; as it turned out, the site's treacherous harbours made it useless for the purpose. Walsingham himself had devised the details of the Newfoundland raid, and they bore a marked similarity to Gilbert's proposals of eight years before. Spanish seamen and their provisions were to be seized and their ships either destroyed, if the Queen should finance the attack, or brought back to England or the Low Countries to defray expenses, if private adventurers were involved. As the action would probably be considered an act of open war by Spain, Walsingham advised that the approval of the king of France be first secured.

The one part of this scheme not wholly aggressive in intent, the Roanoke colony, was implemented in 1585; the raids on the West Indies and Newfoundland might have remained no more than interesting possibilities had not Philip II first concluded the Holy League, and then clapped an embargo on all English shipping within his dominions. The news of the embargo reached England in May 1585. By June Bernard Drake had been diverted from his preparations for a Virginia voyage to go to Newfoundland, there to warn the English fishermen not to sail directly to Spain, and to capture as many enemy fishing vessels as possible.[39] The attack was executed with thoroughness. Drake raided twenty Portuguese fishing and treasure ships, bringing more than half of them back to England as prizes.[40] The unfortunate

38 "A plotte for the anoyeng of the K[ing] of Spayne," c. March 1585, PRO, SP 12/177, no 58; the hand is Walsingham's own.

39 PRO, HCA 13/101: 16 Feb. 1588/89, John Drake. Bernard Drake's commission is in *CSP Dom., 1581-90*, p. 246. In fact two almost identical commissions were issued on the same day, 20 June 1585, the second being addressed to Carew Raleigh, PRO, Signet Office Docquet Book, Ind. 6800, f 24. The purpose of the duplication is obscure, unless it was meant to confuse the Spaniards.

40 PRO, HCA 13/27: 24 Oct. 1588, John Staple and Gilbert Turner; 8 Nov., John Marshall; 25 Nov., Nicholas Hooding; 30 Nov., Henry Browne; 2 Dec., Robert Bragge. HCA 13/101: 15

Portuguese bore the brunt of Drake's fury, as they had done three years before in an apparently private raid set out by a Southampton merchant, Henry Oughtred, in revenge for losses he had suffered in Spain.[41] The Spaniards, having realized that the Avalon peninsula was no longer safe for them, had it seems already moved the base of their activities to the southern and western coasts of Newfoundland, and into the St. Lawrence itself.[42] The effect of Bernard Drake's raid was to kill the Portuguese fishery, and to ensure that the Spaniards did not return to the Avalon peninsula in any great number. More damaging still to the Spanish fishery were the attacks on Spanish vessels in European waters and Philip's decision, fired by English aggression, to revive the plan for the invasion of England and so to impress large numbers of Basque ships and seamen.[43]

By December of 1585 news of the Spanish preparations for invasion had filtered through to England and, in that same month, was produced yet another project for a series of offensives against Spain.[44] Its author was most probably William Herle, a member of Walsingham's highly efficient spy service, who was being used by the Secretary in an attempt to force Burghley to adopt a more aggressive policy towards Spain.[45] Recognizing that a state of war existed even if it had not been formally declared, Herle included Spain's vulnerable spots in Europe as well as in the New World. In America, his proposals combined a Newfoundland raid with the further colonization of Virginia; the one to "starve his [Philip's] country and possess his mariners and shipping, wherein consists his chief strength," the other "to possess King Philip's purse." No further attacks, however, would be made on the Spaniards through their Newfoundland fleet,[46] because the damage inflicted on Spanish shipping in European waters combined with the government's crippling impressment of ships and men rapidly brought about the decline of the Spanish industry. In fact the Spaniard in America was left in peace generally until 1595, while the English concentrated on the defence and blockade of the seas nearer home. By that time the Spanish fishing fleet was no longer England's chief rival, and fear of Spain had in part been replaced by alarm at increasing French activity in the St. Lawrence area.

It was an hostility that contained a strong element of jealousy, for the French, who took their fish home wet and who were not therefore tied to the shore as were the English, soon began to return home with more than cod. In pursuit of the whale, the Basques and Bretons particularly ventured north to the Strait of Belle Isle; they

Feb. 1588/9, Amias Preston; 16 Feb., John Drake. Some 600 prisoners and 60,000 quintals of fish were also brought back to England, *CSP Dom., 1581-90*, p. 273.

41 PRO, HCA 13/24: 25 April 1583, Thomas Peers; 26 April, William Dill; 27 April, John Heimers; HCA 13/25: 16 Oct. 1583, Paulus Dies; 17 Oct., John Ortize and Peter Serano; 6 Nov., P. de Subeaure; 8 Nov., Henry Billingsly and Alonso de Bastarto; 9 Nov., Richard Staper. See also PRO, SP 12/153, no 73; SP 12/165; nos. 39-41; State Papers Foreign, Spain, SP 94/1, no 106; *CSP Sp., 1580-86*, p. 410.

42 In 1594 more than 60 Basque ships, both Spanish and French, were fishing at Placentia Bay, Hakluyt, *Principal Navigations*, VIII, 165.

43 Innis, "Spanish Fishery," pp. 51-70.

44 *CSP For., 1585-86*, pp. 228-30.

45 Conyers Read, *Mr. Secretary Walsingham and the Policy of Queen Elizabeth* (3 vols., Oxford, 1925), III, 117.

46 But such a raid did remain a possibility; see the proposals made by Francis Drake and John Hawkins in 1587 for a series of attacks on Spain from the West Indies and the Gulf of Mexico as far north as Newfoundland, *CSP Sp., 1587-1603*, pp. 20-1.

rounded Cape Ray to reach Newfoundland's west coast; they discovered and exploited the walrus fishery of Ramea (Magdalen Islands); and they penetrated up the St. Lawrence to trade for furs with the Indians. In contrast, no Englishman is known to have rounded Cape Ray until 1594, even though the publication of accounts of Cartier's voyages might have been expected to kindle some interest in the gulf area. The colonizing project of the Marquis de la Roche in 1584, and the award of a trading monopoly in the St. Lawrence to Cartier's nephew, Jacques Noel, and his associates did cause the English some concern[47] – but not enough apparently to make them do anything about it. Distracted by the Spanish war, ignorant of the area, and lacking a knowledgeable pilot to guide them, they allowed the French to gain the initiative.

Then, in 1591, the St. Lawrence region suddenly forced itself into prominence. That year a Breton vessel, the *Bonaventure* of St. Malo, an interloper into the predominantly Basque walrus fishery at the Magdalens, was captured on its way home and brought to Bristol. So notorious was Lord Treasurer Burghley's concern for the welfare of the fishing industry that Thomas James, the mayor of Bristol, sent him a description of the ship's cargo of walrus leather, tusks, and oil. Perhaps as a result of a request for more information from Burghley, the master of the *Bonaventure* was induced to write a description of the Magdalens and their situation.[48] Hakluyt chose to print James's letter at the beginning of his section on English voyages to the west coast of Newfoundland, implying perhaps that he knew this report, Burghley's interest, and the subsequent explorations were connected. Just a few weeks later, news reached Burghley from his agent in St. Jean de Luz, Edmond Palmer, of the capture of a Basque ship coming from Canada with a cargo of fish, train oil, and "greate Store of Riche Fures as beavers, martrenes otters and many other Sortes." Added the wily Palmer, knowing his ageing employer and his ailments, "sometimes they do bring black fox skins – no such things to ease the pain of the gout."[49] The cargoes of the two vessels could not but convince Burghley that the English were neglecting a valuable trade, for that of the *Bonaventure* alone had been worth perhaps some £1,430,[50] and her walrus oil was a particularly attractive commodity now that olive oil from Spain was in such short supply. "If it will make sope," wrote Thomas James whose city had a large soap-manufacturing industry, "the king of Spaine may burne some of his Olive trees."

Even so, it took a little time before an expedition could be organized. Early in 1593 an association was formed between Peter Hill, a Thames-side shipowner with previous experience of the Newfoundland trade, and not surprisingly a group from Bristol which included James. Two ships were prepared: the *Marigold*, belonging to Hill, and another vessel owned and captained by George Drake of Topsham. Through Edmond Palmer the partners procured the services of Stevan de Bocall, a French Basque and a Huguenot with considerable experience of the gulf. Their

---

47 See H. P. Biggar, *The Early Trading Companies of New France* (Toronto, 1901), pp. 34-5, 38-41; and Hakluyt, *Principal Navigations*, VIII, 272-4.
48 Hakluyt, *Principal Navigations*, VIII, 150-4, 155.
49 Palmer to Burghley, 19 Oct. 1591, PRO, SP 94/4, ff 64-6.
50 See D. B. Quinn, "England and the St. Lawrence, 1577-1602," in *Merchants and Scholars*, ed. John Parker (University of Minnesota, 1965), 117-43. I am much indebted to this article for my account of English voyages to the St. Lawrence after 1590.

destination was the Magdalens; their objective the walrus fishery.[51] The ships sailed late in the season but Drake's, piloted by Bocall, reached the Magdalens quickly enough to fish some walrus and to seize part of the catch of a Breton vessel which they found there. Apparently there was no direct sequel to this voyage. The next year, 1594, a ship left Bristol, again with Bocall as pilot, but its destination was the west coast of Newfoundland and Anticosti. This was again new ground to the English. Sylvester Wyet, the ship's master, later wrote an account of the expedition which supplied future voyagers with useful sailing distances and identifiable landmarks.[52]

Bocall subsequently left England, being dissatisfied with the limited scope of the English expeditions. In 1595, however, Palmer was again recommending him to Burghley because of his invaluable knowledge. Bocall had promised to reveal the whereabouts of copper deposits in Newfoundland, as well as to lead the English to the "Grande Baye" where Basque whalers could be captured.[53] If such a voyage were made, Hakluyt evidently did not know of it. But somehow an English privateer named William Craston had managed to acquire a remarkable familiarity with the gulf area before 1597.

But the expedition in which Craston participated in that year differed radically from any yet made. Not only was it designed to give the English a foothold in the St. Lawrence by the establishment of a permanent settlement in the Magdalens and, therefore, control of the walrus fishery, but also to rid England of a troublesome, nonconformist sect, the Brownists.[54] Behind the commercial side of the enterprise was a partnership which included again Peter Hill, Abraham von Harwick, a well-to-do if not over-scrupulous alien merchant resident in London, Stephen von Harwick, probably Abraham's brother, William Craston, erstwhile privateer, and Charles Leigh, merchant and leader of the expedition. Leigh apparently acted as intermediary between the merchant group and the Brownists, who had first requested permission to quit England in 1593, and who now petitioned to be allowed to go to a "foreign and far country ... in the province of Canada."[55]

In 1597 two ships left for the Magdalen Islands under Leigh's command. Each carried two prospective settlers, hardly an adequate advance party for the new colony.[56] It was an eventful voyage. Only one of the vessels, the Hopewell, with Craston as master and Leigh as captain, reached the destination, Basque Harbour. There they found four ships – two Breton, two Basque – peacefully and profitably hunting walrus. Although the Basques offered proof that they did indeed come from the French side of the border, Leigh calmly requested them "for our better securitie in the harborough peaceably to deliver up their powder and munition." Not surprisingly the Basques refused. One of their ships was then seized, and only with difficulty did Leigh restrain his men from pillaging it. Now the Bretons and Basques joined forces against the English and, after four days of violence, Leigh agreed to

51 Hakluyt, *Principal Navigations*, VIII, 157-62.
52 *Ibid.*, 162-5.
53 PRO, SP 94/5, ff 9-10ᵛ.
54 See C. Burrage, *The Early English Dissenters* (2 vols., Cambridge, 1912), I, 118-54.
55 BM, Harleian MS 6849, f 143; PRO, SP 12/246, no 46.
56 Charles Leigh's account of the voyage was printed by Hakluyt, *Principal Navigations*, VIII, 166-82.

withdraw. Daunted by the hold which he now perceived the French to have on the Magdalens, he moved to the gulf in search of an alternative site for the colony. But now Leigh's unruly crew, apparently encouraged by Craston, demanded that the ship resume its career as a privateer. Finally Leigh had to abandon the purpose of the expedition and go to Newfoundland where, after a series of encounters with French fishing ships, his crew finally obtained its prize.

The expedition had failed dismally, but Leigh had not entirely given up his interest. On his return to England he wrote "A briefe platforme for a voyadge with three ships unto the Iland of Ramea."[57] He proposed to make another voyage in 1598 and to establish a colony which might farm and fish, and control not only the Magdalen Islands but the whole gulf of the St. Lawrence, "to the greate preiudice of the Kinge of Spaigne, who were not able to maynteine his ships at sea yf he were not supported by theise fishermen.'" The plan, as Leigh should surely have realized, was impossible. The Magdalens would not be an easy place in which to live, as the Marquis de la Roche's settlers would soon discover to their cost,[58] and it would have been almost impossible for a small English outpost to hold the islands against the hostile French. Fortunately, perhaps, the experiment was never tried.

While the English attempt to shake the French grasp on the St. Lawrence area had failed, English privateers roaming the Atlantic had greater success. Ever since 1585, but particularly in the years 1590 and 1591, the English had lain in wait for Basque fishing vessels returning from Newfoundland and Canada, as the sudden outcrop of complaints in the Admiralty Court reveals. Spanish and French fell victim alike, for Spanish Basques frequently masqueraded as French and the English could not distinguish between them; and of whatever nationality the ships might be, most of their fish would go to victual the Spanish navy. The danger became so great that Basque merchants frequently procured passports from the Lord Admiral of England, swallowing their pride by thus admitting in effect English suzereignty over the fisheries. Theoretically these passports guaranteed them safe passage, but their English persecutors were as likely to ignore them as not.[59]

The English had come far since 1577 when Newfoundland had interested none but a handful of west-country fishermen, and when even they had been greatly outnumbered by French, Spaniards, and Portuguese. But as the industry had grown and become vital, as the war with Spain forced England to take stock of its strategic advantages, so the English had become better informed, more possessive, and above all more aggressive. The Oughtred raid of 1582 had demonstrated to the Spaniard the dangers of fishing in enemy strongholds. Three years later Bernard Drake had found only Portuguese in those harbours most frequented by his fellow-countrymen. Alarmed by English hostility, attracted by other regions and other trades, the

---

57 BM Add. MS 12505, ff 477, 477ᵛ.
58 See Biggar, *Early Trading Companies*, pp. 40-1.
59 PRO, HCA 13/32: 17 Jan. 1595/6, Stephen de Harembilett, who testified that the Basque owners of the *St. Mary St. Vincent* of Ciboure procured such a passport for their voyage in 1595, and a second for their return journey from the English fishing admiral of St. John's harbour. See also PRO, HCA Exemplifications, HCA 14/29, no 27, Feb. 1592/3, list of 6 passports issued to ships of St. Jean de Luz, Caberton, and Bayonne; HCA 14/30, 1594, 4 passports to ships of Ciboure.

French and Spanish Basques, the Bretons, and the Normans moved north and west into the gulf of the St. Lawrence and south to the future "French shore." The Avalon peninsula, though certainly not the whole island, had become an English preserve.

So the situation stood when the war ended and Englishmen found themselves free to turn to more peaceful enterprise. Much was now known of Newfoundland – its climate, resources, and geography. Foreign competition had been removed from the part of the island in which the English were most at home. The fishery had developed into a flourishing and highly profitable business. Now the time had come for capital to move in and try to take over an industry which small west-country merchants had built up slowly over a century. International rivalry faded. It would be replaced by struggle between two groups of Englishmen: the fishermen and the colonists.

IV

The First Colony
1610-31

ENETRATING COLD, frequent fogs, barren soil – hardly the characteristics one might expect to find in what was after all only the second permanent English settlement in North America. Yet there were many reasons why Newfoundland seemed a good choice, many reasons why a colony there might prove a good investment. For more than a hundred years now the island had been the one constant focus of English attention in the New World. With the ending of the Spanish war in 1604 had come the liberation of capital previously channelled into that most lucrative of Elizabethan investments, privateering. There followed a rush to put money into the chartered trading companies, and into colonizing companies the formation of which probably only the war had prevented. Virginia, New England, Newfoundland: within four years companies had been formed to embrace those regions of North America which had long been of greatest interest to the English. With Newfoundland they reached the area which they had known longest and best, where they enjoyed the greatest security, and where, most important of all, the prosaic codfish offered a certain staple. By 1610 a fleet of approximately 200 ships crossed annually to the fishery;[1] the Mediterranean markets were open; a period of great prosperity lay ahead.

Newfoundland then had appeal for practical men, and with these England was richly endowed: merchants with capital, ready to advance their country's commerce and their own fortunes. In the opinion of most of them a chartered company with a monopoly was the most effective and profitable way of exploiting any trade and excluding foreign competition. When the London and Bristol Company for the plantation of Newfoundland was formed in 1610 it attracted 48 members, 36 of whom were merchants of the two cities. Of these 10 came from Bristol, 2 from other provincial ports, and the remaining 24 from London.[2]

The idea of a Newfoundland colony may well have originated with the Bristol subscribers who were among the most eminent members of that city's merchant community. Many of them had already invested in Newfoundland voyages; all

---

1 The figures given by representatives of the company in their petition of incorporation, 9 Feb. 1609/10, Trinity House Transactions, 1609-25, ff 1, 1ᵛ.

2 The names of all the subscribers were enrolled in the patent, PRO, Patent Rolls, 8 Jas I, pt. viii, C66/1826; printed in C. T. Carr, ed., *Select Charters of Trading Companies, A.D. 1530-1707* (Selden Society, 1913), pp. 51-62.

were familiar with the markets of southern Europe.[3] One of them, John Guy (who would be the first governor of the company colony), had visited the island in 1608, apparently to consider possible sites for the settlement. On his return he had written "a Treatise to animate the English to plant there."[4] These Bristol men could not but be aware that their city, despite its long-standing links with the island, now lagged behind other lesser ports in the exploitation of the fishery. A chartered company, combining local expertise with London wealth, might be the means of restoring Bristol's lost eminence.

From the Londoners came the bulk of the capital and much of the work of organization within England. And they included some of the most prominent and prosperous merchants of the day – John and Humphrey Slany, William and Ralph Freeman being perhaps the most notable. All of these, with the exception of William Freeman, served on the company's council, and John Slany was the company's first and only treasurer for eighteen troubled years. A freeman of the Merchant Taylors' Company, John Slany also served twice as its warden and once as its master; he was an important shipowner who, with his partners, received a royal subsidy for building six vessels, all of the then extraordinatary capacity of 200 tons or more; and he was the owner of considerable property in his native Shropshire.[5] But the Newfoundland Company and the East Indian Company were apparently the only extra-European ventures in which he invested. His younger brother, Humphrey, was far less cautious; there was hardly a trading venture of the period with which his name was not linked. A Haberdasher and a Merchant Adventurer, Humphrey Slany traded to Spain, the Atlantic islands, the Levant, Barbary, and Guinea; in the latter place he and his associates established a thriving trade some years before the incorporation of the Guinea Company. An eminent member of the Virginia and Bermuda companies, in 1623 he was among those judged suitable for the governorship of the second organization.[6] The Freeman brothers adventured jointly in a number of overseas undertakings, the Virginia and East India companies among others, but Ralph's enterprises ranged the wider. Besides engaging in the more usual traffic to western Europe and the Levant, he held the monopoly of the Greenland whale fishery. At various times he served on committees of the East India and North-West

3 For the careers of the Bristol subscribers, see especially A. B. Beavan, *Bristol Lists, Municipal and Miscellaneous* (Bristol, 1899); P. V. McGrath, ed., *Records Relating to the City of Bristol in the Seventeenth Century* (Bristol Record Society, 1952), and the same editor's *Merchants and Merchandise in Seventeenth-Century Bristol* (Bristol Record Society, 1955); J. Latimer, *The History of the Society of Merchant Venturers of the City of Bristol* (Bristol, 1903), and the same author's *The Annals of Bristol in the Seventeenth Century* (Bristol, 1900). See also the Bristol port books (PRO E 190), for the early seventeenth century.
4 John Guy to Sir Percival Willoughby from Newfoundland, 6 Oct. 1610, NU, Middleton MS Mi x 1/2; S. Purchas, *Hakluytus Posthumus; or Purchas his Pilgrimes* (20 vols., Glasgow, 1905-1907), XIX, 405.
5 C. M. Clode, *The Early History of the Guild of Merchant Taylors* (2 vols., London, 1888), II, 345; PRO, Signet Office Docquet Book, Ind. 6804.
6 A. Friis, *Alderman Cockayne's Project and the Cloth Trade* (London, 1927), p. 100; PRO, HCA 13/42: 22 Oct. 1613, Lancelot Fisher; 18 Jan. 1613/14, William Cane; J. Blake, "The English Guinea Company, 1618-1660," *Belfast Natural History and Philosophical Society*, 2nd ser., III, pt. 1 (1945-6), 14-27; *APC 1616-1617*, pp. 105, 181-2, 263; A. Brown, *The Genesis of the United States* (2 vols., Boston, 1890), II, 1004; S. M. Kingsbury, ed., *Records of the Virginia Company of London* (4 vols., Washington, 1906-35), IV, 91.

Passage companies, as well as on the Virginia Commission of 1624. By 1620 he was confident enough and wealthy enough to assume, in return for a payment of some £ 12,000, all the assets and liabilities of the Muscovy Company. A member and one-time master of the Clothworkers' guild, Ralph Freeman had been alderman and sheriff of the city of London, and at his death in 1634 he held the office of lord mayor and was about to be knighted.[7] William, his elder brother, although civically less prominent, was nevertheless a highly successful merchant. One of the foremost Merchant Adventurers of the early years of the century, then an exporter of tin on a large scale, in 1611 he and a fellow member of the Haberdashers' Company took over financial responsibility for the whole of that company's share in the London-derry plantation.[8]

Nor were the other London subscribers obscure men. Among their number were some of the foremost cloth exporters of the day: bold, imaginative men who traded to the limits of the known world. Many invested in the proliferation of new or revived companies for overseas trade; the rolls of the Spanish, French, Muscovy, Levant, Virginia, and East India companies contain their names. Officers and bene-factors of their livery companies, aldermen and sheriffs of the City, endowers of scholarships and of charities, they stood at the heart of London's commercial life. Reflected in the Newfoundland Company's membership too was the intimacy of merchant society; here were kinsmen, men related by marriage, close friends, and business associates in other very different projects. And these personal connections were not limited to London but linked the merchant communities of London and Bristol.[9]

Such were the men who made up the majority of the subscribers to the New-foundland Company: practical businessmen, with long experience of judging a promising investment. Although none of the London merchants is known to have participated in the fishery before 1610, they could hardly have been ignorant of the prosperous state of that trade. Their contracts with the west-country and with those of their fellow Londoners who were familiar with the Newfoundland trade, together with their own knowledge of the Mediterranean markets, would all go to convince them that here was an industry ready for greater capital investment, and one that might possibly compensate for the decline in certain of their traditional trades. The establishment of a chartered company was therefore the obvious step if they were to secure a favourable position in the industry.

If the merchant investors hoped to have a monopoly written into their charter, they were wise enough not to ask for it in the petition for a grant of incorporation

7 CSP Col., East Indies, 1513-1616, nos 256, 417, 448, 616, 742; Trinity House Transactions, 1609-25, f 64; Brown, Genesis, II, 893; Friis, Alderman Cockayne's Project, p. 56n.; Memorial of Ralph Freeman, nd, Guildhall, Noble Collection, c 78; Thomas Girtin, The Golden Ram (London, 1958), p. 326.
8 Friis, Alderman Cockayne's Project, p. 101; T. W. Moody, The Londonderry Plantation, 1609-1641 (Belfast, 1939), p. 92.
9 For example, John Slany's will included bequests to three members of the Newfoundland Company, apart from his brother Humphrey: his "brother" (in the Merchant Taylors Company?), Thomas Langton who was also a kinsman of John Langton, a Bristol subscriber; Richard Holworthy of Bristol; and Humphrey Spencer of London. Will dated 17 Aug. 1631, Somerset House, Prerogative Court of Canterbury, 42 Audley.

which they presented to the Privy Council in February 1610.[10] They chose in politic fashion to stress the urgency of preventing "anie forraine Prince or State" from establishing a Newfoundland colony first, "whereby our nation shoulde be debarred from the quiet enioying of the saide harbours & fishing, the losse, and preiudice thereby, woulde be of more Consequence then now Can be imagined."[11] To buttress this argument, they dwelt on the greater security which would be given to the fishing industry, and on the increased revenue from trade which might be expected to result. They hoped also to produce naval stores, trade with the natives for furs, discover iron and copper, and provide a halfway base for ships voyaging to Virginia. More significant than the content of this document was the fact that the Privy Council chose to refer it to Trinity House, the one official organization which might claim to represent the interests of the hundreds of individual small fishermen. The council of Trinity House returned their somewhat unenthusiastic approval, "prouided always that thereby the freedome of Fishing which nowe we enjoy may not be altered."[12] Evidently the Privy Council had felt it necessary to sound the opinions of the fishing interests, and these in turn had shown themselves suspicious of the company's motives. When the patent was sealed, great emphasis was placed on the fact that the fishery was to remain completely open to both English and foreign fishermen:

we doe by theis presentes expresse and declare that there be saved and reserved vnto all manner of persons of what nation soever, and also to all and everie our loueing Subiectes which doe at this present or hereafter shall trade or voiag to the partes aforesaid for Fishing all and singuler liberties powers easementes and all other benifitt whatsoever as well concerning their said Fishing as all circumstances and incidentes therevnto in as large and ample manner as they haue heretofore vsed and enioyed the same, without anye ympeachment disturbance or exaccion, any thing in theis presentes to the contrarie notwithstanding.

Yet clearly settlement could not help but give the company certain advantages in the fishery. Residents would have the prior occupation of the best fishing places, which had previously gone to the first ship to arrive in each harbour; equally, colonists would be able to take advantage of a longer fishing season and to get their catch off to market earlier. Nor did the company's plans simply envisage one official colony. Instead, it was intended to divide the land into lots, to be made available to individual subscribers and developed by them at their own expense. Could a chain of settlement be established along the eastern coast of the Avalon peninsula, the area most popular with English fishermen, then the company might come near to establishing a *de facto* monopoly, no matter what the patent might say. And, could they once gain control of the fishery, then the carrying trade in fish to the Mediterranean – with its rich rewards of wines and fruits, spices and coin – would be theirs too. The whole question of whether England's carrying trade in general should be open to

10 Trinity House Transactions, 1609-25, ff 1, 1ᵛ; this is the only surviving copy.
11 The document mentions an attempt by the French to winter in Newfoundland about the year 1580; perhaps a garbled version of the two La Roche ventures.
12 Reply of the council of Trinity House, 24 Feb. 1609/10. Trinity House Transactions, 1609-25, f 1ᵛ.

all comers or managed through chartered companies was one of the most contro-
versial economic issues of the day, with the right of the west-country fishermen to
transport their catch directly to the Mediterranean being a central point of dispute.
Perhaps the formation of the Newfoundland Company was a part of this debate;
perhaps the merchant members of the company saw the venture as a step towards
taking control of the existing trade. We cannot be certain. Certain it is, however,
that the trend in economic thought was towards regulated trade, and that adventurers of the seventeenth century were nothing if not sanguine of the outcome of
even their wildest speculations.

If such perhaps were the aspirations of the merchants, what did the more socially
prominent subscribers to the company expect in return for their investment? Members within the court circle were few but distinguished. Heading the list came
Henry Howard, earl of Northampton and lord privy seal, followed by Sir Francis
Bacon, then solicitor general. Sir Lawrence Tanfield, chief baron of the exchequer, Sir John Dodridge, principal sergeant-at-law, Sir Daniel Dun, sometime master
of the requests, and Sir Walter Cope, soon to be master of the wards. Their names
are to be found in the subscription lists of many of the trading companies which
nonmerchants could join. Overseas investment was of course the fashion. England
hummed with travellers' tales of exotic goods and fabulous profits, and "all the liquid
world was one extended Thames." But at least in Northampton, Bacon, and Cope,
the Newfoundland Company had more than mere followers of fashion, for these
men were practical and persistent supporters of the expansion of England's trade.
Their genuine concern may well have led them to take a more active role in the
project than the simple lending of their names. Even so the story that Francis Bacon
persuaded James I to grant the company a considerable subsidy is not likely to be
true. English monarchs were not yet sufficiently concerned about overseas colonies
to support them financially and in 1621 the colony's first governor, John Guy,
would grumble that "the plantation of the Newfoundland never had penny help,
but from the adventurers' purses, nor ever had any lotteries."[13]

The gentry members could not, however, afford to be as disinterested as the
courtiers. To them such speculations were not primarily a means of furthering their
country's economic growth, but of bettering their personal fortunes and that rapidly. For, wrote the ever-pessimistic Sir John Oglander, "it is impossible for a mere
country gentleman ever to grow rich or raise his house. He must have some other
vocation with his inheritance ... If he hath no other vocation, let him get a ship and
judiciously manage her ... By only following the plough he may keep his word
and be upright, but will never increase his fortune."[14] The majority of the gentlemen investors in the Newfoundland Company had already taken Oglander's advice.
Two had found themselves a profession, for both Robert Kirkham of Middlesex
and Simon Stone, the third son of a Sussex gentleman, had passed from Oxford to
the Inns of Court;[15] and lawyers, from the time of the elder Richard Hakluyt, had

13 Stock, *Proceedings and Debates*, I, 55. The story of Bacon's involvement seems to originate
with Prowse, *History of Newfoundland*, p. 93, where it is not documented.
14 As quoted in H. R. Trevor-Roper, *Men and Events: Historical Essays* (New York, 1957),
pp. 199-200.
15 Joseph Foster, *Alumni Oxonienses, 1500-1714* (4 vols., Oxford, 1891-92), II, 858; IV, 1428.

been intimately connected with England's overseas expansion. Kirkham later invested in the East India Company,[16] but Stone is not known to have interested himself in any other such enterprise. Another gentleman member, Philip Gifford, was probably drawn into the company through his father-in-law, William Turner, one of the London merchant subscribers to the Newfoundland Company and also a member of the Salters' guild and of the East India Company, as well as a Merchant Adventurer, and an incorporator of the Virginia Company. In 1620 Gifford himself became a member of the Virginia Company when he received one of the Earl of Southampton's personal shares.[17] Two other subscribers described in the patent as gentlemen were the cousins of the same name: John Weld of Middlesex and John Weld of Shropshire. John Weld of Middlesex, the older of the two and the more prominent, would perhaps be more accurately described as a merchant who had invested heavily in land. He participated in most of the leading ventures of the day: the Virginia, East India, Somers Island, and the Levant companies. His younger cousin, later Sir John and town clerk of London, was a Shropshire neighbour of the Slanys, whose sister married Humphrey Slany, and it was probably through this connection that he entered the company.[18]

But of all the gentlemen subscribers the most interesting, because we know most about his motives, is Sir Percival Willoughby. A member of the Kentish branch of Willoughby d'Eresby and a distant cousin of the pioneer Arctic explorer, Sir Hugh Willoughby, Sir Percival made his first sortie into overseas investment when he joined the Newfoundland Company, being named first in the list of council members. He followed it two years later with a subscription to the Virginia Company with which, however, he was never particularly concerned.[19] But his involvement with the Newfoundland scheme persisted for the extraordinarily long period of twenty-one years.

Despite the survival of a substantial group of letters and papers, official and private, on his connection with the company,[20] we do not know exactly how he was drawn into the venture. Most probably it was through his own ties with John Slany to whom he was heavily in debt.[21] In fact, the story of Willoughby's life is one of continuous financial problems which he struggled in vain to resolve. By his marriage to Bridget, daughter and heiress to his kinsman, Sir Francis Willoughby of Wollaton, Nottinghamshire, he inherited extensive but impoverished estates to add to his own smaller patrimony in Kent. The inheritance brought him also a legacy of debts and lawsuits, costing him, so a later member of the family reckoned, more than £38,000 and causing him to come perilously close to being committed to the Fleet prison for debtors.[22] The early years of the century Willoughby, then

16 CSP Col., East Indies, 1513-1616, no 702.
17 J. J. Howard and J. L. Chester, eds., The Visitations of London, Anno Domini 1633, 1634, and 1635 (Harleian Society, 1883), p. 353; CSP Col., East Indies, 1513-1616, nos 256, 281, 288; Friis, Alderman Cockayne's Project, p. 304n.; Kingsbury, Records of the Virginia Company, III, 62.
18 Brown, Genesis, II, 1044; Howard, Visitation of London, p. 336.
19 Brown, Genesis, II, 1053.
20 NU, Middleton MSS Mi x 1/1-66; the papers cover the years 1610-31.
21 See NU, Middleton MSS 1/1/9; 2/713/42; 5/162/56, 58, 62.
22 Cassandra Willoughby, "An account of the Willoughbys of Wollaton," 1702, NU, Middleton MS Mi LM 27, f 159; and by the same author when Cassandra Brydges, duchess of Chandos,

a member of parliament, spent mainly in London where he became well acquainted with the moneylenders, usually merchants, who would willingly advance loans on good security such as land. Such may have been his entry into City circles.

Much of Willoughby's income came from coal mining, a long-standing family interest; over half the total output of the Nottinghamshire coal fields was mined at the Wollaton pits alone. His father-in-law, Sir Francis, "as much industrial magnate and entrepreneur as ... land-owner," had also financed iron works and experimented with the manufacture of glass and the growing of woad at Wollaton.[23] None of these projects, except the mining of coal, had been particularly rewarding, and any profits had been speedily devoured by Sir Francis' wild extravagance in building Wollaton Hall, one of the most impressive manor houses of the late Tudor period. But their modest success must have convinced Percival Willoughby that only by taking chances could he hope to rescue himself from financial disaster; merely "following the plough" for him meant ruin.

At home he plunged into a multitude of speculative schemes spanning the midland counties of England – iron works in Warwickshire and Derbyshire, coal pits in Nottinghamshire, Worcestershire, and Staffordshire, besides the less serious experiments at Wollaton. As coal production in the Nottingham area threatened to glut the local market, he and a group of associates planned to ship coal to London, in competition with the old-established supply from Newcastle.[24] Overly ambitious and ill-considered, the scheme was an expensive failure, but one that well illustrates the bold and desperate nature of Willoughby's business ventures.

Investment in Newfoundland may then have been an overseas extension of Sir Percival's domestic speculations. Both iron and copper had long been rumoured as being among the resources of Newfoundland, and Edward Hayes had added a possibility of silver. The officers of the Newfoundland Company certainly believed that exploitable minerals might be found within their grant of land. Willoughby, buoyed up by optimistic private reports, was sure that iron would be mined on Bell Island in Conception Bay.[25] His expectations would indeed be realized – more than three hundred years later. Any hopes of quick profits must have faded quite early in the colony's history, but Sir Percival nursed his dream for twenty-one years with apparently nothing to show for it – a man of remarkable perseverance, or perhaps just a compulsive and desperate speculator who had adventured too much to dare to withdraw and acknowledge his failure.

And so there came together in the Newfoundland Company a varied group of subscribers, inspired by motives equally diverse. But, if the merchants were interested in the fishery, the courtiers in England's commercial development, and Willoughby at least in his personal fortune, this is not to say that the attempt at settlement was not genuine, or that there was no interest in the island itself. The documents, and particularly the journals of the winter weather which were kept at the

The Continuation of the History of the Willoughby Family, ed. A. C. Wood (Nottingham, 1958), p. 39.
23 A. C. Wood, A History of Nottinghamshire (Nottingham, 1947), pp. 148, 149.
24 See R. S. Smith, "Huntingdon Beaumont: Adventurer in Coal Mines," Renaissance and Modern Studies, I (1957), 115-53.
25 Trinity House Transactions, 1609-25, f I; J. Guy to Willoughby from Newfoundland, 10 Aug. 1610; Crout to Willoughby from Newfoundland, Aug. [1613]; A Report on Bell Island, [1613]; J. Slany to Willoughby, 5 Feb. 1615/16, NU, Middleton MSS Mi x 1/2, 24, 25, 31.

company's command during the first years,[26] show a real interest in Newfoundland as a possible residence for Englishmen. The company colony was not merely a fishing station, for the company could not afford to dissipate whatever profits it might make by fishing on maintaining an entirely uneconomic colony. The two activities had to complement one another, and there was from the very beginning an attempt to make the colony self-sufficient if not actually profitable.

With an adequate number of subscriptions promised and the petition for incorporation presented to and approved by the Privy Council, the charter of the Newfoundland Company received the royal seal on 2 May 1610. In the preamble, England's right to the island was based on the fact that her subjects had been engaged in the fishery for more than fifty years, during which time the island had remained uninhabited. The patent discounted the presence of native inhabitants as had the petition of February 1610. Interestingly enough no claim to sovereignty was presumed from the right of first discovery, or from Sir Humphrey Gilbert's actions in 1583. The company was awarded the whole island, but particular stress was placed upon the area of the Avalon peninsula between Cape Bonavista and St. Mary's Bay. The usual powers, rights and privileges were granted, and in general the terms of the charter were very similar to those of the second Virginia charter of 1609.[27] Under the charter a council of twelve, all of whom had to reside in London, was appointed with the responsibility of conducting the day-to-day business of the company, and of summoning a general assembly when necessary. The council was composed of Sir Percival Willoughby, John Slany, the treasurer, and two John Welds, and eight London merchants: Humphrey Slany, John Stockley, William Turner, William Jones, Thomas Juxon, Thomas Jones, Ralph Freeman, and Richard Fishbourne.[28]

Evidently the company was set up on a joint-stock basis initially. The original shares cost £25,[29] which gave the campany a starting capital of at least £1,200 and more if, as seems likely, subscribers were allowed to buy more than one share. Once the £25 had been paid, each shareholder had the right to participate in the government of the company through the general assembly, a state of affairs which caused some alarm in August 1610 when it was discovered that certain of the Bristol members had paid for only half their share.[30] The fear was expressed that the Bristollians who wished their names to be "sett down in in [sic] the booke heare kept as Free as wee of london ... consideringe ther many voices might heare prevaile against the government of the busyness as it is nowgh established," and hints at a jealousy between the two cities which augured ill for the success of the partnership. As only ten of the original forty-eight shareholders were Bristol men, this apprehension is difficult to understand, unless new members had already been admitted.

26 Only that for the winter of 1612-13 has survived in full, NU, Middleton MS Mi x 1/66; Purchas had copies of those for 1610-11 and 1611-12 which he summarized very briefly, *Pilgrimes*, XIX, 405.
27 Carr, *Select Charters*, pp. 51-62, indicates the exact points of similarity.
28 The William Jones who joined the company was almost certainly the Trinity House warden who was among those approving the company's petition of incorporation.
29 See the notebook of company records, 1610-13, which is among the Willoughby Papers, NU, Middleton MS Mi x 1/1, ff 15ᵛ-16.
30 *Ibid.*

By February 1612 the value of a share had risen to £40, which appears to have been both par and market value,[31] the increase probably representing calls made on the shares and suggesting that further capital amounting to at least £720 had been raised. By this time members could certainly hold more than one share;[32] perhaps they had been able to do so all along, for otherwise the initial capital would have been very small. The Virginia Company, though admittedly operating on a much larger scale, estimated the cost of one of its operations at £10,000.[33] Unfortunately the uncertainty on this point makes it impossible to calculate the total capital available to the Newfoundland Company. By 1616 the market value of a share was £70;[34] there is no evidence on their price after that. Nor is it entirely clear whether this was to be a permanent or a terminable joint-stock. The Willoughby Papers contain references to company voyages, but by the 1620s at least the company apparently allowed individual fishing voyages. This development may well have followed the realization that shared profits were negligible, if indeed there were any at all. Willoughby constantly complained of the amount of money he had invested "as it was required and never yet received pennye."[35]

THE YEARS OF OPTIMISM, 1610-13

But the venture began realistically enough. By July 1610 the newly appointed governor, John Guy, and his thirty-nine colonists had sailed from Bristol,[36] furnished with a detailed and practical set of instructions.[37] The building of a fortified habitation on a healthy site was to be combined with fishing, making salt, and searching for minerals. With remarkable foresight the company had already bought a cargo of fish which the settlers were to send home in the ship in which they had travelled, together with any samples of iron ore that could be found before the ship sailed. Otherwise such ore, together with samples of sarsaparilla, ashes for making glass and soap, and any fish and oil that the colonists might make that summer and

---

31 Deed of sale of shares in the Newfoundland Company by William Lewis of Bristol to the company, 14 Feb. 1611/12, NU, Middleton MS Mi x 1/4. For a company to repurchase its own shares was an unusual procedure, cf T. S. Willan, *The Early History of the Russia Company, 1553-1603* (Manchester, 1956), p. 43. An exception may have been made because the company had assured buyers, the shares being sold the following day to Thomas Cowper and Henry Crout, both associates of Willoughby, NU, Middleton MS Mi x 1/5.

32 *Ibid.*, Mi x 1/4.

33 C. M. Andrews, *The Colonial Period of American History* (4 vols., New Haven, 1934-8), I, 106.

34 Deed of sale of a half share in the Newfoundland Company by John Browne to Edward Willoughby, Sept. 1616, NU, Middleton MS Mi x 1/40.

35 Willoughby to J. Slany, [1616], *ibid.*, Mi x 1/32.

36 Most secondary sources follow Latimer, *Seventeenth-Century Annals*, p. 39, in saying that Guy left Bristol with 3 ships early in May and arrived in Newfoundland only 23 days later. A letter from Guy to Willoughby from Newfoundland, 10 Aug. 1610, NU, Middleton MS Mi x 1/2, proves these dates to be incorrect and shows that there was only one ship. The figure of 39 settlers is derived from a letter which Guy wrote to John Slany, 16 May 1611, printed in Purchas, *Pilgrimes*, XIX, 410-16.

37 "Instructions directed by the counsaile ... to Iohn Guy," 26 May 1610, Notebook, NU, Middleton MS Mi x 1/1, ff 12-14. These instructions were previously known only from the badly damaged version in BM, Cotton MSS, Otho E VIII, 3. There are a number of differences in the two versions, that in the Middleton Papers being longer and more detailed.

not need for their own provision could be sent back in the next ship. Cordial but not over intimate relations with the native population were counselled by the company, learning perhaps from the recent unhappy experiences of the Virginia colonists; and attempts should be made to learn the language and to teach the natives English, so that a fur trade after the French model could be established. A journal of events and of the weather between September and March was to be kept, a remarkably sensible provision when, because of their lack of experience, Englishmen were not even sure that they could survive a Newfoundland winter. Such a report would help the company to victual its colony, as well as to assess the possibilities of a successful and permanent settlement. That the company should require such a record suggests a more scientific approach to the problems of colonization than had been apparent in the first days of the Virginia enterprise.

The only other recommendation of special significance was that the charter should be read to the fishermen, if they appeared to "entertayne anye Ielouzies or Suspicions as though your plantation tended one [sic] there preiudice," to convince them of the continued freedom of the fishery. The company perhaps expected some opposition and this may have been the reason why the colonists did not leave England until July. When they arrived in Newfoundland some time in the following month, the fishermen were about to leave and, because the colonists had "no house built nor any settled habitation effected," John Guy decided not to call an assembly but to leave any announcement concerning his intentions until the following year, when the colony would be well established.[38] If he feared violence from the fishermen, who would have far outnumbered his handful of men, none was offered that year. Their hostility was aroused, however, and later the company would accuse them of burning the colonists' fishing stages and damaging their grist and saw mills.[39]

To John Guy the company gave supreme authority to govern as he saw fit. Only in the event of a capital offence had he to call on twelve of his companions to assist him in judgment; in dealing with lesser crimes he could ask for the advice of four others or not, as he chose. Elaborate provision was made for the succession:[40] John Guy was to be followed by his brother, Philip, and then by William Chatchmaid, although each of them had the right to name his own successor if he preferred. Should Chatchmaid die without naming anyone, the new governor was to be chosen by the remaining settlers.

In their instructions, as in their provisions for the colony's government, the Newfoundland Company showed such down-to-earth awareness of the problems ahead that it seems likely that they knew of the particular difficulties encountered by the Virginia settlers. Many of them, of course, had subscribed to the Virginia venture. That company's instructions to its colonists had dealt almost exclusively with the choice of a site;[41] even so, the lack of familiarity with the James River area had resulted in a poor choice. It was different in Newfoundland. John Guy had gone to

38 Guy to Willoughby, 10 Aug. 1610, NU, Middleton MS X 1/2.
39 PRO, CO 1/1, f 180.
40 "The comission direckted by the Counsaill to Iohn Guy For his government there in newfoundland," 26 May 1610, Notebook, NU, Middleton MS 1/1, ff 14-15ᵛ.
41 John Smith, *Travels and Works*, eds. E. Arber and A. G. Bradley (2 vols., Edinburgh, 1910), I, xxxiii-vii.

the island himself in 1608, had explored Conception Bay, and appears in 1610 to have had a very precise idea of where the settlement should be established. Of his decision he later wrote: [42]

we arrived (God be praised) all in safetie in the bay of Conception, in Newfoundland, in the harbour here called Cupperes coue; which is a branch of Sammon Coue, . . . This harbour is three leagues distant from Colliers bay to the Northeastward and is preferred by me to beginne our plantacion before the said Colliers bay, for the goodnes of the harbour the fruitfullnes of the soyle the largenes of the trees, and many other reasons.

Although he does not say so, Guy may also have been influenced by the fact that Conception Bay was less exposed than the coast south of St. John's and also a little removed from the main centres of the English fishery, where the settlers' presence might have been even more actively resented by the annual fishermen. Cupids Cove proved a wise choice. The harbour was reasonably well sheltered, with good supplies of fresh water and none of the health problems of the James River. Guy would be disappointed, however, in his hopes of its fertility, for Cupids is a region of slate, sandstone and siltstone capable of supporting only such crops as hay and root vegetables. But the only areas with more agricultural potential would have been the immediate vicinity of St. John's, which was too much frequented by fishermen, or St. George's Bay on the west coast, of which the English still knew very little.

Again in their advice on Indian relations, their choice of artisans rather than gentlemen as settlers, and their decision to entrust one man alone with the government, the company seems to have profited from the Virginia Company's mistakes. And the Newfoundland colonists reacted to their situation quite differently from their counterparts in Virginia. Thanks no doubt to John Guy's practical and positive leadership their industry was remarkable. Having built themselves temporary shelters, they took advantage of the mild weather to concentrate on cutting a cargo of merchantable timber for the ship in which they had come out. They searched too for other commodities such as turpentine and "frankincense," presumably gum from the black spruce which Guy hoped would make pitch. By October 1610 Guy had worked out a number of commercial projects for the company's consideration. Timber was an obvious export; pitch and tar might be manufactured. A glass house had already been set up and needed only more workmen to make it a practical proposition; Guy's correspondent, Sir Percival Willoughby, probably found this of particular interest because of his own experiments at Wollaton. Guy also had hopes that iron would be discovered on Bell Island. He had already procured samples of ore from the master of a fishing ship, which he sent home to be tested, the colony's own expert having deserted before they left England. Should iron not be found, then Guy proposed that ore be shipped from England and smelted at Newfoundland. Guy reckoned that iron was now so expensive in England that it could be produced more cheaply in Newfoundland, even allowing for freight costs of ten shillings a ton. The smelted iron could be used as ballast under fish which, being so light, required an extra-heavy ballast.

As for the fishery, Guy reported in the same letter:

42 NU, Middleton MS Mi x 1/2.

Here is a good beach and the fishinge neare, to be assured of a good place to fish and a beach, boats and stage may be worth more then one or tow hundreth poundes yearely ... , which the company may be assured of by the plantacion *because they shalbe sure to be first here every yeare to take what stage they shall haue need of for there own vse* [My italics].

This of course was precisely what the fishermen feared: the inherent contradiction between allowing settlement while insisting on the preservation of an absolutely free unrestricted fishery. Otherwise Guy envisaged the establishment of a triangular trade with La Rochelle in salt, fish, and timber. But he was over-optimistic, because of his lack of experience of winter conditions in Newfoundland, in thinking that three such voyages could be made in a year.

This first letter of Guy's was in fact a blend of hard-headed realism and excessive optimism. But to the company members back in London it would make comforting reading, especially when Guy assured them that by "husbandrie, fishinge, and trade by husbandrie and fishinge, the Colonie wilbe soone able to supporte it selfe and by the fruites of the earth, and cattle vndertakers and tennantes to take land of the Company wilbe in aboundance drawne hether." And the experiences of the first winter did not betray his hopes.[43] Unusually mild weather and only four deaths among the settlers must have encouraged all, whether in London or in Newfoundland. There are no indications that the colonists wanted for food as had the first Virginia settlers, or that they suffered seriously from scurvy as had Champlain's men at Sainte-Croix some six years earlier. The company had evidently kept the venture well within the scale which its resources allowed. And the health of those at Cupids Cove was undoubtedly helped by being able to work outdoors most of the time.

And work they did. By the beginning of December they had built themselves a house, a store room, and a work house, and had enclosed them all within some sort of palisade 120 feet long by 90 feet wide, which they fortified with three guns overlooking the harbour and one on either flank. During the course of the winter they built six fishing boats and a twelve-ton pinnace for use on coasting expeditions; they cleared land and planted seed; they made charcoal, constructed a forge, explored Conception Bay, and began work on a new and larger house. If Champlain was right in believing that inactivity encouraged scurvy, John Guy made sure his men would not suffer from it.

The tiny colony was relieved in the spring of 1611 by the arrival of three company ships which went on to fish. Guy sent some of his settlers home that summer, "for their owne good, and that the vnprofitable expense of vituals and wages might cease." With them he sent samples of charcoal and a hogshead of skins and furs. Guy had already decided to return home himself at the end of the season to report personally to the company. Before leaving, however, he issued a series of regulations for the conduct of the fishery, necessitated, he said, by the disorders and abuses practised by the visiting fishermen. These rules forbade the fishermen to obstruct

43 Reported by Guy in a letter to the company's council, 11 May 1611, Purchas, *Pilgrimes*, XIX, 410-16.

harbours, damage buildings, occupy unnecessary beach space or stages, alter the distinguishing marks on fishing boats, use another's boats without first advising the admiral of the harbour, burn the woods, or receive runaways from the colony.[44] How Guy thought that thirty-odd settlers might impose such orders upon the hundreds of fishermen scattered up and down the coasts of Newfoundland remains a mystery.

As his deputies Guy named his brother, Philip, and William Colston, also of Bristol, to whom fell the task of keeping the official winter journal. Purchas received a copy of this journal, but made the infuriating decision not to print it because he found it "very tedious."[45] Apparently the months passed uneventfully, and the weather was again kind. John Guy came back to Newfoundland early in 1612, bringing with him sixteen women settlers.[46] Shortly afterwards a second group of newcomers arrived, including Sir Percival Willoughby's son, Thomas, in the care of his agent, Henry Crout. Thomas was the third son, then aged about nineteen. Evidently the blackest of the sheep in a large and troublesome family – the youngest son later broke into Wollaton and removed all the silver – Thomas had angered his father to such an extent that he had been packed off to Newfoundland to reform. The nature of his misdemeanour is unknown, and his kinswoman, Cassandra Brydges, was evidently confusing the offence with the punishment when she believed that it was his making a voyage without parental consent.[47] But Thomas Willoughby had the distinction of being perhaps the first in the British empire's long line of remittance men.

Life as a pioneer was a sobering experience for Thomas who, among other trials, was thrown into an icy stream for neglecting to turn the drying fish. Writing home, he expressed suitably penitent sentiments and resolutions to "leaue aside idel vices which is not for my good" and become "a newe man."[48] He was allowed to go home in the late summer of 1613 but returned, or was sent back, three years later. For a brief spell in 1615 Thomas seems to have enjoyed his father's favour, for Sir Percival was then considering transferring the title of his land in Newfoundland to him and to one of his brothers.[49] But after 1616 nothing more is heard of Thomas Willoughby, either in Newfoundland or in the records of his family. In her history of the family, Cassandra Brydges presumed that he had died young but as, in 1631, his name was completely omitted from the family pedigree, it seems possible that he had been disowned.[50]

With Thomas Willoughby and Henry Crout travelled six youths sent out by Sir Percival as apprentices. Three of them would later claim that Sir Percival had

44 PRO, CO 1/1, f 125.
45 Purchas, *Pilgrimes*, XIX, 415, 416.
46 Bristol Record Office, MS Calendar 07831. This eighteenth-century calendar incorrectly gives the date of Guy's return as 1611 and is probably not a very reliable source. The presence of women in the island during the winter of 1612-13 is confirmed, however, by the journal kept by Henry Crout, NU, Middleton MS Mi x 1/66, f 16.
47 Brydges, *History of the Willoughby Family*, p. 41.
48 T. Willoughby to his father from Newfoundland, [Aug. 1612], NU, Middleton MS Mi x 1/16.
49 Draft indenture, 7 Feb. 1616/17, *ibid.*, Mi x 1/63.
50 See Brydges, *History of the Willoughby Family*, p. 41; *Visitations of Nottinghamshire, 1569, 1614, and 1631* ed. G. W. Marshall (Harleian Society, 1871), p. 185.

promised them each fifty acres of land at the end of five years' service, or £30 if they did not like the country. But after little more than three months in Newfoundland, "findinge our vseage far woorse then we expected our labour verie much and harde and with all beinge dubtful of the goodnes of our land," they announced their refusal to serve any longer and their desire to return home at the end of the summer.[51] One of the grumblers, Edward Garton, would never return to England; he died at Cupids Cove that winter. Another of Willoughby's apprentices was perhaps more fortunate; he proved so unsatisfactory that John Guy sent him home just a month after his arrival.[52] The whole system of apprenticeship came under fire from Henry Crout who found the boys quick to "guie an evill report of the country, they will rather filtche and steall at home then they will take any paines hear." Crout believed that it would be very little more expensive to bring out only trained artisans.[53]

Sir Percival also sent out older men to whom he had allotted particular duties: a surveyor called Olney who was to survey the land Willoughby expected to receive from the company; and Bartholomew Pearson who came from the Wollaton estate and whose function seems to have been to assess the agricultural potential of the island. But, like the apprentices, Pearson was unimpressed. The high land, he reported, was rocky and barren, the low ground permanently flooded, and the livestock refused to eat the grass. Only for the island's wild life did he show any enthusiasm, for he was a keen hunter and some of the furs he sent back to Willoughby. Soon Pearson too was asking to come home, "for I haue spent my time I cannot tell how auailinge mee nothinge at all." By 1613 he had got his way.[54]

Only from Henry Crout, his general agent and guardian of Thomas, can Sir Percival have received any comfort as to the soundness of his investment; Crout also had a stake in the colony, having purchased a half share in February 1612.[55] It was Crout's responsibility to explore the lot of land which Willoughby hope to secure from the company, and to report on the likelihood of mineral deposits. Even before he had the opportunity to visit the area himself, Crout relayed to his employer information gleaned from fishermen, who told of tracts of good open land, woods frequented by deer, and harbours teeming with fish. And, according to Crout, he and John Guy had found iron only ten or twelve miles from Renewse, a good augury of the island's mineral wealth.[56]

The lot in which Willoughby was interested comprised that portion of the peninsula between Conception and Trinity bays which lies north of a line drawn from Carbonear to Hearts Content – an area roughly thirty-five miles long and fifteen miles across at the widest point.[57] It included also Baccalieu Island, but not Bell Island for which Willoughby schemed and pleaded for years without success. Lots

51 Thomas Cowper, Edward Garton, and John Harrington to Willoughby from Newfoundland, 23 Aug. 1612 NU, Middleton MS Mi x 1/14.
52 J. Guy to Willoughby from Cupids Cove, 17 June 1612; Journal, ibid., Mi x 1/7, 66.
53 Crout to Willoughby from Cupids Cove, 8 Sept. 1612, ibid., Mi x 1/20.
54 Pearson to Willoughby from Newfoundland, 17 Aug. 1612 and 2 April 1613, ibid., Mi x 1/11, 21.
55 Ibid., Mi x 1/5.
56 Crout to Willoughby from Renewse, 4 Aug. 1612 and from Cupids Cove, 27 Aug. 1612, ibid., Mi x 1/10, 15.
57 Draft indenture, 7 Feb. 1616/17, ibid., Mi x 1/63.

were evidently awarded partly on the basis of a tender and partly according to the size of the shareholder's investment in the company. The value of Willoughby's tender is not known, but by 1626 he estimated that his lot had, together with his general expenses, cost him more than £500.[58] His intention was that, as soon as possible, his own men should leave the company plantation and develop his Trinity Bay lot. But to begin with Crout, Thomas Willoughby, and the rest joined the other settlers under Guy's authority at Cupids Cove.

The summer of 1612 would in fact prove the most trying time yet for the young colony, for the whole island was terrorized by the notorious pirate Peter Easton. Easton's violence was in fact directed against the fishermen rather than the colonists, although one settler was accidentally shot; and Guy, in return for a couple of the colony's pigs, seems to have persuaded Easton to leave his settlers alone.[59] But the indirect harm that Easton did to the settlement of Newfoundland was perhaps more serious than a raid on Cupids would have been. The threat of his presence caused the indefinite postponement of the company's plans to establish a second settlement at Renewse that year. For when Easton came, Guy withdrew all his men to Cupids and removed the livestock which had been landed at Renewse in readiness for the new colony. At Cupids Cove Guy set his men to build a fort, lest the pirates come again the next year; he evidently believed, as did Henry Crout, that it was more "requisitt that the generall and cheefest place should be made strounge for the plantacion first before any other be taken in hand."[60] No second official settlement was ever made and by 1616 the company had transferred Renewse and the surrounding land to Sir William Vaughan.[61] The Newfoundland Company had suffered the first severe setback in its plan to extend its control of the Avalon peninsula and so, perhaps, of the fishery.

Despite Easton's depradations the company fishing ships made successful voyages. In September 1612 John Slany reported to Sir Percival Willoughby that the ships had returned with good cargoes, and that fish was likely to fetch a good price that year because of the failure of the North Sea fishery. Slany intended to store the fish until the Lent market when the price should be even higher.[62] But other Newfoundland fishermen, whether English or continental, had not been so lucky. When Easton sailed south to meet the Spanish treasure ships coming from central America, he left behind him a ravaged fleet. In Harbour Grace alone he took two ships, 100 men, and provisions from every ship there; at St. John's he plundered thirty English ships and despatched his fleet to do the same up and down the coast. Easton planned by the end of the season to have increased his crews to a 1000 men, and in all he was accused of having inflicted £20,400's worth of damage.[63] So much so

58 Willoughby to J. Slany, [Feb. 1626], *ibid.*, Mi x 1/56.
59 Purchas, *Pilgrimes*, XIX, 417; Richard Holworthy to J. Slany, 18 Aug. 1612; Crout to Willoughby from Cupids Cove, 10 April 1613, NU, Middleton MSS Mi x 1/12, 23.
60 J. Slany to Willoughby, 17 July 1612; Holworthy to J. Slany, 18 Aug. 1612; Crout to Willoughby from Cupids Cove, 20 Aug. 1612 and 27 Aug. 1612; J. Slany to Willoughby, 3 Sept. 1612; Crout to Willoughby from Cupids Cove, 10 April 1613, NU, Middleton MSS Mi x 1/8, 12, 13, 15, 18, 23.
61 See below, chapter v.
62 J. Slany to Willoughby, 3 Sept. 1612, NU, Middleton MS Mi x 1/18.
63 Holworthy to Slany, 18 Aug. 1612, *ibid.*, Mi x 1/12; Purchas, *Pilgrimes*, XIX, 417; PRO, CO 1/1, f 179. For details of Easton's attacks on foreign fishermen, see PRO, Privy Council Registers,

that John Slany believed that the west-countrymen would ask the Privy Council for protection at Newfoundland the following year. But if they did, the company was not prepared to share the costs for, said Slany, had the fishermen

bin Ruled by master Guy and sett vppon the pirottes att ther Comminge in they might esely haue taken them beeinge soe weke as they were their men sicke and ther shipps soe leake skant able to swym but now they ar stronge Agen. the chef pirat gooes with his Gard and a noyse of trumpettes and his sett of vialles.[64]

Willoughby approved the idea of requesting government help, and suggested that the Earl of Northampton – the most influential member of the company – be approached to push the scheme at court. But the fishermen apparently took no action, and it was left to the company to ask the Privy Council for a commission to surpress piracy, which they received in July 1613.[65]

Easton had further upset the company's plans by delaying a voyage of exploration which Guy had planned that summer, with the intention of making contact with the Beothuck Indians of Trinity Bay.[66] Not until October could Guy leave Cupids Cove, and then he took with him thirteen men in the pinnace, including Henry Crout, and five in a shallop, among them Bartholomew Pearson.[67] On 7 October 1612 the two boats left Cupids Cove and a fortnight later reached the south side of Trinity Bay, which they proceeded to explore with some care, penetrating into a number of harbours, and noting such things as geographical features, the fertility of the land, and the presence of wild life. In the inlet which they christened Savage Harbour (probably Dildo Arm), they found the first evidence of Indian occupation, but the inhabitants had fled. They probed various harbours at the head of Trinity Bay, hoping to find a passage through to Placentia Bay, and going ashore at several places to inspect the land. Not until they reached Bull Arm on 7 November did Guy's party finally make contact with the Beothucks; presumably the first contact the colonists had ever had with the Indians who seem to have deserted Conception Bay well before this time. Both John Guy and Henry Crout supply charming descriptions of the encounter, the exchange of gifts, the shared meal. They met only once; but the Beothucks left skins – beaver and sable – mounted on poles when they departed. The English did not at first grasp the significance of the action but then, realizing that the Beothucks wished to trade, they took some of the pelts, leaving a hatchet, a knife, and some needles in exchange. The incident suggests that the Beothucks were more accustomed to the fur trade, presumably with the French, than were the English.

PC 2/27, f 41ᵛ; PRO, HCA Examinations, Oyer and Terminer, HCA 1/4, f 314; HCA 13/42: 19 Nov. 1612, Isebrande Dirrickson; HCA 14/42, nos 18, 47.

64 J. Slany to Willoughby, 3 Sept. 1612, NU, Middleton MS Mi x 1/18.
65 Willoughby to J. Slany, [Sept. 1612]; ibid., Mi x 1/19; PRO, PC 2/29, f 47.
66 Crout to Willoughby from Cupids Cove, 20 Aug. 1612, NU, Middleton MS Mi x 1/13.
67 Previously the only known account of this voyage has been that written by John Guy himself, Lambeth Palace MS 250, ff 406-12ᵛ, printed in C. I. A. Ritchie, ed., The New World (for the Lambeth Palace Library, 1957), pp. 52-64, and summarized in Purchas, Pilgrimes, XIX, 419-24. Guy's narrative is now supplemented by descriptive letters from Crout and Pearson to Willoughby, NU, Middleton MSS Mi x 1/23 and 59 (in fact one letter), Mi x 1/21; and by the fullest version of all in Henry Crout's journal for the winter of 1612-13, ibid., Mi x 1/66.

Now, as the weather began to worsen, the group quitted the house which they had begun to build on an island in Bull Arm and set out on their eventful return journey. At Green Bay the shallop was wrecked; its crew of five walked to Carbonear where they found a fishing boat and so reached Cupids. Those in the pinnace had only a slightly less adventurous voyage for, deceived by the strength of the current, they were carried south to Cape St. Francis when they believed themselves to be near Baccalieu Island. They sailed on as far south as Fermeuse before realizing what had happened. With some difficulty Guy and his men made their way north, anchoring at Torbay and Bell Island, before finally regaining Cupids Cove on 25 November, two days after the crew of the shallop. There is no further evidence of contact between the Beothucks and the settlers although, more than twenty years later, Sir David Kirke alleged that the two groups had arranged to meet again in 1613, but that the Indians were shot at by some fishermen and fled before the colonists arrived. The Beothucks, confusing the fishermen with those whom they had come to meet, retired deep into the woods and from that time did whatever harm they could to Europeans.[68]

Now the colony of sixty-two people settled down for its third winter. Thanks to the journal kept by Henry Crout – the only one of three such documents that has survived – we have an extremely full account of events from September 1612 to May of the following year.[69] The journal does not always make the most exciting reading, being primarily a day-by-day record of the weather such as the company had instructed should be kept. The entry for Christmas Day, for example, reads:

in the morninge the winde at north north east freesing verie hard and exstreeme all the daie vntill night but the sune Shining verie faire and clear vntill night the wind still at north east verie cold at night the winde verie calme vntill day but freessing hard all night.

Every day Crout made similar entries, noting wind direction, rain or snowfall, periods of sunshine, and the severity of frost. The terms used are highly subjective: we have no way of knowing what was Crout's standard in distinguishing between "faire sunshininge" and "verie fair sunshininge," between "myld weather" and "something myld weather." Nevertheless Crout was sufficiently conscientious for his journal to reveal the trends of the weather and to make this, despite its limitations, an invaluable document.

The colonists' main occupation that winter, according to Crout, was trapping and hunting; the pelts of foxes, sables, and muskrats all went into the company's stores. In January a group set out overland for Trinity Bay but thick snow forced them to return after two days. The weather was changeable – later that same month Crout and Thomas Willoughby managed to reach Brigus and men were able to work in the woods – but on the whole this winter seems to have been more severe than the previous two. For the first time the colony suffered seriously from scurvy: by mid-February twenty-two people were sick although only eight deaths were recorded. On 27 March, however, the first English child born in Newfoundland was delivered to the wife of a settler, Nicholas Guy. There was a surgeon at Cupids

68 PRO, CO 1/10, ff 112ᵛ-13.
69 NU, Middleton MS Mi x 1/66. Unless otherwise noted, the following account of the events of the winter is taken from this journal.

Cove, and various remedies were tried against scurvy of which turnips, dug up when the snow melted, proved most effective. Although food supplies seem to have been adequate, by January the settlers were forced, much to their disgust, to dilute their beer with three parts of water; two of them would later claim that the death of Edward Garton was caused by hard work and too "much drinking of water in the winter."[70] By April of 1613 stocks of shoes and clothing were also very low. The lakes near the plantation froze at times, but fresh water was usually available. The harbour at Cupids was also frozen over for short periods in February and March, and was once completely blocked when "a verie hudg great Iland of ice" floated in. The hard winter caused the deaths of most of the settlers' livestock: seventy goats besides pigs and cattle were lost mainly because of lack of fodder.[71]

The first of the company's relief ships reached Cupids Cove on 29 March, bringing letters and more apprentices; others soon followed and then dispersed to fish at Ferryland, St. John's, Harbour Grace, and Bell Island. But the coming of spring found the colonists in low spirits which were not helped by the sudden departure of their governor in April. The major journey of exploration which Guy had planned had to be postponed and, when Henry Crout later took a small party to Trinity Bay, they failed to make contact with the Beothucks. The letters written to Willoughby that spring and summer, even those of Crout, express disillusionment and dissatisfaction. Pearson begged to come home; William Hatton and Robert Rossell complained of Guy's harsh rule and demanded that they be given their own land immediately or allowed to leave. Crout and Thomas Willoughby seem to have been prepared to stay another winter, but by August 1613 it had been decided that they too should go home. Only thirty people remained to spend the winter of 1613-14 at Cupids, the smallest group since the colony was established.[72]

THE YEARS OF DISILLUSIONMENT, 1613-1631

As the subscribers to the Newfoundland Company reviewed the state of their investment at the end of 1613, they can scarcely have been other than discouraged. If they had hoped to secure a monopoly of the fishery, they must have begun to realize that this was by no means as straightforward as it had appeared; for the island was large, the fishermen scattered, disorderly, and hostile. What profits the company had made from its fishing voyages, the colony must have more than swallowed in its constant need for provisions, equipment, livestock, and wages. So far the only crops grown successfully were cabbages and turnips; attempts to grow grain had failed each year. Too few furs had been obtained to make this a commercial proposition, and the chances of a regular trade with the Indians seemed slight. Reports of iron and samples of ore still reached England, but no workable deposits had been located. Even the company's conduct of its fishing voyages was criticized by Henry Crout:

me thinks the com[pany ma]keth [too few fishing] viages wch if it were well con-

---

70 Robert Rossell and William Hatton to Willoughby from Newfoundland, 6 April 1613, NU, Middleton MS Mi x 1/22.
71 Crout to Willoughby from Cupids Cove, 10 April 1613, *ibid.*, Mi x 1/23 and 59.
72 *Ibid.*, Mi x 1/21, 22, 23 and 59, 24.

s[idered and g]ood advice taken they might Fr[ay] much of the charge towardes the [colony] vntill such time as the land and ground be mannvred: they [haue] heartofore sent fishermen wᶜʰ haue had no great experience [*sic*] wᶜʰ to my knowledge hath bin a great lost vnto the companye.[73]

Neither merchants nor speculators can have gone into the fourth year of the venture without some misgivings.

In fact the winter of 1613-14 seems to have been a turning point in the history of the Newfoundland Company. By now much of the original enthusiasm had faded, the company was rent by squabbles and jealousy, its difficulties were multiplied as the fishermen became actively hostile. Now too the nature of the documentation changes; we have to rely more on official records and letters written in England as direct reports from Newfoundland become fewer. Very gradually the enterprise was dying.

The colony suffered a great setback in the loss of its very able governor, John Guy. Although Crout expected him back in Newfoundland by the autumn of 1613, Guy was still in Bristol in September and did not apparently return to the colony again.[74] Certainly Guy's relations with the company became strained at this time. Complaining to Henry Crout in December 1614 that the company had neither awarded him his own grant of land nor paid his men's wages, he wrote that his "adventure, personall imployment, & hazarde hath bred [him] nothing but a suite." The whole enterprise, he continued, was likely to fail because those in control

care not, though yt fall to the grownde, yf they, not by theire purse, but by their wites, at other mens adventure, & chardge can not continew. Yt is to be feared, that yt will neaver goe well as long as, soe vngratefull a person, & soe stonieharted a pennyfather is at the helme.[75]

This was presumably an indictment of the treasurer, John Slany, who later accused Guy of deceiving the company about the island's mineral resources.[76] When Guy withdrew, he probably took the Bristol men with him and, by 1617, an independent Bristol settlement had been established.[77] As for John Guy himself, he resumed his active role in the civic life of Bristol, serving as mayor and twice representing the city in parliament where he was particularly prominent in the debates on the freedom of the North American fisheries that took place in the early 1620s. Before his death in 1629 he had received a lot in Newfoundland, which he called Seaforest and which he bequeathed to his sons.[78]

John Guy's dissatisfaction with the company was echoed now by Sir Percival

---

73 *Ibid.*, Mi x 1/24.
74 Guy attended meetings of the Bristol Common Council in September 1613 and throughout the summer of 1614, see Bristol Record Office, Proceedings of the Common Council, 1608-28. According to William Vaughan, *The Golden Fleece* (F. Williams, 1626), sig. Ddd 2, Guy spent only two winters in Newfoundland.
75 NU, Middleton MS Mi x 1/28.
76 J. Slany to Willoughby, [1615], *ibid.*, Mi x 1/30.
77 See below, chapter v.
78 Will of John Guy, 21 Feb. 1625/6, Bristol Record Office, Great Orphans Book III, 276; probate granted May 1629.

Willoughby, who had expected to receive his own land as early as 1612 but who was still waiting in 1617, by which time it would seem that he had ceased to be a member of the company council. To some extent the delay was caused by Willoughby's insistence that Bell Island be included in his lot. Although he constantly denied it in his correspondence with John Slany, Willoughby had received a number of private reports that the island was rich in iron ore, besides being fertile and having a harbour and beaches suitable for the fishery. The most enthusiastic of these had come from Henry Crout, who had stated that "the like land is not in Newfoundland for good earth and great hope of Irone stone." His testimony had so impressed Willoughby that, on the reverse side of the letter, he had personally drafted a grant of the island to himself.[79] Unfortunately for Willoughby the company was itself becoming increasingly convinced that minerals, most probably iron and tin, would be found in Newfoundland and particularly on Bell Island. This prospect, together with the island's proximity to the main settlement at Cupids Cove, made it one of the more valuable lots and one which, according to treasurer Slany, many subscribers were willing to receive as their whole grant.[80]

Reluctantly Willoughby agreed to the exclusion of Bell Island, but even so his grant of "that worst and northerly" lot, as he described it, on Trinity Bay was further delayed.[81] Believing that those individuals who held land on which minerals were discovered would reap enormous profits, both from exploiting the ore and from renting land to those who came to work the mines, the company decided to reserve to itself one-fifth or one-sixth of any minerals found, to forbid the leasing of land to aliens without its consent, and to repossess any land left vacant for more than three years.[82] In vain did Sir Percival try to obtain more favourable conditions, pleading the expenses he had already incurred in the Newfoundland business: "I thinke I am more out in my owne particular then any one man else." In vain did he warn that investors would not be found to accept such restrictions, for

you knowe the companey can not restrayne the fishery to any man, and if you take awaye the mynes which ar but yet in imagination what shall men haue, that aduenture to plant vppon there owne charge, for the land itself if it laye within two myle of my house I woulde not manure it ... if the ayer were sutche as men could liue without anye thinge else, then the companey might looke for rent from thence.

It was, he noted bitterly, difficult enough to extract rents for good land in England.[83]

John Slany remained firm: the company must get the best terms it could, and others were willing to accept its conditions. In fact land was now in some demand. William Payne, soon to be a member of the company's council, and his associates had put in a tender for the St. John's lot, and other grants were being made on Trinity

79 NU, Middleton MS Mi x 1/25.
80 J. Slany to Willoughby, [1615] and 5 Feb. 1615/16, *ibid.*, Mi x 1/30, 31.
81 Willoughby to J. Slany, [1616], *ibid.*, Mi x 1/32.
82 J. Slany to Willoughby, 5 Feb. 1615/16; H. Slany to Willoughby, [1616]; J. Slany to Willoughby, 1 Feb. 1616/17, *ibid.*, Mi x 1/31, 33, 42.
83 Willoughby to J. Slany, [1616], *ibid.*, Mi x 1/32.

Bay.[84] About 1617, too, the company probably from financial necessity departed from its previous policies and began to alienate large tracts of land to independent proprietors who were not company members. During the next three years a group of Bristol merchants, Sir William Vaughan, Henry Cary Lord Falkland, George Calvert Lord Baltimore, and Sir William Alexander all purchased land in this way.[85]

Finding that the company would not make any exceptions in his favour, Willoughby withdrew his threat to abandon the whole undertaking and accepted the lot with the conditions. While protesting always that he was doing the company a favour in taking worthless land off its hands, in reality he was both eager to obtain more and unscrupulous in his methods of doing so. When the death of Thomas Cowper, a shareholder since 1612, gave him the chance to acquire a share from Cowper's widow and her second husband, John Browne, he asked first that the Brownes give it to his son, Edward. As the Brownes insisted that they wanted to recover "that mony which we soe longe since disbursed for the newfound land and neuer yet receued peny profit," Willoughby finally bought half of the share for Edward for £35. A considerable price for a half share, in view of the fact that Willoughby had presented himself to the Brownes as having offered his own share for sale at £10 and as having been told that it was not worth "ten pence."[86] Having secured the half share, he then tried to obtain the St. John's lot for John Browne, without apparently telling Slany that his own son was now Browne's partner.[87] St. John's was perhaps the most valuable lot in the whole island because of its excellent fishery, its position as the centre of the bartering trade between the fishermen, and its relatively good land. But Slany refused on the grounds that Browne had not adventured enough. Browne, he suggested, should try for the lot next to Willoughby's which "willnott be denyed so he seeke nott to much For the Company begins to incline to plantations and willnott be liberall in grantinge of those landes in the bayes neere to the plantation [at Cupids] which are now well knowen."[88]

While the shareholders squabbled in England, very little is heard of the fortunes of the colony at Cupids Cove. About 1615 a new governor, Captain John Mason, had been appointed, probably because of his naval background and his experience in dealing with pirates; for the company suffered increasing alarm at the frequent visits of pirates to the island.[89] Mason had taken up the governorship by 1616, and had begun that exploration of the island which resulted in the publication of the first English map of Newfoundland known to have been compiled in part from personal survey. The summers of both 1616 and 1617 Mason spent in coasting voyages to

---

84 J. Slany to Willoughby, 1 Feb. 1616/17, *ibid.*, Mi x 1/42; PRO, CO 1/1, f 123.

85 See below, chapter v.

86 Elizabeth Cowper to Lady Bridget Willoughby, 3 June 1616; [Willoughby] to Elizabeth Browne, [1616]; deed of sale of a half share in the Newfoundland Company by John Browne to Edward Willoughby, Sept. 1616, NU, Middleton MSS Mi x 1/35, 39, 40.

87 Willoughby to J. Slany, [4 Feb. 1617], *ibid.*, Mi x 1/43.

88 J. Slany to Willoughby, 10 Feb. 1616/17, *ibid.*, Mi x 1/44.

89 J. Slany to Willoughby, [1615], *ibid.*, Mi x 1/30. Mason had been commissioned by James I in 1610 to put down the pirates known as the Redshanks in the Hebrides, see G. P. Insh, *Scottish Colonial Schemes, 1620-1686* (Glasgow, 1922), p. 34. For a full account of Mason's career, see J. W. Dean, ed., *Captain John Mason* (Prince Society, 1887).

the south, and in 1617 he reached Placentia Bay and may even have gone as far as St. George's Bay on the west coast.[90]

These journeys of discovery apart, virtually nothing is known of Mason's activities as governor. It is possible that he devoted so much time to exploration because he was considering moving the colony from Conception Bay, in view of the growing hostility between fishermen and planters. In 1619 a correspondent of Willoughby's, Thomas Rowley, wrote:

master masson is about to cause the Company to enlarge the pattent yf they can; for that when you see him you will quickly know hath to be done; ... its large enough yf it be well managed but the company wants corrage hers rome enough for us & Fyshermen two: we want but a little power to writte the rongs they do us: & the greattest want is settling well; wher we meane to plant, the welch Fooles haue left of ... thers now land enoughe to be had ... [91]

Rowley's meaning is somewhat obscure. He may simply have meant that Mason wished to obtain, as governor, greater authority over the English fishermen. However, his reference to the departure of the Welshman Sir William Vaughan's colonists from Renewse suggests that the company was again thinking of a settlement in that harbour, or perhaps even at St. Mary's or Placentia bays, the second of which at least was beyond the area specifically awarded to the Newfoundland Company in 1610. Of course, had Mason moved from the east to the south coast he might have left behind the English fishermen only to find himself in a centre of the French fishery, a dubious advantage.

However this may be, it is certain that during Mason's governorship the smouldering conflict between settlers and fishermen had flared up into open hostility, with both sides striving to enlist the sympathy of the government. In 1618 the fishing merchants of Devon, Dorset, and Hampshire complained that, whereas the fishermen had traditionally been free to choose their fishing places and leave their equipment in Newfoundland at the end of each season, now the colonists monopolized the best beaches, destroyed their boats and buildings, and stole their salt. The Privy Council, considering "the singular importance of that Newfound land fishing vnto the Westerne partes of this Kingdome," both as a livelihood for its people and as a nursery for the nation's seamen, set up a committee to hear evidence from both sides. Despite the company's counter-allegations that it was the fishermen who were guilty of abuses and who even harboured pirates, the Privy Council decided in favour of the fishermen and admonished the company to respect the terms of its charter, especially that clause guaranteeing the absolute freedom of the fishery.[92]

90 Notes for a letter from Crout to Willoughby from Newfoundland, [1616], NU, Middleton MS Mi x 1/38; John Mason to Sir John Scott from Newfoundland, 31 Aug. 1617, National Library of Scotland, Adv. MS 17.1.19, ff 121, 122ᵛ, incomplete. The map is printed in William Vaughan, *Cambrensium Caroleia* (W. Stansby, 1625), and in the same author's *The Golden Fleece.*
91 Rowley to Willoughby from Cupids Cove, 16 Oct. 1619, NU, Middleton MS Mi x 1/51.
92 PRO, State Papers, Domestic, Jas I, SP 14/103, no 44; PRO, CO 1/1, ff 121, 123; PRO, PC 2/30, ff 10-11, 2/31, f 58.

The victory had gone to the west-country fishing merchants, for they had been able to represent their interests as identical with those of the nation. On this occasion, however, their triumph was short-lived. Perhaps as a result of pressure from Mason – and Mason had influential friends at court notably James' Scottish favourite, Sir William Alexander – the Privy Council reversed its earlier decision. In March 1620 the company again brought its case before the Privy Council, requesting that Mason be appointed king's lieutenant in Newfoundland with authority to put down the piracy which endangered both colony and fishery.[93] This time the company attempted to play the role of guardian of the national welfare. The fishery, it said, now employed some 300 English ships and 10,000 seamen annually, besides supporting 20,000 residents of the west-country and providing the crown with £20,000 in customs revenue. In all some 500 ships – English, French, Basque, and Portuguese – frequented the island, without protection from pirates and without any sort of government such as existed in the Danish, Scottish, and home fisheries. Should the present state of anarchy continue, it was entirely possible that the French or Spanish kings would send warships to protect their subjects. Lest this should happen, a lieutenant should be appointed, he and his ship being maintained by a levy of five nobles – the price of 500 fish which was perhaps one-fiftieth part of one boat's catch – collected from each fishing vessel. Only in this way could the piratical raids, which in the past eight years had inflicted £40,800's worth of damage on the fishery, and the fishermen's malicious destruction of property be prevented. The Privy Council responded immediately by addressing letters to the mayors of the major fishing ports, ordering them to warn all Newfoundland-bound vessels to commit no further offences against the colony, but to establish friendly relations with it.[94] Two months later, in May 1620, Mason received the Lord Admiral's commission to go to Newfoundland as commander of a ship of 320 tons to suppress piracy and restore order.[95]

Whilst in England John Mason probably supervised the publication of his *Briefe Discovrse of the New-found-land* which appeared in 1620.[96] Mason devoted the greater part of this rare and attractive pamphlet to a description of the geography and climate of Newfoundland, as well as of its flora, fauna, and natural resources. To correct earlier accounts, "some too much extolling it [Newfoundland] some too much debasing it," he wrote only of what he knew from his own experience during his three and a half years' residency. His purpose seems to have been to interest his Scottish acquaintances in the island, and he was apparently successful, for the petition for his appointment as king's lieutenant in Newfoundland was presented by "the Treasurer and Company with the Scottish vndertakers of the plantations."[97]

In a tantalizing conclusion to his brief tract Mason wrote:

93 PRO, CO 1/1, ff 178-80.
94 PRO, PC 2/30, f 453.
95 PRO, SP 12/237, ff 30-2; the document has been filed with a group of Admiralty papers among State Papers, Domestic, Elizabeth.
96 Printed in Edinburgh by Andro Hart.
97 PRO, CO 1/1, f 178. The work was dedicated to Sir John Scott of Scotstarvet who was also an acquaintance of Sir William Alexander.

I might heare further discourse of our discoueries, conference with the Saluages by Master *Iohn Gye* their maner of life. Likewise of the managinge our businesse in our plantations with the descriptions of their situations in 2. places 16. miles distant from other on the northside the bay of conception, of the manner charge and benefite of our fishings ... , projects for making Yron, Salt, Pitch, Tarre, Tirpintine, Frank-Incense, Furres, Hope of trade with Saluages and such like, with many accidents and occurences in the time of my gouerment there, but these may suffice ...

So was lost the most authoritative account that we might have had of the settlement at Cupids Cove; and after 1613 the papers of Sir Percival Willoughby do not fill the gap very satisfactorily. Henry Crout and Thomas Willoughby did not return to Newfoundland until 1616 and then seem to have stayed only one year. From this period no complete letter from Crout to Willoughby survives, but evidently their relationship had so deteriorated that Crout felt the need to be absolutely meticulous in accounting for provisions and in justifying his conduct. Even so Willoughby, ignoring both his son's and Henry Crout's explanations that they could not leave Cupids Cove because their labourers had deserted, grumbled about their failure to begin to develop his own land at Carbonear.[98]

After this disagreement Crout apparently left, or perhaps was recalled from, Newfoundland for, by 1619, Willoughby had a new agent, Thomas Rowley. Rowley had considerable experience of the island, having been there at least since 1612, when he had been a member of John Guy's expedition to Trinity Bay, and perhaps since the beginning of the colony in 1610.[99] In 1618 Sir Percival had taken both Rowley and William Hannam into partnership with him, making over half his land to them in return for a peppercorn rent.[100] Rowley and Hannam were to settle on his lot on Trinity Bay and to endeavour to support themselves by farming, trading with the Indians, and hopefully by discovering minerals. Strangely enough Willoughby never seems to have been much interested in the island's obvious resource: fish. He disregarded his son's warning that "if efver you looke for monney agayne in this country, you must send fisher men,"[101] perhaps believing that the erratic Thomas could never give sensible advice.

In January 1619 Thomas Rowley was in Bristol hiring a ship and men for Willoughby's service, but Willoughby, always impecunious, was having difficulty in raising enough money to cover the expense. Nothing came of their plans for Rowley to settle first at Carbonear, then at Heart's Content. Rowley and Hannam quarrelled constantly and, by 1620, Rowley was threatening to withdraw from the whole enterprise because, he maintained, he had neither received any land from Wil-

98 T. Willoughby to his father from Newfoundland, 4 Aug. [1616]; notes from Crout to Willoughby [1616]; Willoughby to Crout, 15 March 1616/17, NU, Middleton MSS Mi x 1/36, 38, 45.

99 "From the first plantation [Rowley] hath lived in Newfoundland, little to his profit," Robert Hayman, *Qvodlibets, Lately Come Over from New Britaniola, Old Newfovnd-Land* (E. All-de for R. Michell, 1628), sig. F 1.

100 An indenture between Willoughby and Rowley and Hannam, 1618, NU, Middleton MS Mi x 1/64; another copy, *ibid.*, Mi x 1/65.

101 T. Willoughby to his father from Newfoundland, 4 Aug. [1616], *ibid.*, Mi x 1/36.

loughby nor any commission to prove his authority.[102] Willoughby seems to have been incapable of sustaining a good relationship with any of his associates; his distrust and his constant grumbling alienated them all, and soon Thomas Rowley too had broken the connection.

Unfortunately Rowley's letters are mostly concerned with his squabbles with Hannam and with Willoughby; they are almost silent about the affairs of the Cupids Cove colony. The company was still active, as the disputes with the fishing merchants between 1618 and 1620 show, but its members were becoming desperate in their search for some way to make the colony pay. In April 1620 they successfully applied for permission to transport iron ore to be smelted in Newfoundland, so assuring England of a supply of iron at a time when the domestic industry was threatened by a shortage of timber and providing the settlers with employment when the fishing season ended.[103] That such a bulky commodity could be shipped economically across the Atlantic, even if used as ballast for empty fishing vessels, must be dubious; and we have no proof that the company ever in fact made the experiment.

Mason may have returned to Cupids Cove, but about 1621 he relinquished his connection with the Newfoundland Company to begin a new career in New England.[104] His wife, Anne, may well have influenced his decision to leave, for another Newfoundland resident, Robert Hayman, poet and governor of Bristol's Hope, addressed this verse to her and to "all those worthy Women, who haue any desire to liue in Newfound-Land":

> Sweet creatures, did you truely vnderstand
> The pleasant life you'd liue in Newfound-land,
> You would with teares desire to be brought thither:
> I wish you, when you goe, faire wind, faire weather:
> For if you with the passage can dispence,
> When you are there, I know you'll ne'r come thence.[105]

If a third governor was appointed we have no record of him; and, while the Newfoundland Company did not die with Mason's departure as has sometimes been alleged, it is evident that it survived only because of the enthusiasm of a small group of individuals, notably the Slany brothers. In 1623, for example, Humphrey Slany set out a fishing voyage to Newfoundland, and his agent procured fish from the colony and elsewhere which he sold at Malaga.[106] Sir Percival Willoughby also persevered, even though as late as 1626 he had not succeeded in finding anyone who would settle on the Trinity Bay land. John Slany wrote that he had difficulty per-

---

102 See the series of letters from Rowley to Willoughby written between January 1619 and February 1620, *ibid.*, Mi x 1/48-51, 53.
103 PRO, CO 1/1, f 162; PRO, PC 2/30, f 477.
104 There is a reference in an Admiralty Court deposition to the presence of a governor at the colony in the summer of 1621, see PRO, HCA 13/43: 30 Nov. 1621, Humphrey Randell.
105 Hayman, *Qvodlibets*, sig. E 4.
106 Richard Newall to Humphrey Slany and William Clowberry from St. John's, 8 July 1623; a bill of lading for the *Luke* of London, 28 Aug. 1623, Bodleian Library, Malone MS 2.

suading the company to allow Willoughby to keep the lot, because he had not fulfilled the conditions under which it was awarded. There were now, said Slany, "plantations in St. Iones & other places and people incline to the Cuntrey & suerly in short time land wilbe ther in some Esteeme."[107] But these are the same hopes that Slany had advanced ten years earlier, and now his determined optimism begins to sound both forced and pathetic. Willoughby, who still owed him considerable amounts of money, he reproached as having left him "ingaged so Far as I am in my ould age when I shud be att peece with the world." Peevishly Willoughby replied:

for my lott in newe founde lande I thancke you, it hathe cost me in particular and withe the generall aboue five hunderde pounds, and hope in there iustice, and iudgements will not take it from me without satisfaction, you knowe how manye courts and meetings there was before I coulde gett anye graunte beinge vppon sutche conditions and restrictions, as noe man will adventure withe me, to lye open to all manner of outrages of saylors and pirates, without ether peace or protection from the company ...

If the company would only relax its restrictions he was convinced that he would be able to get others to adventure with him.[108]

Yet not only Willoughby and Slany still nursed hopes of finding new investors. In 1627 William Payne, one of the partners in the St. John's lot – "the principall prime and chief lot in all the whole countrey" – tried to interest Secretary Sir Edward Conway in the enterprise, for "as it now standes the yce being broken and some howses allreddy built it will require no great charge." Payne, who held nine of the twelve shares, offered six of them to Conway if he could obtain the necessary consent of John Slany, "th[e] Governour of the wholle land." According to Payne, he and his associates were making a profit from fish, furs, and sarsaparilla, and had great hopes of iron and silver which they were confident that the mining expert on Sir William Alexander's Nova Scotia expedition had discovered on their land in 1623. Although Slany signified his willingness to accept Conway, the completion of the business had to await the return of the fishing ships, for Slany correctly feared that the French had inflicted severe losses on the English fleet that year.[109] We do not know whether Conway ever purchased the shares. Even if the threat of French aggression and the precipitate departure from Newfoundland of his friend, Lord Baltimore, did not deter him, Conway may well have wondered why Payne, who according to his own reports was making such profits from the St. John's lot, should be so anxious to unload most of his shares.

We hear no more of Payne, of the St. John's colony, or of treasurer John Slany who died in 1632. Amazingly enough, in 1631 Sir Percival Willoughby was negotiating yet again to have someone settle on his land. This time it was Nicholas Guy, who had been in Newfoundland since 1612 when his wife had given birth to the first English child known to have been born on the island.[110] A single letter from Guy

107 J. Slany to Willoughby, 13 Feb. 1625/6, NU, Middleton MS Mi x 1/55.
108 Willoughby to J. Slany, [Feb. 1626], ibid., Mi x 1/56.
109 Payne to Lady Conway, 2 Nov. 1627; James Meddus to Lady Conway, 27 June 1628; Payne to Meddus, 30 June 1628; Meddus to Lady Conway, 25 July 1628, PRO, SP 16/84, no 13, 16/108 nos 37, 61, 16/111, no 11.
110 Journal, NU, Middleton MS Mi x 1/66, f 16.

to Willoughby reveals that Guy had already moved from Cupids Cove to Carbonear, where he claimed to be farming and fishing successfully enough to have made a profit of between £50 and £100 the previous year. He was silent about the fortunes of the Cupids colony, though he did suggest that Willoughby send out the two men and the provisions he needed in "the plantation ships that vseialle [usually] come." Guy may, however, have been referring to the Bristol colony close by at Harbour Grace, for he also reported that the settlers there were contesting Willoughby's title to the land about Carbonear.[111]

Nicholas Guy's letter is the last Newfoundland document among Willoughby's papers, and provides the last information of any kind that we have on the Newfoundland Company and its subscribers. Willoughby was already an old man in 1631. Though he lived on until 1643, even his interest may have faded now. One imagines that the Newfoundland Company must have failed finally and completely along with the two optimistic, stubborn, and querulous old men, John Slany and Percival Willoughby, who had for so long struggled to keep it alive.

As testimony of the hopes that had run so high in 1610 there remained but a handful of settlers who continued to exist through their own enterprise. At the outset the company had not grasped what it would cost in ships, in men, in chains of settlement, above all in money to colonize Newfoundland and to exploit the fishery on a large scale. Although the investors had exhibited a shrewder understanding of the problems of overseas colonization than many of their contemporaries, they were still over-optimistic in their hope that the colony could quickly become self-supporting. The cost of even the modest settlement at Cupids Cove swallowed up the profits from the fishery, until gradually the company had to surrender control of large areas of land as the only means of raising fresh capital. Had a second major commodity such as iron been discovered, then the fate of the company might have been different; then perhaps they could have afforded the wide-spread settlement so essential for any monopoly of the fishery. When, in 1620, the company was reduced to considering shipping iron to be smelted in Newfoundland, the desperate state of its finances was revealed.

About the same time that the company admitted the unlikelihood of minerals being found on the island, it was forced to recognize another unpleasant fact – the unchanging hostility of the fishermen to settlement, let alone monopoly. As the New England Company fought and won its battle for control of that fishery in the twenties, the determination of the fishermen to preserve their rights at least in Newfoundland must have become ever more entrenched. Given this unyielding westcountry attitude, firmly backed in the House of Commons, and the ambivalent position of the government which never dared endanger its reserve of ships and seamen, however it may have felt about the greater efficiency of trades conducted under a monopoly, the idea of establishing a monopoly was never feasible.

Nor did the individual speculator, such as Sir Percival Willoughby, perceive how ephemeral were his dreams. Even if iron had been found on his land, he could never have afforded to transport men and equipment across the Atlantic; he could never

111 Nicholas Guy to Willoughby from Carbonear, 1 Sept. 1631, *ibid.*, Mi x 1/57.

have borne the expense of establishing an industry on that remote and totally un-developed island. Why he did not become disillusioned earlier is mystifying. But nagging Slany, fighting the company, persecuting his associates – he persisted; per-haps because he had invested so much money that it was impossible for him to withdraw. He and the company as a whole failed to appreciate that the task they had set themselves was gargantuan and their resources pitiful. Indeed the difficulties and costs of any scheme involving colonization could not yet be understood by Englishmen with their limited experience. They only knew that the world had opened up before them. Into their chosen adventure they plunged, with little doubt of their ability to realize their undertakings, and with little realization of what they had undertaken.

V

Further Experiments in Settlement 1616-37

HERE MUST HAVE COME a time, some five years or so after the establishment of the colony at Cupids Cove, when the officials of the Newfoundland Company faced the fact that they had to find new sources of capital. The sums they could raise simply by making calls on the stock were just not enough to allow them to expand the scope of the venture. By now perhaps the number of shareholders had fallen off; almost certainly those who remained would object to putting up more money when they had as yet seen no return on their investment. The maintenance of the settlement at Cupids was as much as the company's resources would bear, and the development of land by individuals such as Sir Percival Willoughby had proved a dishearteningly slow business. Yet, in the face of the fishermen's mounting hostility, the area of settlement must be extended and that soon. Otherwise the very survival of plantation in Newfoundland was doubtful, let alone the realization of any dreams of monopoly. The obvious remedy, and one adopted by the Virginia Company at about the same time,[1] was to tap fresh reserves of capital by disposing of land to private individuals or associations to develop at their own expense. The Newfoundland Company might hope to find in such patentees valuable allies against the west-countrymen, as well as potential suppliers of fish to their sack ships.

Between 1616 and 1621, then, five such grants of land were made to independent patentees. All but one of these were awarded to individual proprietors who desired land rather than trading privileges, and a society more perfect than they found at home rather than a commercial centre. The aims of these four proprietors, therefore, had more in common with those of Sir Ferdinando Gorges and the Council of New England, than with those of John Slany and the original Newfoundland Company. Only one grant was made to a group whose interests were primarily commercial; and the colony set up at Harbour Grace by these practical Bristol merchants for practical reasons was probably the most successful and certainly the most long-lived. Whether these patentees had first to take shares in the common stock, as did the Virginia associates, is not clear.

Of all the adventurers who offered to take land from the company, the first and

---

1 W. F. Craven, *The Dissolution of the Virginia Company: the Failure of a Colonial Experiment* (reprint, Gloucester, Mass., 1964), pp. 57-64.

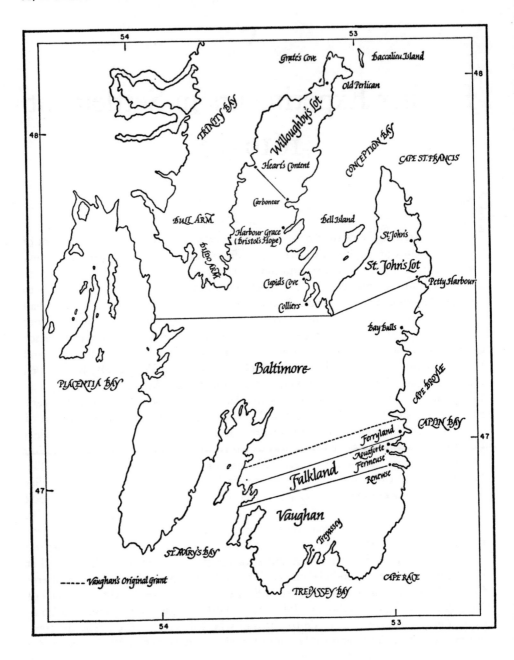

surely the strangest was William Vaughan, MA, DCL.[2] Welsh gentleman, scholar, poet, romantic, he dreamed of a new Cambriol – a second and more prosperous Wales – in the New World. To cure the poverty and apathy he found in Wales where, he wrote with his customary gift for overstatement, the land lay neglected while the people starved, where maritime enterprise was ignored while just across the Severn commerce brought prosperity to the county of Devon – such were his ambitions. To Vaughan, Newfoundland was the land divinely reserved for Britons, easier of access than Virginia, and with a staple commodity – fish – on which the economies of the French and Spanish nations already depended. "This," he declaimed with a fine sense of the dramatic if not perhaps of the ridiculous, "is our *Colchos*, where the *Golden Fleece* flourishethe on the backes of Neptunes sheepe, continually to be shorne. This is *Great Britaines Indies*, neuer to be exhausted dry."[3] That William Vaughan was not the man to transform such fantasies into reality became apparent in the very first year of settlement.

In 1616 he received his land from the company: that portion of the Avalon peninsula lying south of a line from Caplin Bay to Placentia Bay, and including the popular fishing harbours of Ferryland, Fermeuse, and Renewse.[4] He chose the area around Renewse, and not, I believe, Trepassey Bay, as the site of his colony. In fact it is difficult to understand why D. W. Prowse, who published in 1895 what has become the standard history of Newfoundland, fixed so definitely upon Trepassey as the location of Vaughan's colony when the evidence is so vague.[5] Strangely enough Vaughan, in all his writing about Newfoundland, never identifies the site. He did include in two of his books, *Cambrensium Caroleia* (1625) and *The Golden Fleece* (1626), almost identical maps of the island, attributed to John Mason. Both contain a number of placenames which have obvious links with Vaughan. But only one of them, "Colchos," is in the Trepassey area, the name being written across the opening of the bay. Of the rest, "Vaughan's Cove" and "Glamorgan" are on the east coast of the Avalon peninsula between Renewse and Cape Race; "Golden Grove," which was also the name of the Vaughan family estate in Wales, is inland from Renewse; and "Cambriola" is printed across the width of the southern part of the peninsula. The evidence of these maps then is inconclusive, but perhaps is slightly in favour of the east coast. It is Richard Whitbourne, governor of Vaughan's colony in 1618-19, who pinpoints the location more precisely:

And aboue the foresaid Iland [in Renewse harbour], it is the most commodious place for Geese, Ducks, and other Water-fowle, winter and summer, as there is not the like in any other harbour on the East side of that Land, to the Southward of the Bay of Conception; whereof those men, which I left there all the winter season, in *Anno* 1618, made good proofe, and so likewise the winter before that time.[6]

2 There are biographies of Vaughan in *DNB; Dictionary of Welsh Biography; Dictionary of Canadian Biography*, I, 654-7.
3 Vaughan, *Golden Fleece*, sigs. Dd 3-Ee 2ᵛ, Aaa 3, Bbb 1, Bbb 2ᵛ.
4 *Ibid.*, Mason map facing sig. A 2ᵛ.
5 Prowse, *History of Newfoundland*, pp. 110-11. He has been followed by J. D. Rogers, *Newfoundland* (Oxford, 1911), p. 60; Innis, *Cod Fisheries*, pp. 63-4; E. Roland Williams, "Cambriol: the Story of a Forgotten Colony," *Welsh Outlook*, VIII (1921), 230-3, and many others.
6 *Discovrse Containing a Loving Invitation* (1622), sig. C 1.

And in all the promotion literature which Whitbourne published between 1620 and 1623 he always writes his most detailed and most favourable descriptions of the land around Renewse and Fermeuse.

Vaughan sent out his first colonists in 1617, according to the inscription on the Mason maps. We do not know how many he sent or what kind of people they were but, as pioneers in an unsympathetic land, they proved totally inadequate. Moreover, Vaughan seems to have provided them with no experienced leader, for not until 1618 did the capable Richard Whitbourne take up his appointment. A seaman since the age of fifteen and familiar with the island of Newfoundland ever since 1579, Whitbourne had become in 1615 the first Englishman commissioned to hold vice-admiralty courts in Newfoundland for the purpose of investigating charges of abuses against the visiting fishermen. The following year he had been back at his more accustomed occupation of master of a fishing ship bound for Newfoundland and Lisbon; and on his return from Portugal he had been approached by William Vaughan.[7] When Richard Whitbourne reached the little settlement in 1618, he found that the colonists had not even exerted themselves to build a habitation, but had endured the cold of a Newfoundland winter with only the fishermen's summer shacks for shelter. He had brought with him two ships with new colonists and more provisions, paid for by himself, Vaughan, and other unnamed adventurers. One of the ships was intended for the fishery, but the plans went awry when the vessel was attacked by one of Sir Walter Raleigh's "erring" Guiana captains. Whitbourne sent most of the settlers home, as being unsuited to the life, keeping only six whom he organized so that they spent the winter of 1618-19 in comparative comfort.[8] But not unnaturally Whitbourne had found these experiences discouraging. By 1619 it was reported from Cupids Cove that "the welch Fooles" had given up and left the island;[9] and by the following year Whitbourne was back in England, the first edition of his *Discovrse and Discovery of Newfoundland* was ready for the press, and his connection with Vaughan was apparently at an end.[10]

After this misadventure William Vaughan, "finding the burthen too heauy for my weake Shoulders," assigned first a part of his grant to Henry Cary, later Lord Falkland, and then, at the instigation of his brother the Earl of Carberry, a further portion to Sir George Calvert.[11] There remained to Vaughan the land south of a line drawn from Renewse due west to Placentia Bay. The precise nature of his involvement in Newfoundland after this date is somewhat dubious. It has been generally believed that he was actively supporting a colony in Trepassey Bay during the 1620s, that he himself visited it in 1622 or shortly thereafter, returning to England to publish two books in 1625 and 1626, and that he was probably back in Newfoundland from 1628 to 1630.[12] The only real verification for the existence of

---

7 See *Dictionary of Canadian Biography*, I, 668-9 for details of Whitbourne's career.

8 Whitbourne, *Discovrse and Discovery* (1620), sigs. C 1ᵛ, G 2-3; *Ibid.* (1623), sigs. A 2ᵛ, B 2ᵛ-C 1.

9 Thomas Rowley to Sir Percival Willoughby from Newfoundland, 16 Oct. 1619, NU, Middleton MS Mi x 1/51.

10 *APC Col., 1613-80*, pp. 29, 38-9. *DNB* says that Whitbourne remained at Vaughan's colony until 1622; in fact by that year Whitbourne had formed a new connection with Lord Falkland, see below, pp. 89, 91.

11 W. Vaughan, *The Newlanders Cvre* (T. Constable, 1630), sig. A 5.

12 See Prowse, *History of Newfoundland*, p. 111; Rogers, *Newfoundland*, p. 60; Williams,

a Vaughan colony after 1619 seems to be a statement in Richard Eburne's *A Plaine Path-Way to Plantations*, published in 1624: "Master Vaughan ... hath within these two or three years last sent thither diuers men and women that doe inhabite there, and prosper well."[13] Eburne's dates, however, are not particularly reliable, and the weight of the rest of the evidence seems to be against him. Above all, there is the fact that nowhere in the two books in which Vaughan writes extensively of his interest in Newfoundland – *The Golden Fleece* (1626) and *The Newlanders Cvre* (1630) – does he himself say that his colony still exists. On the contrary, in *The Golden Fleece* he puts the following words into the mouth of his friend, Sir William Alexander, who himself held land in Newfoundland and Nova Scotia:

Only like a wary Politician you [Vaughan] suspend your breath for a time, vntill you can repaire your losses sustained by some of Sir Walter Raleighs company in their returne from Guiana [in 1618] while your Neighbours the Right Honourable the Lord Viscount Falkland, and my Lord Baltimore ... doe vndergoe the whole burthen[14]

Again in *The Newlanders Cvre* Vaughan refers to his activities of 1617 to 1619, but gives the impression that, since then, his involvement has been confined to encouraging others through his writings.[15] As for having gone to Newfoundland himself, here again the loquacious Vaughan is silent, except for one phrase which is open to interpretation. In the title of *The Golden Fleece* Vaughan claims that the book has been "transported from Cambrioll Colchos, out of the Southernmost Part of the Iland commonly called the Newfoundland." In a work published under the pseudonym "Orpheus Junior" and written throughout in a high, fantastic style, it is entirely possible that the word "transported" was not meant to be taken literally. Moreover, when Robert Hayman, sometime governor of the Bristol merchants' colony, published a book of verses in 1628, he encouraged Vaughan to adventure further "with person, purse and penne," lamenting that Vaughan had not yet gone to Newfoundland because of ill-health and assuring him that he would recover best in "Cambrioll."[16]

As a writer, then, Vaughan seems to have been more active and effective than as a colonizer; certainly he combined the two interests in the most extraordinary way. In 1625 he published the first version of John Mason's map of Newfoundland in his *Cambrensium Caroleia*, a work written to celebrate the accession of Charles I. The next year appeared surely one of the strangest works of propaganda for the New World ever produced before or since. *The Golden Fleece* stands in vivid contrast to the more prosaic tracts on Newfoundland recently published by the two sea captains, John Mason and Richard Whitbourne. Its purpose, as stated by Vaughan,

"Cambriol," pp. 230, 232; J. J. Jones, "*The Golden Fleece*," *The National Library of Wales Journal*, III (1943-4), 58-60; Sir D. Ll. Thomas, "Iscennen and Golden Grove," *Trans. Honourable Society of Cymmrodorian*, (1940), 115-29; *Dictionary of Welsh biography*; *DNB*. In writing the biography of Vaughan for the *Dictionary of Canadian Biography*, I, I realized that the 1617-19 colony was at Renewse but accepted that there was a later settlement at Trepassey, although I doubted that Vaughan ever visited it himself.

13 sigs. Q 1-1ᵛ.
14 sig. B 1ᵛ.
15 sigs. A 5-5ᵛ.
16 *Qvodlibets*, sigs. E 4ᵛ-F 1.

was simple and ordinary enough – to promote the island as a place for settlement, with the objectives of relieving over-population at home, trebling England's present annual income of £20,000 from the fishery, allowing the development of Newfoundland's other resources, and ending the lawlessness now prevalent on the island.[17] In none of this did *The Golden Fleece* differ very much from other promotion literature. Rather, it was Vaughan's method of presentation which was unique. He imagined Apollo holding court as arbiter in all matters – religious, political, economic, and moral. In that section of the book dealing with ways to increase Britain's wealth, Apollo summons those most intimately connected with the colonization of Newfoundland, among them John Guy and John Mason, to testify as to the island's resources; to prove, in fact, that the golden fleece is to be found there. Much of what Vaughan has to say here is sound and practical – his debt to Whitbourne is obvious though unacknowledged – if not very original, and as always over-optimistic. Such passages, however, are so well concealed among pages of fantasy, history, and hysterical anti-Catholicism, that its impact as propaganda must have been blunted.

Even if he were not now actually investing in Newfoundland, Vaughan's interest in the island was still alive in the late 1620s when he recruited a number of new adventurers, notably his brother-in-law, Sir Henry Salusbury of Llewenni.[18] By 1628 Vaughan seems to have been considering reviving his colony. Certainly Robert Hayman suggests as much, though he suggests too that Vaughan's wife, Anne, was opposed to the whole idea. Hayman addressed one of his verses to her to convince her of the healthfulness of Newfoundland. Whether she found all his lines reassuring may be doubted:

> Yet scuruy Death stalks here with theeuish pace,
> Knocks one down here, two in another place.[19]

In 1630 Vaughan was still hoping that Salusbury, "with some *Gentlemen of North-Wales*, will the next Springe proceede to doe somewhat in that Country, which with open armes awaites for their coming."[20] It may be that Salusbury, taking warning from his brother-in-law's fruitless expenditure and from the recent failure of Lord Baltimore's plantation at Ferryland, decided that it would be wiser to stay out of Newfoundland. Nor do the Englishmen to whom Vaughan had assigned land and who had "faithfully promised to *Plant* in their seuerall Diuisions. The which, if they performed, my costly Cares for Sacrifice would be the lesse,"[21] appear to have taken up their grants. *The Newlanders Cvre* of 1630, a book of medical advice for emigrants, containing remedies for such ailments as seasickness and scurvy and perhaps occasioned by the sufferings at Ferryland, was the last book which Vaughan wrote on the subject of Newfoundland. Apparently he devoted the remainder of his life to his family, his estates in Wales, and the two religious tracts which he published shortly before his death in 1641.

17 sigs. Bbb 1-Ccc 1.
18 Vaughan, *Newlanders Cvre*, sig. A 7.
19 *Qvodlibets*, sig. F 1.
20 Vaughan, *Newlanders Cvre*, sig. A 7.
21 *Ibid.*

Soon after the establishment of Vaughan's second Cambriol, in 1617, came the planting of Bristol's Hope on Conception Bay, another colony optimistically and romantically named but apparently more efficiently managed. The split between John Guy and the Newfoundland Company in 1614 seems to have destroyed the alliance between London and Bristol, perhaps a partnership which had always been based on self rather than on common interest. By February of 1616 some of the Bristol men had evidently left Cupids Cove, either to return to England or to live elsewhere in Newfoundland; and a year later John Slany reported that "the bristoll men are Comminge vp to have a lott amongst them all."[22] Presumably these negotiations were completed some time during the year 1617-18, when a group of merchants belonging to the Bristol Company of Merchant Venturers and very probably including some of the original subscribers of 1610, received a grant of land on Conception Bay, including Harbour Grace which they made their headquarters.[23] The exact boundaries of the grant are not known; but it evidently adjoined Sir Percival Willoughby's lot and included the south side of the harbour of Carbonear, while Willoughby held the north shore. It could not, therefore, have comprised the whole of the peninsula between Conception and Trinity bays, as the Mason map suggests.[24] The terms of the grant are also unknown to us, but the Bristol group evidently held its land as freely as did Vaughan and the other independent proprietors and not under the restrictive conditions imposed upon company shareholders.

The only known governor of the Bristol plantation was the versifier, Robert Hayman,[25] who was himself a native of Exeter but whose brother-in-law was John Barker, master of the Bristol Merchant Venturers at the time the grant was made. This relationship makes it likely that Hayman was the colony's first governor, appointed when the colony was founded about 1618. His first visit to Newfoundland lasted fifteen months and, by his own account, he later spent several summers there,[26] but he evidently avoided a second Newfoundland winter. The colony flourished. In 1622 it was reported that the settlers, after five years' residence, had "builded there faire houses, and done many good seruices, who liue there very pleasantly and they are well pleased to entertaine vpon fit conditions, such as wilbe Aduenturers with them."[27] But Bristol's Hope evidently prospered in spite of, rather than because of, Hayman's direction. His practical responsibility he took somewhat lightly. "Haueing only had the ouerseeing others hard labour" as distraction,[28] he employed much of his time in writing verses and in translating works of Rabelais and John Owen, all of which he published in the curious *Qvodlibets*,

---

22 John Slany to Sir Percival Willoughby, 5 Feb. 1615/16 and 10 Feb. 1616/17, NU, Middleton MSS Mi x 1/31, 44.

23 Grant printed in McGrath, *Records*, 200.

24 Nicholas Guy to Sir Percival Willoughby from Carbonear, 1 Sept. 1631, NU, Middleton MS Mi x 1/58; Vaughan, *Golden Fleece*, facing sig. A 2ᵛ.

25 For the fullest biographical account of Hayman see David Galloway, "Robert Hayman (1575-1629): Some Materials for the Life of a Colonial Governor and First 'Canadian' Author," *William and Mary Quarterly*, 3rd ser., XXIV (1967), 75-87.

26 "A Proposition of Profitt and Honor Proposed to my Dread and Gratious Soueraigne Lord, Kinge Charles, By his humble Subiect Robert Hayman," [1628], BM, Egerton MS 2541, ff 164-9ᵛ.

27 Whitbourne, *Discovrse and Discovery* (1622), sig. A 3.

28 BM, Egerton MS 2541, f 165.

Lately Come Over from New Britaniola, Old Newfovnd-land (1628), a work designed to encourage the promoters of the various Newfoundland plantations. One poem he addressed to all the investors in the Bristol colony:

> When I to you your Bristoll-Hope commend,
> Reck'ninge your gaine, if you would thither send,
> What you can spare: You little credit me:
> The mischiefe is, you'le not come here and see.
> Here you would quickly see more then my selfe:
> Then would you style it, Bristol's Hope of wealth.[29]

Other verses were dedicated to Bristol merchants and their wives, including John Doughty who had invested in the Newfoundland Company in 1610, his brother-in-law John Barker, and Elizabeth Guy, the widow of Philip Guy.

About the same time that he published this book of verses, Hayman proposed to Charles I that he should take a hand in the plantation of Newfoundland, by building a city to be named in his honour, granting the inhabitants privileges in the fishery, and establishing a free market in fish there. The proposition was prefaced by a letter to the Duke of Buckingham, begging him to bring it before the attention of the king.[30] But 1628 was hardly an auspicious year to try to interest either the king or Buckingham in colonial affairs. Despite all his literary enthusiasm, Hayman evidently severed his connection with Newfoundland in 1628, for in that year he left with Robert Harcourt for Guiana. In November 1629 he died "of a burning fever and of a fluxe" while on an expedition up the Oyapock river.[31] The colony at Harbour Grace survived his departure, however, and was reported to be thriving in 1631.[32]

A Welsh romantic, an English merchant association – such were the first independent proprietors to hold land from the Newfoundland Company. In 1620 a third adventurer came forward with a plan for a colony, this time to benefit Ireland. Henry Cary, soon to be Lord Falkland and lord deputy of Ireland, had long been more than usually interested in overseas ventures. In 1609 he had been appointed to the king's council for Virginia, and three years later had subscribed to the North-West Passage Company. He became a privy councillor in 1617 and thereafter his name appeared frequently on committees appointed to consider colonial problems. Moreover, as his later activities in Ireland were to show, he had developed a number of theories on colonization.[33] His west-country origin and connections – his brother was bishop of Exeter – and his marriage with Elizabeth, daughter of Sir Lawrence Tanfield who had been one of the original subscribers to the Newfoundland Company, may explain his choice of Newfoundland as the site for his own colonial venture.

---

29 sig. F 2^{v}.
30 BM, Egerton MS 2541, ff 162-3^{v}.
31 Anderson, *Examinations and Depositions*, II, 65-9.
32 Nicholas Guy to Sir Percival Willoughby from Carbonear, 1 Sept. 1631, NU, Middleton MS Mi x 1/58.
33 For Falkland's career in Ireland, see R. Bagwell, *Ireland under the Stuarts*, I (London, 1909), 176-8.

About 1620 Falkland obtained from the company a vast tract of land, running from the east to the west coast and situated between the latitudes of Trinity Bay and Penguin Island.[34] In making this, its largest alienation of land, the company had virtually renounced any interest in the island outside a very restricted area on Conception Bay. About the same time Falkland received a second grant, this time from William Vaughan, who very probably needed the company's consent before he could dispose of his land. Vaughan gave, or more likely sold, to Falkland, a narrow strip of territory – it was only six miles wide from north to south – stretching from the east coast of the Avalon peninsula across to Placentia Bay; its northern limit was a point midway between Ferryland and Aquaforte, its southern limit the harbour of Renewse.[35]

By 1622 Falkland had joined forces with that ever-active promoter of Newfoundland, Richard Whitbourne, to whom he evidently entrusted much of the organization of the business. In that year Whitbourne published *A Discovrse Containing a Loving Invitation ... to All Such as Shall Be Aduenturers ... For the Aduancement of his Maiesties Most Hopefull Plantation in the New-fovnd-land, Lately Vndertaken*, which was dedicated to Falkland. As a site for the colony Whitbourne favoured Renewse, already proved habitable by Vaughan's men, as having a good fishing harbour and some of the best and most open land in the whole island. The land to the north on Trinity Bay would also provide bases for the fishery, besides iron, naval stores, and other commodities.[36] In a letter written to his patron in December 1622, Whitbourne proceeded to outline the course of the venture. As it was too late to begin that year, preparations should be made during the winter so that a ship of forty to fifty tons could leave by the following April. At least twelve settlers, all craftsmen – two carpenters, a brickmaker, a stone mason, a tile maker, a smith, a husbandman, a gardener, a shipwright, a seaman, a lime burner, and a cooper – should be recruited in England; Whitbourne evidently wanted no more experiences with unskilled men such as he had had under Vaughan. The rest, "such a greater nomber of people, as are not to be provided heere, may be shipt from Ireland," together with supplies of meat, corn, and butter. To avoid the expense of sending the ship back to England in ballast, a cargo of fish should be obtained – and Whitbourne suggests that the fishing ship which Sir George Calvert intended to send out in 1623 would have a surplus – and sold at Bordeaux. As for the financial arrangements, he recommended that Falkland encourage subscribers to put up one-third of their money immediately, a second part in September 1623 to provide for the main group of settlers who would go out in 1624, and the remainder in March 1624.[37]

During the winter of 1622 the terms of investment and land allotment were more fully worked out and published in a propagandist tract for Falkland's colony, which appeared in Ireland in 1623. This pamphlet provides the only information we have on the alienation of land by any of the proprietors. The provisions were substantially the same as those proposed by Whitbourne; briefly they were these: any investor

---

34 Whitbourne, *Discovrse Containing a Loving Invitation* (1622), sig. c 1ᵛ.
35 Vaughan, *Newlanders Cvre*, sig. A 5.
36 Whitbourne, *Discovrse Containing a Loving Invitation* (1622), sigs. B 3ᵛ-c 1, c 2ᵛ-3.
37 Richard Whitbourne to Falkland, 24 Dec. 1622, BM, Sloane MS 3827, ff 15-18.

who subscribed £ 100 was to share in the profits from the company fishery and from the labour of the company servants. He would also be given one shore of a harbour on the north side of Trinity Bay, together with 2,000 acres adjoining for which he would pay a nominal rent of one penny a year for each acre. Finally he would receive land near Fermeuse or Renewse, on which to build a house and erect fishing rooms sufficient to deal with the catch of a ship of 80 tons. Had it been carried out, of course, this provision would have effectively excluded the annual fishermen from two of the most popular fishing harbours in the island. Eight or more people had to be settled on this southern land within three years of the grant being made, and an annual rent of ten shillings was to be paid; failure to introduce settlers or to pay the rent would make the land forfeit. Those who invested greater or lesser sums were to be rewarded proportionately. The adventure was to be paid in two parts, one to finance the first year's voyage, and the second a year later. Any labourer with capital who was willing to go to the plantation in person should receive an annual wage, and 100 acres of land after five years' residence.[38]

The remainder of the tract set out the familiar inducements to plantation, differing only from its predecessors in that it was designed to show how the venture would benefit Ireland, "from whence the plantation is to be undertaken." Some of the standard English arguments could be transferred easily enough to Ireland – a colony would foster an increase in shipping, seamen, and customs revenue. Others applied more specifically to Irish conditions. Ireland's surplus products, particularly food-stuffs, could be sold to the colony; and an expansion of the Newfoundland fishery would stimulate employment in the ship-building industry and in the manufacture of fishing equipment, perhaps attracting as emigrants the English craftsmen which Ireland so badly needed.[39]

Falkland provided for both English and Irish investors by appointing Sir Samuel Smith of Dublin as company treasurer and Lionel Welstead as his agent in London.[40] Although T. C.'s tract asked only that the adventurers' money be in the treasurer's hands by November 1623, Welstead was actively seeking support in London early that year. He claimed to have interested a "master Bawle," whom he described as a gentleman of the privy chamber and ambitious to be

either a gouerner there or in the next place of Eminency which to obteyne he would adventure both his person to the best parte of his estate. Other gentlemen there be of his quallity with desire to be adventurers some in person others estate, they desiring to vnderstand your Lordships Condicions which you shall please to propound & send hither by the next retorne that a preparation be made to sett forward with the first of the next Springe.[41]

But Falkland preferred as governor Sir Francis Tanfield, probably a second cousin to his wife, who established the colony that very year, 1623.[42]

38 T. C., *A Short Discovrse of the New-Fovnd-Land* (Dublin, Society of Stationers, 1623), sigs. C 4ᵛ-D 2ᵛ.
39 *Ibid.*, sigs. B1-1ᵛ.
40 *Ibid.*, sig. C 4ᵛ; Whitbourne, *Discovrse and Discovery* (1622), sig. A 3.
41 Welstead to Falkland, 8 Jan. 1622/3, BM Add. MS 11033, ff 18-19ᵛ.
42 Whitbourne, *Discovrse and Discovery* (1623), sig. A 2.

For the scheme was not as abortive as Prowse and subsequent writers have imagined,[43] and both Tanfield and Falkland remained actively involved for some years. A settlement was still in existence in 1626, by which time Richard Whitbourne had visited it twice and had had dealings with Tanfield there. Although clearly out of favour with his patron now, Whitbourne wrote in February 1626 of his endeavours to interest Falkland's brother, the bishop of Exeter, and other west-country gentlemen in the enterprise. But the combined circumstances of a parliamentary session and their fear of Spanish reprisals against English shipping discouraged them from attempting anything that year.[44] By November 1626 Whitbourne had been released from Falkland's service and was seeking fresh employment.[45]

Strangely enough the only investor who is known to have taken land under Falkland's conditions was neither English nor Irish, but Welsh. Sir Henry Salusbury of Lleweni was William Vaughan's brother-in-law, and doubtless owed his interest in Newfoundland to him; indeed Salusbury's connection with the island has hitherto been known only from a brief reference in Vaughan's *The Newlanders Cvre*.[46] In fact, about the year 1626, Salusbury received two grants of land from Falkland under the terms set forth three years previously in T. C.'s pamphlet. His adventure must have been substantial, for he received in South Falkland a narrow lot of land bounded to the north by Baltimore's province of Avalon and to the south by the harbour of Fermeuse. A more extensive grant in North Falkland included land on Trinity Bay and stretched across to the "westerly sea." At this time Salusbury was evidently very serious in his intentions to establish a colony. Instructions were prepared for a colony situated on the strip of land between Placentia and Trinity bays. They recommended that only a few settlers be sent out at first

such as are Husbandmen which will [take] paines in the grownde and such as will not live idle & [waste] vittells & Cattell ... & therfore of gentreye n[oe] more to be sent thither then soe much as shall bee tho[ught] fitt to Comaunde the husband men.

Salusbury got advice on the provision of settlers from John Guy, who estimated that it would cost £94 15s. 6d. to provide a year's supply of food for eight people, and who recommended that they also be supplied with seed, cattle, goats, and pigs. From Nicholas Guy came advice on the equipment and men necessary for participation in the fishery.[47] There was evidently a strong link between the Vaughan group and Lord Falkland for, among Salusbury's papers, is a petition, perhaps dating from 1628 and addressed probably to the Duke of Buckingham, which groups Salusbury, Sir William Vaughan, Walter and Henry Vaughan with Sir Francis Tanfield and others as being "ingaged and interested in the Plantacions."[48] But Salusbury's schemes never seem to have got beyond the paper stage and, by 1628, Robert Hayman was

---

43 See Prowse, *History of Newfoundland*, p. 120. Prowse also confuses Lawrence and Francis Tanfield.
44 Whitbourne to Falkland, 27 Feb. 1625/6, BM, Sloane MS 3827, ff 67-8ᵛ.
45 Petition to the Duke of Buckingham, 10 Nov. 1626, PRO, CO 1/4 no 16.
46 sig. A 5.
47 National Library of Wales, MS 5390 D.
48 *Ibid.*, MS 1595 E.

regretting the failure of Falkland's enterprise and counselling him to try again "With wise, stayd, carefull honest-harted men."[49]

When Vaughan assigned land to Lord Falkland in 1620, he also disposed of further territory to Sir George Calvert, later Lord Baltimore. Bounded to the south by Falkland's land, Calvert's grant stretched north from a point midway between Fermeuse and Aquaforte as far as Caplin Bay.[50] Like Falkland, Calvert too had a long-standing interest in overseas ventures: a subscriber to the Virginia Company at the time of the second charter, he had also invested £1,000 in the East India Company in 1614.[51] He too tested his theories on colonization in Ireland, in confiscated lands around Baltimore, County Longford.[52] But Calvert's Newfoundland plantation was not intented as a cure for economic ills, as were Falkland's and Vaughan's; rather his colony seems to have been a personal, family undertaking – a refuge for the Calverts and their fellow Catholics.

While Calvert remained secretary of state, he was unable to go to Newfoundland himself; but in 1621 he sent out his first colonists under the governorship of a Welshman, Captain Edward Winne. Ferryland was the chosen site, and there the settlers spent an industrious and successful first year. By November of 1621, according to Winne, they had completed their first habitation: a building forty-four feet by fifteen feet, comprising a hall, a cellar, and four other chambers. By Christmas they had erected a stone kitchen with another room above it. The rest of the winter they spent fortifying the harbour, planting wheat, and preparing the ground for a spring sowing of barley, oats, and vegetables. The winter weather proved milder than expected and brought very little sickness. Even Newfoundland's freshwater streams had been found, to the writer's evident amazement, to quench the thirst "as well as any Beere . . . and neuer offended our stomacks at all." Summer found the crops flourishing, a store room built, and a salt works already in production. All this had been achieved by only twelve men.[53] In 1622 Calvert sent out a second group of settlers and the first discordant note amidst all the optimism came from the leader of this new group. Captain Daniel Powell – his name suggests that he too was a Welshman – reported that Ferryland had the reputation of being the coldest harbour in the whole island, and advised that a second settlement be established at Aquaforte the following spring.[54] One wonders whether Calvert recalled this prophesy after the disastrous winter that he spent in Ferryland some six years later. But meanwhile a colony of seven women and twenty-five men remained to try another winter at Ferryland.

Thus encouraged, Calvert, who still held his land only from a patentee of the Newfoundland Company, decided to set his tenure on a more formal and secure footing. Initially he received from the crown in December 1622 a grant "of the

49 Hayman, *Qvodlibets*, sig. F 1[v].
50 Vaughan, *Newlanders Cvre*, sig. A 5; Vaughan, *Golden Fleece*, map facing sig. A 2[v].
51 Brown, *Genesis*, II, 841.
52 See Hamill Kenny, "New Light on an Old Name," *Maryland Historical Magazine*, XLIX (1954), 116-21.
53 Winne to Calvert, 28 July 1622; the same to the same, 17 Aug. 1622; N[icholas] H[oskins] to W. P., 18 Aug. 1622; printed in Whitbourne, *Discourse Containing a Loving Invitation* (1622), pt. 2, sigs. A 1-3, B 1-C 1[v].
54 Powell to Calvert, 28 July 1622, *ibid.*, pt. 2, sigs. A 3[v]-4[v].

whole country of Newfound lande."[55] Three months later, perhaps after a protest by the Newfoundland Company, this was amended; and the charter of Avalon passed the great seal in April 1623.[56] This assigned to Calvert not only the land allotted to him by Vaughan, but further territory stretching north to Petty Harbour, where it was bounded by the St. John's lot, northwest to Conception Bay, and west to Placentia Bay. The province of Avalon did include, then, land previously held by the company. And it may be that the company decided to accept this infringement of its own charter in the hope that Calvert could establish a permanent settlement to the south and, through his very considerable influence at court, help to ensure the future of plantation in Newfoundland.

In 1625 Calvert resigned as secretary of state, declared himself a Roman Catholic, and received the title of Baron Baltimore. Now he was free to devote himself personally to his Newfoundland colony which, according to all contemporary reports, was the most flourishing on the island. His settlers, now numbering a hundred,

both for building and making triall of the ground haue done more than euer was performed by any in so short a time, hauing already there a broode of Horses, Kowes, and other bestial, and by the industry of his people he is beginning to draw back yeerly some benefit from thence already.[57]

With everything going so well, Baltimore tried to attract "any that will aduenture with him, or serue under him."[58] One such apparently was George Cottington who later, however, bitterly regretted the money he had invested in a fishing voyage with Baltimore and above all his "aduenture by land which I shall euer account desperat."[59]

But the colony meanwhile was without a governor, Edward Winne having left about 1624,[60] and Baltimore formed the intention of going out himself. His first frustration came when his two ships were impressed for the King's service. It took personal intervention on the part of Buckingham to get the ships released; and even then they were only allowed to sail on condition that they left Newfoundland within ten days of their arrival and brought home a cargo of fish for the royal navy.[61] Similar difficulties the following year, 1626, delayed the departure of his governor, Sir Arthur Aston, for Ferryland.[62] Not until 1627 was Baltimore able to pay a short visit to Newfoundland

which it imports me more then in Curiosity only to see; for, I must either go and settle it in a better Order than it is, or else give it over, and lose all the Charges I have been at hitherto for other Men to build their Fortunes upon. And I had rather be esteemed a

55 PRO, SP 14/141, f 351.
56 *CSP Dom., 1618-23*, 543; PRO, CO 1/2, no 23.
57 Sir William Alexander, *An Encouragement to Colonies* (W. Stanley, 1624), sigs. E 1.
58 R. Eburne, *A Plaine Path-Way to Plantations* (G. P[urslow] for John Marriott, 1624), sig. Q 1.
59 George Cottington to Sir John Finest, 7 April 1628, BM, Sloane MS 3827, ff 124-5ᵛ.
60 Vaughan, *Golden Fleece*, sig. Ccc 2ᵛ.
61 HMC, *Cowper*, I, 187.
62 Baltimore to Edward Nicholas, 7 April 1626, PRO, CO 1/4, no 19.

Fool by some for the Hazard of one Month's Journey, than to prove myself one certainly for six Years past, if the Business be now lost for the want of a little Pains and Care.[63]

What he saw, however, encouraged him to return the next year, taking with him his wife and all his children with the exception of his eldest son, Cecil.[64]

Although Baltimore had gone to Newfoundland "to builde and sett, and sowe," he soon found himself cast in the role not of planter but of protector of the English fishery. For the war with France had crossed the Atlantic and the old rivalries broke out again as the English attacked the French in the St. Lawrence, and the French raided the English at Newfoundland. In 1628 the Marquis de la Rade with three ships and four hundred men harassed English fishermen at their trade up and down the coast. In reprisal Baltimore captured six French fishing ships in Trepassey Bay and sent them home as prizes. Subsequently Baltimore requested protection for the fishery from two men of war, reporting that the fishermen were prepared to contribute towards the expense. Charles I's reply was to send one of the French prizes back to defend the island.[65] Nor were the French the only enemies that Baltimore made that summer. Among "the many crosses and disasters" that he had to bear was an Anglican clergyman, Erasmus Stourton by name, who so quarrelled with Baltimore that he was expelled from Ferryland. On his return to England Stourton proceeded to complain to the Privy Council of his treatment, accusing Baltimore of bringing two Catholic priests to Ferryland in 1627 and another priest and forty Catholic settlers in 1628; mass had been said, and a Protestant forcibly baptised.[66]

Perhaps it was these experiences which decided Baltimore to apply to the King for a grant of land in Virginia sometime during 1628;[67] perhaps he was simply dissatisfied with the results of seven years' work and investment in Newfoundland. However this may be, the experience of the winter of 1628-9 definitely convinced him that this was not the home for himself and his family. On 18 August 1629 he wrote a bitterly disillusioned letter to his friend, Sir Francis Cottington. He had, he said, already sent his family home "after much suffrance in this wofull country, where with one intolerable wynter were we almost undone. It is not to be expressed with my pen what we have endured."[68] The following day, 19 August, he informed the King[69] of his decision to

quit my residence, and to shift to some other warmer climate of this new world, where the wynters be shorter and lesse rigorous. For here your Majesty may please to

63 Baltimore to Sir Thomas Wentworth, 21 May 1627; printed in W. Knowler, ed., *The Earl of Strafforde's Letters and Despatches* (2 vols., London, 1739), I, 39.

64 Manuscript account of Baltimore's colonizing ventures in North America, 1670, BM, Sloane MS 3662, ff 24-6.

65 Baltimore to the King, and to Buckingham from Ferryland, 25 Aug. 1628; Sir Francis Cottington to Lord Treasurer Weston, 13 Dec. 1628; Petition of William Peasely on behalf of Baltimore, Dec. 1628; Memorial of Baltimore [to Secretary Dorchester], Dec. 1628, PRO, CO 1/4, nos 56, 57, 60-2.

66 *Ibid.*, no 59; Anderson, *Examinations and Deposition*, III, 38-41. For a biography of Stourton, see *Dictionary of Canadian Biography*, I, 614.

67 He had done so before December 1628, see PRO, CO 1/4, no 62.

68 Printed in L. C. Wroth, "Tobacco or Codfish: Lord Baltimore Makes his Choice," *Bulletin of the New York Public Library*, LVII (1954), 523-34.

69 PRO, CO 1/5, no 27.

vnderstand, that I haue found by too deare bought experience ... from the middest of October, to the middest of May there is a sadd face of wynter vpon all this land, both sea and land so frozen for the greatest part of the tyme as they are not penetrable, not plant or vegetable thing appearing out of the earth vntill it be about the beginning of May nor fish in the sea besides the ayre so intolerable and cold as it is hardly to be endured.

That winter fifty out of one hundred colonists had been sick at one time – Vaughan suggests from scurvy[70] – and nine or ten had died. Consequently he had resolved "to committ this place to fishermen that are able to encounter storms and hard weather," and himself move south to Virginia. Despite Charles I's advice that he abandon his colonial plans altogether, and despite an investment in Newfoundland later estimated at £20,000 to £30,000,[71] Baltimore returned to England only to secure a new charter. He was to die, however, before it passed the great seal, leaving it to his heir, Cecil, to establish the more successful plantation in Maryland.

Ferryland, however, was not abandoned, despite its reputation as "the coldest harbour of the Land, where those furious Windes and Icy Mountaynes does [sic] play, and beate the greatest part of the yeare."[72] In a protest against the award of a patent to Sir David Kirke and his associates in 1637, Cecil Calvert maintained that his father had left there "a sufficyent Colony, with a Governour."[73] According to a long-time inhabitant of the island this governor was a man named Hoyle "whoe was afterward carried away by one Ralph Morley." Sometime after this mysterious disappearance Cecil Calvert appointed a new governor, Captain William Hill, who took up residence in Baltimore's stone "mansion house" about 1633 or 1634 and there remained until expelled by Kirke in 1638.[74] The Calverts never completely renounced their interest in the island and, when David Kirke was recalled to England during the Interregnum, they revived their claim to proprietorship of the island, the suit being finally decided in their favour by Charles II.[75]

Cambriol, Bristol's Hope, a colony for the relief of Ireland, a haven for Catholics, even a new Scotland was thought of. For, about the year 1621, Sir William Alexander purchased from the company a large grant on the south coast of the island, west of Placentia Bay. But in the end the mainland rather than Newfoundland became the site of Nova Scotia.[76] It was perhaps as well, for the island – its severe climate, poor soil, lack of resources – defeated idealistic proprietors just as it had the original colonizing company. However industrious settlers might be, they could not make themselves self-supporting; and fishing alone it seemed could not cover the expenses of a large, uneconomic colony. Neither the chartered company nor the private association, then, had proved the answer to the problem of how to colonize Newfoundland.

70 Vaughan, *Newlanders Cvre*, sigs. F 2-2ᵛ.
71 PRO, CO 1/5, no 39; CO 1/14, no 9; PRO, HCA 24/110, no 329.
72 Vaughan, *Newlanders Cvre*, sigs. F 2-2ᵛ.
73 PRO, CO 1/9, no 43. And see below, p. 116.
74 Maryland Historical Society, Calvert Papers, evidence taken by commissioners at Ferryland, August 1652, testimony of William Poole; PRO, HCA 13/65: 12 March 1651/2, James Pratt; 29 March 1652, Robert Alward.
75 PRO, CO 1/14, no 9, i, ii, and see below, pp. 121-3.
76 Alexander, *Encouragement to Colonies*, sigs. E 1-1ᵛ.

And yet the energy and the money had not been completely wasted. The record of financial loss was balanced by the absence of major tragedy. And for some years now, continuously since 1610, there had been settlers in some part of the island; and many remained even when the official venture collapsed. In 1652 there were people still living in Ferryland who had been there with Lord Baltimore;[77] and there must have been similar groups in Cupids Cove, Renewse, and Harbour Grace. Not only had they proved that Newfoundland was habitable, but also that subsistence agriculture, supplemented by fishing, could provide a possible if meagre way of life. What had failed was collective settlement on a large scale, sponsored from England. Settlement then was possible, and in future it would be undertaken more by individuals than by organizations.

---

77 Maryland Historical Society, Calvert Papers, evidence taken by commissioners at Ferryland, August 1652.

VI

Prosperity and Crisis
1604-30

FREE TRADE VERSUS MONOPOLY

NPRECEDENTED COMMERCIAL EXPANSION awaited England in the decade that followed the peace of 1604. The markets of Spain and the Low Countries were open again. Restraints on shipping and exports had been lifted. Trade routes were relatively secure. Above all, capital had been released for investment in trades old and new. But the way in which English commerce should develop became the centre of one of the most heated economic debates of the day; the issue – regulated trade versus free trade; the protagonists – London capitalists versus outport merchants and their allies, the gentry.[1]

Not only had the war severely restricted trade and, for Londoners and west-countrymen especially, provided the powerful counter-attraction of privateering, but it had so disrupted the normal conditions of commerce as to allow interlopers to invade markets previously closed to all but members of certain chartered companies. When the war ended, the outport merchants were loath to surrender these markets to London-dominated companies. And comparatively few traders from the provinces possessed the extensive capital reserve necessary for participation in a regulated trade. For economic expansion, therefore, the west-countrymen and other outport merchants needed free trade, and the greater opportunities and higher prices which they were convinced would result from an absence of restriction.[2] To the wealthier Londoners, however, who could afford to have their money tied up for lengthy periods, the regulated company was the one effective way of maintaining prices, securing favourable conditions of trade, and shutting out foreign competition. Consequently they could not tolerate the encroachment of the west-country merchants into the Mediterranean, especially as these southern markets increased in value while their traditional outlets in northern Europe declined. The trade in New-foundland fish, prosperous despite the war, dominated by the west-country but

---

1 On the reasons for the alliance between certain members of the gentry, notably Sir Edwin Sandys, and the outports, see T. K. Rabb, "Sir Edwin Sandys and the Parliament of 1604," *American Historical Review*, LXIX (1964), 646-70, who offers a revision of the standard interpretation given in Friis, *Alderman Cockayne's Project*; and also R. Ashton, "The Parliamentary Agitation for Free Trade in the Opening Years of the Reign of James I," *Past and Present*, no 38 (Dec. 1967), 40-55, who takes issue with Dr. Rabb's conclusions.
2 See Sir Edwin Sandys, "Instructions Touching the Bill for Free Trade," in A. E. Bland, P. A. Brown, and R. H. Tawney, eds., *English Economic History, Select Documents* (London, 1914), pp. 443-53.

dependent upon markets which London wished to control, could not help but become a factor in the dispute.

The irreconcilable attitudes of the two sides became clear in 1604 when, perhaps as a result of a rumour that the Spanish Company's charter would soon be confirmed, an unsuccessful bill was introduced into the Commons which would have given all merchants freedom of trade to all countries. And when the Spanish Company did receive its new charter, even though it had been modified in favour of the outports so that their merchants were in the majority, the whole question of free trade was reopened by a west-country member, Sir George Somers of Lyme Regis. The Spanish Company, being primarily interested in cloth and opposed to the trade in victuals, complained that the Newfoundland fishermen could undercut their price for fish by half. Only reluctantly did it concede that the fishermen made a valuable contribution to the nation's economy by exchanging their fish for Mediterranean goods and specie.[3] Despite the company's opposition, the parliament of 1606 passed a bill freeing trade with Spain, Portugal, and France, on the grounds that shipowners, seamen, and fishermen were impoverished by being excluded from these, their most valuable markets. Interestingly enough, during the bill's preliminary stages, it was suggested that the charters of Exeter and Bristol for trade to France and Spain respectively should be upheld; but these proposals were dropped as revealing too clearly the outports' jealousy of the capital.

The disputes on free trade did not end with this outport victory. The west-country merchants, consistently supported by their influential and vocal representatives in the Commons, opposed any move to limit their freedom in the Mediterranean. In 1609, when Salisbury proposed the formation of a new democratically organized French Company, the scheme was severely criticized in the Commons, despite the provision that all fishermen should be at liberty to transport their fish to France and to trade there. A proposed revival of the Spanish Company in 1616 met with less success, even though the Londoners themselves suggested that the restrictions should apply only to those trading from the capital. The west-country merchants still objected and referred the matter to the Commons where, as expected, they found vociferous support. The question was raised again in 1619 and 1620, but still with no result. Nevertheless by 1620 the London merchants had so strengthened their grip on the Spanish trade that, while the west-country retained its control of fish exports, five-sixths of all other trade to and from Spain, Portugal, and the dependent islands was channelled through the capital.[4]

The outports' jealousy, therefore, had some foundation and they neglected no opportunity to challenge London's predominance. When, in 1617, the Levant Company attempted to extend its control, especially over imports of Levantine goods, by the direct authority of Sir William Garway, the outport merchants' refusal to accept the company's authority forced the question before the Privy Council. In fact, few outport merchants traded directly with the Levant, but many exchanged their Newfoundland cod, their pilchards, and other fish for Levantine goods in Genoa, Leghorn, Civitavecchia, and other ports on the west coast of Italy which were open to all. Even the paralyzing commercial depression of the latter part of

3 PRO, SP 14/21, no 2.
4 For a more detailed account of the struggles to revive these two companies, see Friis, *Alderman Cockayne's Project*, pp. 149-67, 169-71.

James I's reign could be, and was, blamed on the companies and the crippling impositions which they placed upon trade.[5]

By 1620 the question of free trade and the rights of the west-country fishermen had become in effect synonymous. In these arguments, as in those between the Newfoundland Company and the fishing interests, the latter could raise the cry of the national welfare. Not only was the fishery a nursery for seamen and an encouragement to shipbuilding, but the trade in fish accorded ideally with current economic thought – for a minimal capital outlay it brought a high return in costly Mediterranean goods and above all in specie. This was a fact which could not be circumvented, however much the Privy Council might believe in the long-term effectiveness of regulated trade. The whole issue reached a crisis with the discussion of the New England Company's monopoly of the fishery,[6] for this dispute in reality concerned not only the control of the New England grounds but also the future of the Newfoundland industry. The recent troubles between the Newfoundland Company and the fishermen had concluded with the Privy Council's pious wish that both groups coexist in friendship, hardly a satisfying result to either side. A decision on the New England issue, whether in favour of the fishermen or the company, was obviously relevant to the situation in Newfoundland.

Sir Ferdinando Gorges' decision to revive the scheme for the colonization of "North Virginia," and to obtain a new patent with some restriction of fishing rights to the patentees, brought a swift reaction in the House of Commons. There a mention of monopolies was enough to light the fuse of explosive debate. This particular issue created a formidable alliance between the west-country members and Sir Edwin Sandys, treasurer of the Virginia Company and now the most influential advocate of free trade. His bill to guarantee the complete freedom of all the North American fisheries, introduced first in 1621, occasioned discussion in each session of parliament for the next seven years.[7]

For the first three years, the debates dealt as much with Newfoundland as with New England. Thus, while Sandys attacked Gorges' patent for opening the shores of New England to aliens while closing them to Englishmen, the representatives of Plymouth and Dartmouth dwelt upon the Newfoundland fishermen's complaints of abuses, and accused the Londoners of imposing restraints simply to foster their own dominance of the fishery. "London merchants by restraining trade, and imposing upon trade, undo all trade," declared William Nyell of Dartmouth. As opponents of the bill stood the members of the Privy Council, including Sir George Calvert and John Guy, now member for the city of Bristol. Initially both sides could agree on the necessity of ending the disorders prevalent in the island; but any grounds for agreement were soon forgotten. The issue resolved itself thus: should the colonizing companies be allowed reserved space on the beaches, or should the harbours remain open each year until the annual fishermen arrived? Guy argued that to guarantee the fishermen complete freedom of beach space was simply to abolish that of the settlers, and so to overthrow settlement altogether, leaving the

5 *Ibid.*, pp. 183, 406.
6 The issue as it affected the New England Company is very fully discussed in R. A. Preston, *Gorges of Plymouth Fort* (Toronto, 1953).
7 The following account of the parliamentary discussions is based upon Stock, *Proceedings and Debates*, I, 30-88 *passim*.

island open to foreign occupation. There were not now, he maintained, and never would be enough colonists to endanger the fishermen's prosperity. The west-countrymen challenged this conclusion. To give the settlers' privileges in every harbour would so favour the colonizing companies as to enable them to increase their membership until they could exclude the fishermen completely. And if the fishery were overthrown, threatened John Glanvyle of Plymouth, the nation would lose an annual income of £120,000 which it received in return for nothing more than a few provisions.

The bill twice passed the Commons but the Lords, less subject to pressure from the fishing interests and more amenable to royal direction, never discussed it. After 1624 the importance of the Newfoundland question declined. The energy had gone out of the company; it had become apparent too that the other patentees would never be a very formidable threat to the fishermen's existence. Guy and Calvert furthermore had ceased to be members of the House. Attention was now focused on Gorges' patent. The threat to the Newfoundland merchants had passed, at least for the time being.

PROSPERITY, 1604-24

While in London their members of parliament and agents fought for the right to fish and to sell fish without restriction, in the west-country the fishermen made the most of the boom in England's commerce. A fleet of perhaps 150 ships in 1604 had grown to approximately 200 in 1610, and to 250 five years later when Richard Whitbourne estimated that the Newfoundland fishery annually employed some 5000 men and produced 300,000 quintals of fish, worth £120,000, and 1250 tuns of train oil, worth £1500.[8] A glance at Table XI shows the increase in the number of vessels returning directly from Newfoundland to England after 1604. In the earlier period, 1577-1604, it was comparatively rare for the total number entering one port to reach double figures (see Table IV), whereas now in one year thirty-two ships and in another sixty-six ships entered Plymouth alone.

Only a small proportion of this fish would be purchased by Englishmen. The ending of the war on land and sea had destroyed an extensive market, and the government had by now realized the error of Burghley's earlier assessment of domestic consumption. After 1604 it relied upon an expanding overseas market to provide the necessary demand, and ceased trying to safeguard the security of the industry by artificially stimulating demand at home. The coastal port books reveal no significant increase in the volume of Newfoundland fish distributed by this means, nor any change in the overall and restricted pattern of the trade as compared with the pre-1604 period. Fish continued to reach London, but otherwise very little passed beyond the west-country itself.[9] Some fish would be moved by road, though again probably not far beyond the immediate locale. About 1606 it was estimated in Southampton that twenty ships could satisfy the English demand for Newfound-

8 Trinity House Transactions, 1609-25, f 1; Whitbourne, *Discovrse and Discovery* (1620), sig. E 2ᵛ.
9 This assessment is based on an examination of all the surviving coastal port books for the period 1604-1660, from the ports of Barnstaple (7 books), Dartmouth (3), Exeter (4), Plymouth (4), Bristol (7), Southampton (5), Portsmouth (9), Poole (4), Weymouth (3)

land fish.[10] Most of the fish, then, remained in the ports, where a considerable amount would be required as ships' victuals, and from which the surplus could be re-exported.

The expansion of this re-export trade, perceptible even during the closing years of the war with Spain, continued without setback until 1620. In that year English commerce, at least as measured by the trade in cloth, was gripped by a severe depression which lasted for the next four years. The depression, however, apparently affected London much more than the outports,[11] and the evidence of the port books suggests that the level of trade in Newfoundland fish was roughly the same in the early 1620s as in the previous decade (see Tables XII-XIX).

Predominant in the trade, now as in the earlier period, were the two ports of Plymouth and Dartmouth, which consistently sent most ships to the fishery and despatched the largest quantities of Newfoundland fish to a wide area of distribution in both English and alien shipping (see Tables XI-XIII and Figs. III, IV). The pattern of the re-export trade in fish from these two ports reflects that of their trade in general. Both were popular centres with alien merchants and shipping. Neither specialized heavily in one particular product: exports of local cloth formed the bulk of the trade, but other west-country goods such as lead, calfskins, provisions including herrings and pilchards, stockings, and small wares, as well as Newfoundland cod and oil, were of considerable importance. France, Spain, and Portugal were the most popular destinations for ships leaving either port. In 1609-10, for example, 40 per cent of all Plymouth shipping was destined for France and 20 per cent for the Iberian peninsula; in 1616-17 the figures were 60 per cent and 20 per cent respectively.[12] In the years 1614-15, 1617-18, and 1623-4 between 59 per cent and 64 per cent of Dartmouth's shipping went to France and about 20 per cent to Spain and Portugal.[13] Less important to both were markets in Italy, the Low Countries, Ireland, the Channel Islands, the Baltic, and later the West Indies and New England.

It is significant that William Nyell of Dartmouth and John Glanvyle and Thomas Sherwill of Plymouth were the most vocal representatives of the outports in any parliamentary issue affecting either the fisheries or the trade in fish.[14] The only other outport member to speak on Sandys' bill for the free fisheries was John Guy of Bristol, who was of course one of the bill's staunchest opponents. Bristol and Exeter too were in a rather special position, for the trade of the former to Spain and of the latter to France was controlled by chartered companies, both of which concentrated on the traffic in cloth. Both Bristol and Exeter had had a larger and more

which are in the PRO, and also of the customs records of the city of Chester (Town Hall, Chester), from 1605 to 1624. As so little change apparently took place, the coastal trade will not be discussed in detail again.

10 "A Declaration on Trade to the Straights," [addressed to the Privy Council, 1606], SRO, Second Book of Instruments, 1597-1689.

11 See McGrath, *Merchants and Merchandise in Seventeenth-Century Bristol*, p. xix, and W. B. Stephens, *Seventeenth-Century Exeter* (Exeter, 1958), p. 8. On the causes of the depression and its effects on the cloth trade, see B. E. Supple, *Commercial Crisis and Change in England, 1600-1642* (Cambridge, 1959), and Friis, *Alderman Cockayne's Project*.

12 PRO, E 190/1023/18; 1028/11.

13 PRO, E 190/942/12; 944/2; 945/10.

14 Stock, *Proceedings and Debates*, I, 26-84 *passim*.

valuable export trade, in terms of customs revenue, than either Plymouth or Dartmouth.[15] Bristol shipped valuable cargoes of coal, iron, wax, and soap, besides the usual west-country commodities; but according to the scanty evidence of the port books, the trade in fish was so small as to be negligible, despite the considerable number of ships returning from Newfoundland (see Tables xi, xv). In the export of fish Exeter ranked third after Plymouth and Dartmouth, but fewer alien merchants were involved (see Fig. v), perhaps because the existence of the French Company made the port a less attractive centre. Cloth, however, was undoubtedly Exeter's most important export and most of it was destined for France; in 1624, for example, "the last representative year of Exeter's traditional economy," 45 out of 94 ships leaving the port sailed for France, the remainder being fairly equally divided between Spain and the Atlantic islands.[16] The Newfoundland fishery itself was never as essential to Exeter's welfare as to that of other west-country ports (see Table xi), and few Exeter merchants specialized in it.[17]

Although ships were entering Southampton from Newfoundland during this period, the re-export trade in fish shows no increase over the earlier period, and was almost entirely restricted to France (see Tables xi, xvi). The overall decline of the port which had begun in the mid-sixteenth century continued throughout this period, and was not in fact reversed until the nineteenth century.[18] In 1619, when the Privy Council asked the ports for contributions to fit out a fleet against pirates, Southampton was required to raise only £300, less than the sum requested from the small ports of Weymouth and Barnstaple.[19] The port books reveal that Southampton's major markets in all trades were northern France, Ireland, and the Channel Islands, with only occasional voyages being made to Spain, Portugal, Italy, and the Low Countries. The surviving books show that between 56 per cent and 74 per cent of all shipping leaving Southampton in 1612-14, 1615-16, and 1618-19 went to France.[20] Southampton's smaller neighbours, Poole and Weymouth, were both more important in the fishery and in the re-export trade in fish (see Tables xi, xvii, xviii). In 1619 the mayor of Poole claimed that the Newfoundland fishery and one other trade together occupied all the port's shipping; and three years later the mayor of Weymouth reported that the town had sent only 11 ships to Newfoundland instead of the more usual 39.[21]

That the markets which the London merchants sought to restrict were vital to the prosperity of the fishing merchants is obvious. The Baltic market for fish was supplied by the Dutch and, to a lesser extent, by the Scots.[22] France and Spain,

15 Stephens, *Seventeenth-Century Exeter*, p. 8, Table 1.
16 *Ibid.*, pp. 9-10.
17 See also W. B. Stephens, "The West Country Ports and the Struggle for the Newfoundland Fisheries in the Seventeenth Century," *Trans. Devon Association*, LXXXVIII (1956), 90-101, and the same author's "Economic and Commercial Development of the City and Port of Exeter, 1625-1688" (PHD thesis, University of London, 1954).
18 Ruddock, *Italian Merchants*, p. 272.
19 Anderson, *Examinations and Depositions*, I, viii.
20 PRO, E 190/819/14; 820/6, 9; 821/2.
21 *CSP Dom., 1619-23*, pp. 25, 385. On Weymouth's trade, see M. Weinstock, *Studies in Dorset History* (Dorchester, 1953).
22 The transcripts of the Sound registers show no fish from the west-country going to the

however, were natural outlets for the west-country. Both their religion and their maritime activities created an enormous demand for fish which their domestic fishing industries could not satisfy. Even when commercial depression hit England in the early twenties, the damage to these markets was much less than to trade with the Levant and the east, both of which suffered heavily from the effects of the Thirty Years' War and from Dutch competition.

The trade in Newfoundland fish to France consistently occupied the largest number of ships, although it was not necessarily the most valuable. The ships involved tended to be small, averaging about 20 tons, and so no bigger than the ordinary coastal vessel. They plied across the Channel bringing canvas and coarse cloths from northern France, salt and wine from La Rochelle and Bordeaux, and carrying mixed cargoes of west-country products to France, mainly to Normandy and Brittany. In 1615, for example, 20 out of 28 ships sailing from Dartmouth to France with Newfoundland fish were bound for those two northern provinces, only 4 for La Rochelle and 4 for Bordeaux.[23] In a four year period only 1 out of a total of 17 vessels making that voyage with fish from Southampton sailed as far south as La Rochelle.[24]

A little surprising, perhaps, in this period of relatively safe and rapidly expanding trade through the Straits is the rarity of voyages to the Mediterranean ports of France, especially to Marseilles. In the early years of the seventeenth century, Marseilles served as the entrepôt for fish in the western Mediterranean. There the English, then the dominant foreign traders with their own merchant colony, exchanged their Newfoundland cod, their pilchards, herrings, lead, calfskins, and manufactured goods for wine, fruit, oil, and all the products of the Mediterranean and the Levant.[25] Yet, between 1604 and 1624, years which coincided with Marseilles' greatest popularity with English traders before Dutch competition and a tax on salt fish drove them to Leghorn, the surviving port books reveal only 4 ships carrying Newfoundland fish from England to that destination. Of these, 2 came from Plymouth in 1617 and one from Barnstaple the following year; the fourth was a Dutch vessel which left Dartmouth for Marseilles in 1624.[26] Presumably then most of the English-made Newfoundland fish reached Marseilles by way of the triangular trade.

The two ports of Plymouth and Dartmouth predominated in the trade to the Iberian peninsula, and its character was quite different from that of the trade to France. The ships making the longer voyage tended to be larger, averaging 40 to 70 tons, and they carried more valuable cargoes. In 1618, for example, 28 ships left Dartmouth for France with fish worth £2479 whereas the fish taken to Spain in only 10 ships was worth £4810 (see Table XIII). Alien merchants and shipping were involved, although not to the same extent as in the French trade. Londoners and

---

Baltic; see N. E. Bang, ed., *Tabeller over Skibsfart og Varetransport gjennem Oeeresund, 1497-1660* (2 vols., Copenhagen, 1906-22).

23 PRO, E 190/942/12.

24 PRO, E 190/819/14; 820/6, 9; 821/2.

25 See G. Rambert, ed., *Histoire du commerce de Marseille* (I-VI, 1949-66, Paris, 1954), IV, 123-5, 163.

26 PRO, E 190/1028/11; 944/1; 945/10.

their ships also participated, especially in the trade from Dartmouth (see Figs. III, IV). From the smaller ports, though this is not true of Exeter, the patterns of the Iberian and French trades did not differ greatly. The low tonnage of the ships employed restricted the quantity of fish carried, and made the nearer ports such as St Sebastian and Bilbao more popular destinations than the Mediterranean ports.

The only other market which regularly received large shipments of Newfoundland fish was Italy. The west-coast ports, not being controlled by the Levant Company, were all popular with English traders and Leghorn perhaps the most popular of all. A free port since 1593, Leghorn could be reached fairly quickly from England, ryals could be purchased cheaply, and Florentine cloth could be bought for resale elsewhere in the Mediterranean.[27] Not surprisingly then it was Leghorn which later absorbed those English merchants who at the beginning of the seventeenth century had preferred Marseilles. But Genoa, Civitavecchia, and later Naples[28] also received Newfoundland fish, west-country goods, exports from the Baltic, and Norman canvas – all shipped from southwestern England. In return the English purchased almonds, fruits, silk, currants, spices, and all the other luxury products of Italy and the eastern Mediterranean. A very valuable trade then would have been killed had the Levant Company succeeded in its desire to restrict to its members the importation of Levant goods, even when they had not been obtained from ports in which the company held a monopoly.

Throughout the Mediterranean English traders met with severe competition from the Dutch, whose developments in merchant shipping enabled them to transport cargoes from northern Europe swiftly and cheaply. So successful were the Dutch that in 1621 a bill was introduced into the Commons designed to tighten the navigation system so as to exclude aliens from the carrying trade in general. The bill was rejected as likely to discourage trade, but in the following year and again in 1623 royal proclamations were issued imposing restraints on the use of alien shipping and on the activities of foreign merchants.[29] In all this agitation much was made of the part played by aliens in the carrying trade in fish, so much so that in 1624 the total exclusion of aliens from the export trade in fish and from the fishery off the southern coast of England was discussed.[30]

Consequently the evidence which the port books afford of the participation of aliens in the re-exporting of Newfoundland fish is somewhat surprising. The most striking feature of Figs. III-VI is the high percentage of French merchants and shipping engaged in the trade to France. The Dutch, then, should not have been the sole objects of the Londoners' campaign. In fact Dutch ships have been found carrying fish only from the ports of Plymouth and Dartmouth, and then not in great numbers. Before 1624, on the evidence of the port books at least, there is no known instance of an English merchant employing a Dutch ship, though some of them did use French vessels. Nor was the Londoners' accusation that the west-countrymen

27 Millard, "Import Trade of London," p. 197.
28 See H. Koenigsberger, "English Merchants in Naples and Sicily in the Seventeenth Century," *English Historical Review*, LXII (1947), 304-26.
29 Lounsbury, *British Fishery*, p. 65.
30 *CSP Dom., Add., 1580-1625*, pp. 661-2.

did not charter their shipping entirely accurate; London ships were used on occasion as, for example, in 1624 when John Lynne of Exeter freighted 4 London ships with Newfoundland fish for Portugal.[31]

But, if the Dutch were less important in the carrying trade in fish than might have been expected, both they and the French were serious competitors in the triangular trade. The French, of course, were old rivals. The Dutch apparently began to make the direct voyage to Newfoundland about the turn of the century,[32] although more often to buy fish than to catch it themselves. A typical voyage was probably the one made in 1620 by David de Vries, who bought fish at Newfoundland, sold it at Cartagena, and then proceeded on a long Mediterranean trading voyage.[33] Nevertheless the growth of England's own triangular trade must have kept pace with the development of the industry, for there is a great discrepancy between the port book figures of ships returning directly to England and the contemporary estimates of the size of the fleet, even after due allowance has been made for exaggeration by propagandists such as Whitbourne. Nor could the re-export trade alone have satisfied the European market and have accounted for the £10,000 in customs revenue which England was reported to earn annually from the Mediterranean goods exchanged for Newfoundland fish.[34]

This impression of a sizeable triangular trade is borne out by the evidence. So, in the early seventeenth century, English vessels brought more Newfoundland cod directly to Marseilles than those of any other nation: 13 in 1612, 15 the following year, 7 in 1614, and 8 in 1615.[35] And, whereas before 1604 only the occasional reference to the trade can be gleaned from the records of the High Court of Admiralty, after that date there are a great many cases concerned with the triangular voyage and they frequently involve not just a single ship but large groups sailing in consort. Between August and September 1611, for example, a small fleet of pirate ships attacked no fewer than 17 Newfoundlanders on their way to the Mediterranean.[36] Five years later 7 ships bound for Italy also fell victim to pirates, while 7 more wisely formed a consortship at the fishery for their voyage to Malaga.[37]

Pirates, in fact, were the one great threat to the prosperity of the Newfoundland trade in this period – not so much at the island itself, although Peter Easton and Henry Mainwaring inflicted considerable damage there, but from Europeans in home waters and especially from the Barbary pirates in the Mediterranean. The Admiralty Court records contain innumerable references to their plundering of Newfoundlanders and, in 1622, the mayor of Weymouth reported that almost every ship which had left that port for Spain and the Straits had been lost, so that only 11

---

31 PRO, E 190/945/10.
32 By 1593, according to Innis, *Cod Fisheries*, p. 52n. No references, however, can be found in Dutch sources before 1600, see D. Glerum-Laurentius, "A History of Dutch Activity in the Newfoundland Trade from about 1590 till about 1680" (MA thesis, Memorial University of Newfoundland, 1960), pp. 13-14, 19.
33 D. P. de Vries, "Voyages from Holland to America, 1632-44," trans. H. C. Murphy, in *New York Historical Society Collections*, ser. 2, III, pt. 1 (1857), 3-129.
34 *CSP Col., 1574-1660*, p. 25.
35 Rambert, *Marseille*, IV, 132.
36 PRO, HCA 1/47, ff 261-1ᵛ.
37 *CSP Dom., 1611-18*, p. 426; PRO, HCA 24/77, no 34.

ships had gone to the fishery that year.[38] Piracy, however, soon became only one of the problems facing the west-country fishermen.

CRISIS, 1625-30

In 1625, with the outbreak of war with Spain, the west-country entered a period of commercial chaos from which it did not begin to emerge until the 1630s. Even before the actual declaration of war the fishing merchants were made to realize what the conflict would mean to their trade, and the older men may have recalled unhappily the restrictions of thirty years ago. In December 1624 all ships laden with corn and Newfoundland fish, bound for Spain and Portugal, were stayed until the victualler of the navy had secured all the provisions he needed.[39] By January 1625 watch was being kept on the ports to ensure that no fish reached the potential enemy although, as Sir John Suckling pointed out, Spain could always obtain fish from other sources.[40] Moreover the English were likely to be the chief losers if Spain retaliated by forbidding entry to their exports of woolens; and, should restraints be imposed on the Newfoundland trade, then English navigation must suffer. Nevertheless, all ships were forbidden to leave port before 1 April 1625, a prohibition which the fishermen had evidently anticipated and which some had evaded by sailing unusually early.[41] Although the Newfoundland-bound fleet escaped more lightly than some – by order of the privy council one master, one bosun, and his mate were left to every ship – protests at the delay flooded in from the ports.[42] Probably even more damaging than the stays of shipping and impressment of men was the embargo which, as Suckling had foreseen, Spain promptly placed on English shipping. In the autumn of 1625 a number of vessels which had made the direct voyage from the fishery were detained in Spanish ports,[43] and west-country exports to the Iberian peninsula declined dramatically. Worse was to follow. In 1626 came unofficial commercial war with France, the west-country's second major market. When their goods were confiscated in French ports, the English retaliated by forbidding trade to France. Open war was declared the following year.

The effect of these two wars on the commerce of the west-country was disastrous. In 1625 Exeter's trade to Spain declined by a third, but the loss of the French trade hit the port even more severely. By 1628 the total volume of Exeter's exports was negligible; and in that year just one French vessel collected a cargo of fish for La Rochelle.[44] That year Dartmouth sent no ships at all to France, Spain, or Portugal; just four years before 65 had gone to France, 12 to Spain, and 10 to Portugal. Dartmouth tried to compensate for the loss of these markets by increasing trade with

38 CSP Dom., 1619-23, p. 304.
39 APC Col., 1613-80, pp. 80-1.
40 CSP Dom., 1623-25, pp. 439, 474.
41 APC Col., 1613-80, pp. 83-4.
42 Ibid., p. 84; CSP Dom., 1623-25, pp. 491, 494, 496.
43 PRO, HCA 13/45: 13 Sept. 1626, Robert Staunton; 29 Nov., James Stonehouse; HCA 13/46: 17 Feb. 1626/27, John Arnold. Three Poole ships had not returned by 1628, "A Note of Shipping Belonging to the Towne of Poole," 6 May 1628, PRO, SP 16/103, no 43.
44 Stephens, Seventeenth-Century Exeter, pp. 14-15; PRO, E 190/947/3.

Italy and Ireland, but even so the total number of ships engaged in the export trade dropped from 111 in 1624 to 31 in 1628.[45] Weymouth and Poole had both enjoyed a fairly regular trade in Newfoundland fish to the Iberian markets. During the war years this vanished completely (see Tables XVII, XVIII).

At the same time the danger of attack by pirates increased. Emboldened perhaps by the preoccupation of the English, Spanish, and later the French navies, the Barbary pirates now ventured out of the Mediterranean into the Channel and even into the Atlantic. In 1625 they lay in wait for a Newfoundland fleet estimated at 250 vessels, and within ten days had captured 27 of them. All during the summer the representatives of the west-country ports voiced their fears to the Privy Council until, for the first time, they united in a petition requesting naval protection for their ships, something they usually shunned because of the restrictions which an escort placed upon their freedom. The following year pirates ravaged the fleet as it left in the spring, and again on its return.[46] In 1627 the Privy Council allotted a convoy to the Newfoundlanders as they neared Land's End, but the fleet still suffered badly not only from Barbary pirates but from French privateers. Poole, which had once sent 20 ships a year to the fishery, could send but 3 in 1628, for the port had lost 20 ships in the last four years and had now only a total of 16 left. Early in 1629 it was reported that only 40 west-country ships were at Newfoundland, and even there they were threatened by the French.[47]

Gone then was the prosperity of the early years of the century, meaningless the fishermen's victory in the fight to keep open Mediterranean markets. Both had been destroyed by war and piracy. To fight these wars, to rid the seas of the Barbary pirates, ships were stayed and men impressed. Although some special care was taken to protect the fishing industry above all others, the government of Charles I boasted no William Cecil to watch paternally over his nursery for seamen. With English traders unable to enter Spanish ports, the French and Dutch were free to take over the market. In France itself only the Huguenot ports remained open to the English. The Newfoundland trade suffered now as it had never done during Elizabeth's wars; its peak of prosperity had been reached before 1620, it would not be regained before 1660.

45 PRO, E 190/945/10; 947/1.
46 CSP Col., 1574-1660, p. 75; CSP Dom., 1625-26, pp. 79, 81, 82, 83, 85, 86, 320, 480; PRO, HCA 13/45: 24 Aug. 1626, Nicholas Hollegrove.
47 CSP Dom., Add. 1625-49, p. 217; PRO, HCA 13/46: 7 Nov. 1627, Thomas Turckey; Anderson, Examinations and Depositions, II, 1-3; PRO, SP 16/103, no 43; PRO, CO 1/5, no 3.

VII

The Beginnings of
Government Intervention 1630-60

THUS FAR the efforts of individuals had shaped the history of Newfoundland. Of their own initiative the west-countrymen had adopted the new industry, developed the trade in fish, and established a rough if inadequate form of order at the island. Only in times of national emergency had the government taken positive action to encourage or protect the fishery. And the fishermen preferred it this way: preferred to put up with disorder rather than have their fishing interrupted by inquiries such as that made by Richard Whitbourne in 1615;[1] preferred to risk danger at sea rather than be escorted by naval convoys which meant that their departure was delayed while the fleet assembled, that the ships sailed at the pace of the slowest vessel, and that they all reached their destination together – so flooding the market and lowering the price. To the fishermen government interest meant only interference, government action only restriction.

Colonization, although authorized by royal charter, had also been a private matter. When, in 1618 and 1620, the disputes between the fishermen and colonists had been forwarded to London, the Privy Council had shown itself indecisive, giving support first to one side then the other. The coming of settlers had raised a vital question: would the nation benefit most if the industry were conducted in the old way by independent fishing merchants, or if it were controlled by a chartered company? The same basic issue – free or regulated trade – had already come up in a number of different guises. It seemed that, while favouring the more efficient regulated trade, the government hardly dared to enforce it in face of the Commons' opposition and for fear of upsetting the always precarious stability of the country's trade.

There was no sudden and dramatic change in 1630, no introduction of a consistent policy towards Newfoundland. What can be discerned between 1630 and 1660 is an attempt by successive governments to find and enforce a commercial policy and, within this policy, to reconcile the apparently conflicting interests of a free fishery and a regulated trade.

The administration of Charles I never did succeed in adopting a coherent policy, but its sympathies and its ineffectiveness are revealed as the disputes over the carrying trade in fish reached their climax in the thirties. Agitation to make the carrying

---

1 In 1615 Whitbourne had gone to Newfoundland with a commission from the Admiralty Court to inquire into the disorders prevalent on the island. The fishermen had been uncooperative, resentful of the interruption to their short fishing season. Whitbourne, *Discovrse and Discovery* (1620), sig. C 1; PRO, CO 1/1, f 121.

trade an English monopoly had begun in the twenties and, when the Commons had refused to strengthen the navigation laws in 1621, James I had placed some restrictions on alien merchants and shipping and forbidden the export of bullion by royal proclamations of 1622 and 1623. These and other factors had combined to end the pre-eminent position which aliens had held in English trade since the time of Elizabeth.[2] Even so, as English merchant shipping could not compete with the Dutch in cheapness of freight costs or in sailing ability, foreign bottoms remained popular, especially in trades involving bulky commodities such as fish.

The west-countrymen were indifferent as to who bought or transported their fish as long as it sold well and was shipped quickly and cheaply to market. Although they, like the Londoners, had resented the alien merchants' earlier domination of many branches of trade,[3] they were prepared to wink at it where it did not clash with their own interests. To the London merchants, the flow of foreign shipping from the western outports was a last stumbling block to their domination of the carrying trade, in which the export of fish played no small part. In 1624 the total exclusion of aliens from the export trade in fish and from the fishery on the southern coasts of England was discussed.[4] Two years later an order in council decreed that all English-caught fish, whether taken off the coasts of England, Newfoundland, or New England, be transported only in English shipping.[5] In 1629 the decay of English navigation was blamed on the fact that bulky commodities such as sea coal, Newfoundland fish, herrings, and pilchards were usually exported in foreign vessels.[6]

The whole issue was given new urgency by the trade depression of the late twenties which threatened the lucrative and extensive trade which London had developed with Spain and the Mediterranean since 1604. In the early thirties London pressure on the government to take action increased. When in 1631 it was decided that an order in council of the previous year should be strictly enforced and the use of alien shipping totally forbidden,[7] west-country reaction was immediate. For the next two years both sides appeared before hearings authorized by the Privy Council. The London merchants, represented by the master and wardens of Trinity House, complained that English shipping could not find cargoes because of the employment of alien vessels.[8] To this argument the fishing merchants made their standard reply: that they could not sell their fish at all unless they sold it to foreigners who would transport it themselves. If this trade were disrupted, great hardship would be caused to the many thousands who relied upon it for their livelihood.

The council was in a dilemma. Its members knew, from the constant stream of petitions from the fishing ports and from the representations of local members of parliament during the troubled twenties, how heavily dependent was the west-country on the Newfoundland trade. On the other hand the encouragement of

2 Millard, "Import Trade of London," pp. 207-10.
3 *Ibid.*, p. 110.
4 *CSP Dom., Add., 1580-1625*, pp. 661-2.
5 *APC Col., 1613-80*, pp. 111-12.
6 HMC, *Cowper*, I, 395.
7 *CSP Dom., 1631-33*, p. 123.
8 The officials of Trinity House to the Privy Council, nd, Trinity House Transactions [1613-58], p. 43.

English trade and navigation was their traditional concern. Their only relief was that parliament was not in session and therefore they were freed from the interference of the House of Commons. The council temporized and allowed the west-countrymen to use foreign bottoms that year, in return for a vague promise of greater co-operation with English shipowners in the future.[9] But apparently 1632 saw no great change in the fishermen's habits, for the following year London agitation was renewed.

In the hearings that took place in 1633, the shipping interests claimed that 10,000 tons of English shipping lay idle while almost 30 foreign ships had bought fish at Newfoundland, 16 or 18 had already sailed from the west-country with cargoes of fish for the Mediterranean, and more Dutch vessels waited at London and Plymouth.[10] The defence offered by the merchants of Plymouth must have represented the opinions of all their neighbours. They freely admitted selling their fish to French and Dutch merchants, but denied chartering foreign ships themselves. They protested that the availability of an assured market had allowed the fishing industry to develop until the numbers of ships and men involved had doubled; consequently they claimed that in a normal year, which 1633 had not been, both aliens and Londoners could be supplied. Were alien merchants to be excluded, the Londoners would be unable to carry even half the fish available and would demand it at their own price, as the fishermen knew from experience. Nor could the west-countrymen carry their own fish to market, as most of their ships were Dutch-built and so prohibited in Spain, their chief market. The consequences of a ban on alien shipping would be formidable: not only would the industry decay, but the nation would lose annually the £40,000 which aliens paid for the fish, besides the customs levied on their exports. The Dutch would then be driven to participate in the Newfoundland fishery themselves. The council could hardly afford to ignore this last threat, for the efficiency with which the Dutch could take over an industry had already been experienced in the home fisheries. By stressing the advantages to navigation in the growth of the Newfoundland fleet, and the money which the alien merchants brought into the country, the fishing merchants had shrewdly countered the Londoners' arguments. In all, said the west-countrymen, some 26,700 tons of shipping and 10,680 men were employed in the Newfoundland trade, the annual gross profit from which was about £178,000 and the net profit £24,000.[11]

What measure of truth was contained in the claims and accusations of the two sides has not before been checked against the port books, which reveal the nationality of both ships and their freighters. In this study the trade of Plymouth and Dartmouth has been most closely examined, for these ports were the main exporters of Newfoundland fish. The graphs of Plymouth's re-export trade in Newfoundland fish between 1605 and 1640 (see Figs. III, VII) show the proportion of English to foreign bottoms as well as the nationality of the merchants. As always the occasional nature of the evidence detracts from its value, but the run of figures for three consecutive years (1632-4), coinciding as they do with the period of controversy, is particularly fortunate. In fact the evidence indicates that only in the trade to France

---

9 HMC, *Third Report and Appendix*, p. 71; *APC Col., 1613-80*, p. 170.
10 *CSP Dom., 1633-34*, p. 367.
11 *Ibid.*, pp. 318-19; *ibid., 1634-35*, p. 393.

did alien ships and merchants regularly predominate. Most of this trade was in French hands, although the appearance of Dutch vessels in the thirties does suggest that the Anglo-French war did benefit their Dutch rivals. Remarkable features of the Spanish trade are the absence of Dutch ships in 1632 and 1633, and the generally low level of alien participation, both quite unexpected in view of the west-country-men's assertion that they had to employ foreign bottoms in this trade particularly.

Plymouth of course was a market for fish other than Newfoundland cod; hake, dried conger, herring, and above all pilchards were regularly exported. In 1633, for example, 33 ships sailed with fish other than Newfoundland cod, 11 with various types of fish including Newfoundland cod, and 7 with only Newfoundland fish. Out of this total of 51 vessels, 15 were Dutch (only one of these being partially freighted by an Englishman), 6 were from London (none of these carried New-foundland fish, and only 2 were chartered by local merchants), and 21 were local vessels.[12] Thus the Londoners had estimated Dutch participation fairly accurately, but the west-countrymen's protestation that they rarely employed foreign bottoms also seems to be true enough. When they did use alien ships, they were more likely to hire French than Dutch vessels. However, they used London ships even more rarely, and rather to carry other types of fish than Newfoundland cod.

The Dartmouth port books reveal very similar trends: heavy French participation, little employment of London ships except in the Spanish trade, and Dutch pre-dominance in traffic to Italy (see Figs. IV, VIII). Dartmouth had a much smaller re-export trade in other types of fish than Plymouth, and the trade in Newfoundland cod alone was usually as big or bigger than the total of the rest. Again the pattern was similar to Plymouth's, although London ships, whether freighted by London or by local traders, were employed even more rarely.

Both sides then seem to have stated their positions with some accuracy, and with no more misrepresentation than might be expected from interested parties. It seems doubtful, however, that even the complete removal of alien shipping and merchants from the west-country trade in fish could have resulted in the employment of all the London vessels supposedly idle because of foreign competition.

The outcome of the prolonged inquiries held during the winter of 1633-4 was apparently a victory for the west-country fishing merchants. The debate on the use of foreign bottoms was adjourned inconclusively, with the fishing merchants being allowed to continue to employ alien shipping "for this tyme onely" until alternative buyers and transportation could be found. At the same time the Privy Council appointed a committee of thirty-eight – both Londoners and west-country-men – to devise a scheme to exclude aliens from the carrying trade.[13] Two meetings were held and the west-country representatives did submit their report, but most of the agents from other English and Irish ports failed to do so and no definite recommendations were made. Soon the west-countrymen asked leave to return home as the Newfoundland fleet was about to sail.[14] Once again the fishing merchants had managed to evade any definite commitment to a change in their trading habits. Figures VII-X show that the pattern of trade did not alter radically after 1633, and

---

12 PRO, E 190/1033/26.
13 *APC Col., 1613-80*, pp. 198-9; HMC, *Ninth Report and Appendix*, pt. i, 271.
14 *CSP Dom., 1633-34*, pp. 532-3.

the decline of the volume of re-exports was probably more the result of the general commercial depression than of the attempt to make the carrying trade an English monopoly.

After more than ten years of debate then the problem of carrying trade had still not been resolved. The measures which the government had taken clearly showed their wish to uphold the London merchants in the interest of the national economy. The failure to enforce them revealed the hold which the idea of a free fishing industry as a nursery for seamen had over the minds of Englishmen.

The fishermen's unofficial victory here was probably more valuable to them in immediate effect than the granting of the Western Charter in January 1634. The charter gave the west-countrymen powers that were impressive on paper but, like other charters before it, its worth was perhaps greater as a document which could be invoked and reinterpreted by future generations than as a practical instrument for its contemporaries.[15] For the charter can be seen as a sop to the fishing merchants whose position in the Newfoundland industry was challenged, and not only by the Londoners. In 1633 two schemes had been proposed to counteract French and Dutch competition: one had suggested the formation of a company to manage both the foreign and domestic fisheries and the establishment of settlements in North America, the other the imposition of customs duties on Newfoundland fish.[16] Both were endorsed by a council member – the first by Sir John Coke, the second by Sir Edward Windebank – and both implied the curtailment of the west-countrymen's absolute freedom and the presence of officials, if not new settlers, in the island. The idea of a customs duty foreshadows the later activities of Sir David Kirke and perhaps indicates that he was already lobbying members of the government. These two proposals may well have motivated the west-country merchants to demand confirmation of their ancient privileges in the Newfoundland fishery in the hope of safeguarding their position.

In January 1634 the Privy Council ordered that the charter be circularized in the fishing ports.[17] The terms of the charter have been so often recounted at length that they will be no more than summarized here. The majority of its provisions attempted to remedy the old alleged abuses of which fishermen and colonists had accused each other ever since John Guy had first drawn up laws for the regulation of the island in 1611. Many of the charter's provisions were in fact reminiscent of Guy's laws, for they concerned the protection of property and the prevention of damage to the island and its harbours. It was reaffirmed that the first-comer to any harbour should be admiral for the season with the privilege of extra space for one boat on shore. New were provisions forbidding ships' masters to reserve ground in more than one harbour for longer than forty-eight hours, and prohibiting the establishment of taverns selling alcohol or tobacco. The most radical change came in the first clause which authorized the arrest of any person committing either murder or a theft worth more than forty shillings, and his transportation to England where he might be executed on the testimony of two witnesses. To facilitate action the

15 Two versions of the charter were issued by Charles II, the first almost identical with the original, PRO, Patent Rolls, 12 Charles II, pt. 17, no 30; the second slightly more amended, Patent Rolls, 27 Charles II, pt. 2, no 12.

16 CSP Col., 1574-1660, pp. 170-1; PRO, SP 16/252, no 45.

17 APC Col., 1613-80, pp. 193-7.

mayors of the chief fishing ports were empowered to take cognizance of all complaints, examine witnesses on oath, award compensation to the plaintiff, and punish
the offender by fine or imprisonment. Vice-admirals in Hampshire, Dorset, Devon,
and Cornwall were admonished to proceed against offenders at sea. The charter
was to stand until otherwise decreed, and admirals in all Newfoundland harbours
were to publish its provisions during the coming season. The order in council was
sent out before the patent was enrolled, presumably so that it would reach the west-
country before the fleet sailed. Copies of the letters patent, two of which may be
found in the Chancery warrants and the Plymouth city archives, were issued on 10
February 1634.[18] For some reason the charter was not put on the patent rolls. It has
been suggested that the omission may have been intentional as its provisions were
intended to be temporary.[19] The supporting documents, however, would seem to
indicate that the failure to enroll it was simply accidental.

But the victory of the fishing merchants was more apparent than real. Their old
customs had received formal confirmation and an attempt had been made to ensure
greater order on the distant island. But how much meaning could these provisions
have when the fishing admirals had been given authority but not the means to enforce it, and the west-country officials had been given power but at such a remove
that their ability to employ it was doubtful. Moreover Attorney Noye's words
before charter was granted: " ... his Majesty may give laws, and some *that may
serve for the present* I have presumed to present,"[20] can hardly have given the fishermen any great feeling of security.[21]

Meanwhile Sir David Kirke was probably already a suitor to the king for a charter
which would authorize a new colonizing venture in Newfoundland. Kirke's interest
in the St. Lawrence region may well have originated during his boyhood when his
family lived in Dieppe, a centre both of the Breton fishing industry and of the
French fur trade to Canada. More recently in 1627 David Kirke's father, Gervase,
had joined a company of merchants whose intention it was to oust the French from
the St. Lawrence. In two expeditions – the first in 1628 financed by Gervase Kirke
and other London merchants, notably William Berkeley, the second a joint venture
with Sir William Alexander in 1629 – David Kirke had succeeded in capturing
Quebec and that part of Canada then occupied by the French. Until forced to
restore it in 1632, the Kirke family held Canada for England, and profited personally
from trading voyages to Canada, Newfoundland, and the Mediterranean.[22]

---

18 PRO, Chancery Warrants, ser. II, Charles I, C 82/2106; copy, Plymouth City Archives, MS
  360/68.
19 Lounsbury, *British Fishery*, p. 73.
20 *APC Col.*, *1613-80*, p. 193. My italics.
21 As the authority given to the fishermen did have these limitations, it seems an overstatement
  to say that the charter placed the settlers in a "subordinate position," Lounsbury, *British
  Fishery*, p. 77; or that it gave the fishermen an "overwhelming victory," C. B. Judah, *The
  North American Fisheries and British Policy to 1713* (Urbana, Ill., 1933), p. 79.
22 See T. H. McGrail, *Sir William Alexander, First Earl of Stirling* (London, 1946), pp. 108-12;
  Insh, *Scottish Colonial Schemes*, pp. 75-8. Testimony given by persons involved may be
  found in PRO, HCA 13/48: 8 Jan. 1628/9, David Kirke; 9 Nov. 1629, Samuel Champlain; 18
  Nov., David and Thomas Kirke; HCA 13/49, ff 373ᵛ-4ᵛ. See also HCA 13/50: 10 Aug. 1632,
  Alexander Rice; 22 Sept., John Crosthwaite; 13 Aug. 1633, Thomas Wannerton; HCA 13/52, ff
  24-5ᵛ, 251-2.

The origins of the scheme which united Kirke and his fellow-merchants with the Marquis of Hamilton and the Earls of Pembroke and Holland are obscure. Presumably the idea was conceived by the merchant group. The capital which it could mobilize combined with Kirke's experience would enable it to attract the courtiers whose support in turn ensured the royal approval. Yet these three noblemen were probably more than mere figureheads. True all were or had been Stuart favourites; but Hamilton already held land in New England, Pembroke had been interested in colonization since he joined the Virginia Company in 1612 and more recently he had planned a colony in the West Indies, while from 1630 to 1639 Holland served as an unusually active governor of the newly formed company for Providence Island.

The objectives of the group were probably very similar to those of the earlier London and Bristol Company: to participate in the fishery and to gain a predominant position in the carrying trade in fish to Europe, if not a monopoly of it. David Kirke, in a cautious statement of his plans made in September 1639,[23] claimed that his company had capital "far aboue all the mean[s] that the West Country Marchants euer had." But he wanted another advantage yet: permission to levy a 5 per cent tax on all fish and oil purchased by aliens at the fishery, "for the present ... one of our principall hopes of profitt." In the early days such a tax would supply revenue towards the cost of the colony; and, even if it did have the effect of driving away foreign merchants, Kirke may have hoped that he and his associates could then dominate the market and control the price of fish. But, if such were his dreams, he was wise enough not to make them public. His organization was, he protested, "well enclined to increase the fishinge and the nomber of fishermen his Maiestes subiectes," and any attempt to discourage them would be an "iniury done to the State." Publicly at least he preferred to concentrate on those other sources of income which his settlers might develop. Farming, making salt and potashes, smelting iron, providing food and facilities such as brew-houses for the fishermen were all possibilities. So was trade with the "gulfe of Canada," and here remembering the conquest of 1629 he may well have cherished greater ambitions than he dared express. On the subject of the potential fur trade with the Newfoundland Indians such as the French already enjoyed he was more explicit, and he dismissed as nonsense the west-countrymen's assertions that there were no native inhabitants of the island.

However moderate, however tactful Kirke might try to be, he could not prevent opposition forming to his project. In February of 1637 Kirke and his associates submitted a petition for incorporation. That petition has not survived, but reaction to it followed swiftly. Cecil Calvert, the second Lord Baltimore and now proprietor of Avalon, and Trinity House, now as in 1609 acting as spokesman for the west-country interest, prepared to object. Self-interest had made curious allies.

Evidently the association had expected opposition and, to quiet it, had offered in advance to protect the industry with convoys and by fortifying certain popular harbours. Neither offer was appreciated by the fishermen who, in their anxiety to forestall further settlement, dropped all charges against the existing colonists, insisting that the Western Charter had established perfect order and harmony. The officials of Trinity House, who almost thirty years before had questioned the possibility of a Newfoundland colony, could now with evident satisfaction point to a long list of failures to buttress their argument:

none of all th[ose] which haue attempted in the Nufoundland to settle there to liue, and draw others to them, never thryved, the Lord Baltimore, Captaine Mason, Master Guy of Bristoll and other men ingenious and of excellent partes, yet wearye[d] and soe removed.[24]

Strangely enough they made no mention of what later appeared their main objection – the 5 per cent levy on aliens, which they feared would drive away their best customers. It was left to Baltimore to take up this point, and indeed his concern seems to have been more for the infringement of his financial rather than of his territorial rights. Claiming that all customs collected in Newfoundland had been granted to his father in 1623, he made a desperate appeal for the Privy Council's sympathy by asserting his intention to revive a project of his father's by which revenue from a duty on fish would be used to maintain sea and land forces in defence of the industry.[25]

Little attention seems to have been paid to Baltimore's pleas but the west-country-men, as managers of a trade vital to the nation's economy, had a stronger claim to the government's protection. The next three months were taken up with consultations to reach a compromise acceptable to both sides. The patentees finally undertook not only to maintain the complete freedom of the fishery but also to buy any surplus fish which, from the average sales of the previous seven years, the fishermen might have expected to sell to aliens. As a further safeguard to both sides it was later agreed that the fishermen should declare in advance the amount of fish which they would expect the patentees to take and that, in return, they should be given securities drawn upon certain London merchants. Until these arrangements were completed each year the company's ships were forbidden to sail.[26]

With the opposition thus grudgingly silenced or ignored, the patent passed the great seal in November 1637.[27] In the preamble the claims of all former grantees including Baltimore were swept aside, and the whole island between forty-six and fifty-two degrees north was awarded to the new proprietors. This then was the most extensive grant of land made since 1610, when the Newfoundland Company had been awarded the entire island but with special emphasis on the Avalon peninsula. The general terms of the patent were fairly standard: to the crown, the usual reservation of one-fifth of all minerals or gems that might be discovered; to the proprietors, powers to legislate with the assent of the assembled freeholders, to execute justice but not over the fishermen, to appoint magistrates, and to impose martial law if necessary; and to the settlers, the privileges of all English denizens. But certain of the clauses related to the peculiar conditions of Newfoundland. One of these imposed for the first time what appeared to be crippling restraints on the planters by forbidding them to build or even to cut wood within six miles of the shore

24 PRO, CO 1/9, no 41.
25 *Ibid.*, nos 42, 43.
26 *APC Col.*, *1613-80*, pp. 214-20.
27 PRO, CO 1/9, no 76. An objection by Baltimore in May 1637 to a *quo warranto* proceeding against part of his father's charter was also waived, *ibid.*, no 55.

between Capes Race and Bonavista, or on any island within ten leagues of the shore. This, of course, comprised the entire area of major interest to the English, within which all settlement had so far taken place. As the planters were, however, to be allowed to build forts wherever they chose, the effects of this clause were somewhat nullified. Severe limitations were also placed on the proprietors in that their authority did not extend to those who, for over half the year, made up the greater part of the island's population. The fishermen were subject only to the King and to the Privy Council, and they might disregard any law made by the proprietors which might be deemed prejudicial to the fishery. The final clause permitted the 5 per cent tax to be levied on aliens buying fish, and to be collected by officials supervised by the patentees but answerable to the crown. For fifty-one years the proprietors were to enjoy the profits from the tax, except for the one-tenth payable to the crown.

For the past seven years there had been more continuous interference from the government in matters affecting the fishery than ever before. Through hearings and through the terms of both the Western Charter and the patent to the Kirke group, the administration had attempted to bring some order to the island, and to discover some compromise between the fishermen and planters. But here the patent was no more successful than the charter. There was still no one on the island with authority over both fishermen and colonists, and no one to enforce the ban on settlement within six miles of the shore. Kirke's silence on this last question – it never seems to have been raised in the negotiations before the patent was sealed – suggests that, rather than make an issue of it, he preferred to ignore it in both London and Newfoundland.

Certainly his actions showed a fine disregard for any restraints. In 1638 he sent his agent, Captain Henry Tilliard, directly to the harbour of Ferryland where lived a number of settlers, who had been there since Baltimore's time, and the Calvert family's agent, Charles Hill.[28] When Kirke himself arrived a month later, he promptly expelled Hill and made Calvert's "mansion house" his own residence. The one hundred settlers who had joined him by October 1639 also seem to have made Ferryland their base. Perhaps to justify this settlement and others on the coast, Kirke later claimed to have taken with him "aboue twenty peeces of Ordnance which hee there planted in severall places & Forts in Avalon for ye better securitye of that place."[29] It may be that both sides tacitly realized the impractibility of the restriction on settlement on the coast, and that the fishermen were for a time willing to accept its nonobservance in the hope that Kirke would find it impossible to collect the imposition from aliens and so would be unable to continue his plantation.

In a further attempt to discourage Kirke, even after the patent was sealed, the fishing interests laboured not the difficulties of the scheme, resulting from the widely scattered nature of the fishery, but its unprofitability because of the few foreign vessels visiting Newfoundland. Had this been true, it would have made nonsense of the fears of losing their foreign customers which the fishermen had so vociferously expressed during the negotiations of 1637. Indeed, as Kirke commented dryly, "a strange thinge it is that men so longe experienced in this course of fishinge, should

28 PRO, HCA 13/65: 12 March 1651/2, James Pratt; 29 March 1652, Robert Alward; HCA
   13/67: 15 Feb. 1652/3, William Hill; Maryland Historical Society, Calvert Papers, evidence
   taken by commissioners at Ferryland, August 1652.
29 PRO, CO 1/10, no 40.

labour with such vehemence to ingrosse to thems[el]ues a Trade so vnprofitable." But the fishermen maintained that no more than 30 or 40 French and Basque ships came to the island whereas Kirke put the annual figure at 200 vessels, each with a cargo worth about £1000.[30]

Kirke was well aware of the practical difficulties of his undertaking, and in the early years at least the fishermen were disappointed in their hopes of his failure. The year 1638 found his brother Lewis, who had acted as governor of Quebec after its conquest by the English, in Trinity Bay exacting the levy from both Dutch and Basque ships so effectively that the French ambassador in London complained to the Privy Council.[31] That body, referring him to the recent impositions placed upon English merchants in France, gave him no more satisfaction than it had a year before when he had protested the award of a charter to Kirke. Then both the French ambassador and the Dutch States General had claimed to believe that Kirke was to receive a monopoly of the North American fishing grounds from New-foundland to Virginia.[32] In 1639 Kirke and his associates set out ships to police the fishery and hired at least one other vessel, paying the freighters by selling them fish cheaply. The next year a Captain Cranfield was busy collecting the tax from Basques fishing in Trinity Bay.[33]

After 1640 Kirke's activities in Newfoundland become obscure. Nothing is heard of the success or failure of the association, or of the settlers' farms and other employments. It is not clear whether the colony at Ferryland remained an organized venture, or whether it distintegrated into a group of individual families, each fending for itself. Kirke apparently continued his efforts to collect the imposition and to exercise control over the planters,[34] but with what success we do not know. The situation is curiously reminiscent of that some twenty years earlier, when the positive achievements of the Newfoundland Company faded from view and all that remained were the sterile quarrels between fishermen and planters. By 1640 one has heard it all before: the west-countrymen's complaints of the colonists' destruction of their property and of their favouritism towards foreigners; Kirke's denial and his countercharge that it is the fishermen who are guilty of the abuses; the Privy Council's authorization of an inquiry and their letter to Kirke instructing him to respect the terms of his patent and of the Western Charter.[35] The wrangling would probably have continued after 1640 but that the civil war distracted the government's attention and forced the fishermen to concentrate on the uncertain business of getting their ships safely to and from Newfoundland.

In fact the fishermen had enjoyed very mixed fortunes since 1630, for the reopening of the Spanish and French markets by no means removed all their difficulties. Not only had they the worry of the dispute over the carrying trade and of Kirke's activities, but of piracy at sea and commercial uncertainty and growing tension at home.

30 *Ibid.*, no 38.
31 PRO, HCA 13/58, ff 1-1ᵛ, 9-10, 15-16; PRO, SP 16/421, no 31.
32 *CSP Ven., 1636-39*, pp. 187-8; Judah, *North American Fisheries*, pp. 88-9.
33 PRO, SP 16/403, no 68; SP 16/421, no 31; PRO, HCA 13/58, ff 9-10.
34 See PRO, State Papers, Domestic, Charles II, SP 18/223, no 125, and below, p. 122.
35 PRO, CO 1/10, nos 46, 76, 77; PRO, SP 16/442, no 47; SP 16/447, no 35; *APC Col., 1613-80*, pp. 278-80.

Throughout the decade the Barbary pirates continued to lie in wait for the Newfoundland fleet, both in the spring and in the autumn. Men-of-war stationed in the Channel afforded some protection, but even so a fishing ship was lost in 1636 just three leagues out from Dartmouth harbour.[36] That same year pirates were bold enough to enter the Severn to attack ships bringing goods to the Bristol fair. In desperation the west-country ports appointed a special representative, John Crewkerne, to impress upon the government " yᵉ danger yᵉ Newfoundland men are like to be in att their returne about Michaelmas 1636 ... If timely prevention be not vsed yᵉ Newfoundland fleet must of necessity suffer by them in an extraordinary manner."[37] The threat to ships taking fish to the Mediterranean was even greater; the records of the Admiralty Court reveal constant losses among vessels going to France, Spain, Portugal, Italy and the Levant. So great was the pirates' desire for English ships and seamen that in 1633 it was rumoured that they would even raid the fleets at Newfoundland and Virginia.[38]

Nevertheless the fishermen do seem to have recovered somewhat from the depression of the late twenties and to have been moderately prosperous. In 1630, 40 ships prepared to sail to Newfoundland from Dartmouth alone. Just one year later Alderman John Clements of Plymouth claimed to remember the time when his city sent only 2 or 3 vessels to the fishery each year whereas now Plymouth set out 60 and Dartmouth 80 vessels annually. In 1634 fishing merchants testified that some 26,700 tons of shipping and 10,680 seamen were employed yearly in the trade.[39]

As Table xx shows, there was plenty of fish available for resale in the west-country, and Tables xxi-xxvii do not suggest that there was any marked decrease in the volume of the re-export trade during the thirties. The periodic slumps of that decade did not apparently affect the trade in victuals as seriously as they disturbed the export of cloth.[40] With all markets again open, the fishermen were prepared to run the risk of encounter with pirates to trade freely throughout the Mediterranean. It was estimated by a fisherman that, in September 1635, no fewer than twenty-two ships left Newfoundland together for St. Lucar and neighbouring ports.[41] This was probably but a fraction of the total number of vessels making the triangular voyage that year. Apparently the fishermen could prosper despite adverse conditions provided that Spanish and French ports remained open to them, and that their ships were not subject to stays and impressment at home.

But this period of uneasy calm did not last. In 1636 and again in 1637 the departure of the fishing fleet was delayed and seamen were impressed. The next year all fishing ships were supposed to obtain licences before they sailed, and only because the fishermen had prophesied national disaster if their voyage were forbidden were they allowed to leave at all.[42] The outbreak of civil war brought disaster to the west-

36 CSP Dom., 1635, pp. 396, 401; ibid., 1635-36, p. 205; ibid., 1636-37, pp. 71-2; HMC, Cowper, II, 137, 165, 192.
37 Weymouth Municipal Archives, Sherren MSS, s. 236.1-6.
38 John Delbridge to the mayor of Barnstaple, 5 Feb. 1632/3, Plymouth City Archives, MS 360/29.
39 CSP Dom., Add., 1625-49, p. 368; CSP Dom., 1634-35, p. 393; HMC, Third Report and Appendix, p. 71.
40 On the cloth trade in the 1630s see Supple, Commercial Crisis and Change, pp. 120-31.
41 PRO, HCA 13/52, ff 460-60ᵛ.
42 CSP Dom., 1635-36, pp. 298, 300; ibid., 1636-37, p. 495; ibid., 1637, pp. 20, 22, 24; John

country. The county of Devon became a battlefield, its ports occupied first by one side and then by the other. Fishermen setting out in the spring from a royalist port would return in the autumn to find it held by the parliamentarians, and their ships subject to seizure. The *Handmaid* of Torbay, for example, left that harbour in 1643 when it was held by the crown; returning to Dartmouth that autumn, the ship's master found parliamentary forces in possession and the town beseiged by Prince Rupert.[43] Even worse was the plight of the *Elizabeth Constant* of Dartmouth, a vessel owned by parliamentary sympathizers. In 1643 the ship left for Newfoundland and Spain. On his voyage home the master was advised that Dartmouth was in royalist hands and that he should take his ship to Holland. On the way the *Elizabeth Constant* was captured by a royalist ship and taken to Dartmouth. At great expense her owners secured her release and the unlucky ship sailed for the safety of London, only to be seized by the Earl of Warwick because she came from a port held by the crown.[44] Royal and rebel fleets both regularly lay in wait for ships putting out from a port then occupied by the enemy. Trade between ports held by opposing sides was forbidden, and traffic to the continent was dislocated because of the constant danger to shipping. Very few port books from the years of the civil war and the Interregnum have survived, but something of the damage done to trade may be gauged from the fact that the canal receipts for Exeter-Topsham dropped from £230 in 1643 to £33 in 1645.[45] In 1644 it was reported that ships from the ports then held by parliament would be seized at the Atlantic Islands, Virginia, New England, and Newfoundland to form a royalist fleet. The following year vessels with letters of marque awarded by the parliament were at Newfoundland.[46]

The civil war also brought changes in the situation in Newfoundland itself. As the fortunes of the King fell and with him those of Kirke and all but one of his court patrons, so the confidence of the west-countrymen rose. They appealed to their old ally, parliament, for support against David Kirke. In March 1646, shortly before Charles surrendered to the Scots, a group of Plymouth fishing merchants complained of Kirke's oppressions, his corruption of their crews, and his recent threat to seize fishing ships for the royalist cause. The question was referred without debate to the committee for foreign affairs and no immediate action was taken.[47]

Parliament had many things to deal with more pressing than the grumblings of the fishermen. But, even so, this response or lack of it is interesting and significant. The Commons was no longer prepared to leap to the defence of the west-country-men, automatically identifying their cause with the good of English navigation, as they had done in the twenties. The old alliances – Commons and fishermen, crown and colonists – were dead, killed by changing circumstances. The concern of the new administration was to evolve a coherent commercial policy which would bring about the expansion of English trade and the elimination of the Dutch from the fisheries and the carrying trade. This could best be achieved by the continuation of

Winthrop, *History of New England, 1630-1649*, ed. J. K. Hosemer (2 vols., New York, 1908), I, 271.

43 PRO, HCA 13/60: 30 Jan. 1645/6, Cevill Watson.
44 PRO, HCA 13/59, ff 269-72.
45 Stephens, *Seventeenth-Century Exeter*, p. 63.
46 HMC, *Portland*, I, 168; HCA 13/60: 13 Nov. 1645, Nicholas Browne.
47 Stock, *Proceedings and Debates*, I, 176-7, 178.

many of the policies which Charles' administration had conceived but failed to implement with any consistency.

Throughout the Interregnum period there runs a triple strand of policy towards Newfoundland: the protection of the trade in fish through the enforcement of navigation acts; the defence of the industry by convoys, with consideration being given to the fortification of certain harbours, both measures long opposed by the fishermen; and the orderly administration of the island through commissioners appointed by the central government. None of these steps was hostile to settlement; indeed some of them had been recommended by promoters of settlement ever since 1610. Another man, in David Kirke's position but without his royalist connections, might have been able to profit from the new situation to establish settlement on a firmer basis than ever before.

The first step towards the goal of a regulated trade was taken in January 1647 with the passage of a navigation act. Its two main provisions freed goods destined for any American colony, with the single exception of Newfoundland, from all customs duties over a period of three years, and prohibited the shipment of the produce of the colonies in alien bottoms. It is not clear that this second prohibition was to apply to Newfoundland, but the island's specific exclusion from the first provision suggests that it did not have the same status as the other colonies.[48] The ruling may also have been intended to discriminate against the royalist Kirke.

The navigation act of 1651 went much further in prohibiting the import into England of all foreign goods which were not carried in English ships manned mainly by commonwealth subjects, the only exception being European goods which might be carried in vessels belonging to the country of export. Two clauses directly affected the Newfoundland trade: one forbade the import of all fish and oil not caught and transported by commonwealth subjects; the other, the export of any salt fish whatsoever except in commonwealth shipping. With one blow the administration had struck at the Dutch domination of the carrying trade and of the fisheries in European waters, and had achieved much that Charles I's government had tried so ineffectively to do in the early 1630s.

Here at least the London shipping interests had triumphed, and the west-countrymen's silence was probably a sign of their preoccupation with their many commercial worries rather than of their acquiescence. Restricted trade with France, the constant problem of the Barbary pirates, then the first Dutch war all affected the prosperity of the southwest. And just as trade had begun to revive came the outbreak of war with Spain in 1656. Many things the fishermen could survive but not apparently the loss of their Spanish market. Cries of hardship, demands for the relaxation of the act of 1651 were heard immediately. Despite considerable opposition, the Devonshire members of parliament successfully sponsored a bill in 1657 which allowed the export of certain types of fish from the British Isles in alien shipping, and which also permitted the duty-free transportation of fish purchased by foreigners at Newfoundland and New England. The act was to continue in force for two years and would have been some compensation to the fishermen for the damage done to their trade.

Meanwhile it had become clear that the commonwealth government could no

48 See Lounsbury, *British Fishery*, pp. 94-5.

longer tolerate David Kirke's authority in Newfoundland. In 1649 came reports that he had attracted some 400 seamen to the island to the detriment of recruiting for the commonwealth navy. A few months later fears were voiced that Prince Rupert intended to attack the fishery, and the government ordered two ships to defend and convoy the fleet.[49] Convoys were also provided in 1650, but only three ships chose to keep the rendezvous for vessels going to Spain.[50] The complaints against Kirke were renewed in 1650 and the following year the whole position of the Newfoundland colony and its administration came under review, with Kirke being ordered home to attend an official inquiry.[51] The real issue was not the rights and wrongs of Kirke's conduct, but the far bigger question: was settlement detrimental to the fishery, and if so should it be prohibited? To provide the committee of inquiry with information the Council of State appointed commissioners, three civilians – John Littlebury, John Treworgie, and Walter Sikes – and three convoy captains – Thomas Thoroughgood, Thomas Jones, and William Haddock. The commissioners were authorized to receive complaints against Kirke. They were also to collect evidence as to the profits he had made from the fishery, from rents, from the licencing of taverns, from furs and other trading, and from the imposition on alien merchants. Meanwhile the commissioners were to take over the collection of the 5 per cent tax themselves, and to seize all Kirke's possessions on the island.[52] So began the custom of using commissioners, usually convoy captains, to keep order during the fishing season and to report to the government on the conditions in Newfoundland.

The evidence collected by the six commissioners has not survived but in all probability it was not favourable to Kirke. Certainly the witnesses who, in the summer of 1652, testified in a suit brought against Kirke by Cecil Calvert, the second Lord Baltimore, were almost uniformly hostile to him.[53] Baltimore had taken advantage of Kirke's uncertain position to dispute his authority in Newfoundland and to accuse Kirke of seizing the "mansion house" at Ferryland and other property belonging to the Calvert family. The hearings were held in Newfoundland and the witnesses were settlers who had been there at the time of Kirke's arrival in 1638; some of them in fact had been there since George Calvert's time. One witness testified that she had known Kirke "a little to well and wisheth she had not knowne him"; another said that he did not know the present Lord Baltimore but that he had known Kirke for thirteen years and "as far as hee knowes my Lord Baltemore may be as bad." The only favourable opinion came from a settler who preferred Kirke because he was a Protestant whereas Baltimore was a papist. They agreed that Kirke had collected an imposition from foreigners at the fishery, although there was no agreement on the amount he might have received, and some accused him of having taxed the settlers too.

49 PRO, Interregnum Entry Books, SP 25/62, 263; SP 25/87, 7.
50 Stock, *Proceedings and Debates*, I, 207, 208; *CSP Dom., 1649-50*, pp. 18, 19, 83, 185-6; *ibid., 1650*, pp. 8, 17; HMC, *Popham*, pp. 18, 61-4; PRO, HCA 13/64: 5 Feb. 1650/1, Christopher Frayry.
51 *Winthrop Papers* (Massachusetts Historical Society, 1871), pp. 499-501; PRO, SP 25/17, 29, 65; SP 25/69, 114. And see A. M. Field, "The Development of Government at Newfoundland, 1638-1713" (MA thesis, University of London, 1924).
52 PRO, SP 25/65, 243-4.
53 Maryland Historical Society, Calvert Papers, evidence taken by commissioners at Ferryland, August 1652.

A similar inquiry was held some fifteen years later, in 1667, and again the evidence was hostile to Kirke.[54] The witnesses then were mainly elderly fishermen with long years of experience in the Newfoundland trade, but two of them had been independent settlers in the island. One of these, Thomas Cruse, had settled at Bay Bulls in about 1635 and had lived there for eighteen years. The other, Gabriel Viddomas, had gone to Newfoundland on a fishing voyage about the year 1627 but "by persuasions of a widow" had stayed on as a servant at Carbonear for twenty-four years. But all the witnesses, whether fishermen or settlers, were agreed in their dislike of Kirke. Their testimony painted an idyllic picture of the island before Kirke's arrival and either ignored the earlier colonists or dismissed them as too few to be significant. Before 1637, they claimed, fishermen of all nations had lived together in perfect harmony, free to leave their equipment at the island from one year to the next without fear of damage or theft. Before 1637 the authority of the fishing admiral had been unquestioned, the rights of the first-comer undisputed, and the trade had flourished to "the great encrease of navigation & seamen."

Kirke's arrival had shattered this peace. Now the most skilled fishermen were encouraged to desert their ships and settle in Newfoundland; or they were debauched by the taverns which Kirke had so temptingly provided. The rights of the first-comer were ignored as space on the beaches was seized, sometimes violently, by Kirke, his settlers and his favourites. The fishermen's property was stolen and destroyed; their voyages were delayed and so made unprofitable. Not even the independent settlers were safe. According to the testimony of Thomas Cruse, Kirke imposed taxes and collected annual rents on their houses and fishing places. Cruse had paid £3 6s. 8d. a year on his house, besides "a Fate hogg or 20 shillings in lew thereoff." He accused David Kirke of forcing the inhabitants to take extra land which they did not need but for which they had either to pay rent or be expelled from the island. Kirke even compelled them to take out licences for taverns; Cruse had held such a licence and paid £15 a year for it. All the witnesses agreed that Kirke's terrorizing of the fishermen was likely to cause the decay of the whole industry, and that his presence as governor was of no benefit whatsoever. Nor had he fulfilled his promise to fortify the most popular fishing harbours, although the witnesses claimed that such fortifications were unnecessary as the fishermen could unite to protect themselves during the summer and, during the winter, when the harbours were blocked by ice, no invader could enter.

With such black reports of Kirke's actions reaching London, it would hardly have been surprising had the government expelled him and his settlers forthwith. But they did not. In 1652 Kirke came back to England to appear before the inquiry to answer the fishermen's complaints and to produce his accounts for examination. He also gave evidence before the Admiralty Court in Baltimore's suit against him.[55] In June of 1652 new commissioners, Walter Sikes, Robert Street, and Captains William Pyle and Nicholas Redwood, were appointed to consider how the interests of

---

54 PRO, SP 18/223, no 125; copy, Plymouth City Archives, MS 360/76.
55 PRO, SP 25/66, 103, 179, 192, 272, 280, 348, 533; SP 25/67, 7, 17. Baltimore and Kirke's libels, PRO, HCA 24/110, no 329; HCA 24/111, no 120. The depositions are in HCA 13/65: 12 March 1651/2, James Pratt; 29 March 1652, Robert Alward; HCA 13/67: 15 Feb. 1652/3, William Hill; and the personal answer of David Kirke is in HCA 13/124 [Feb. 1652].

the state might best be served and the fishery encouraged. Their instructions were very similar to those issued the previous year, but the new officials were specifically commanded to defend the fishery against Prince Rupert, and to assume the government of the settlers, previously Kirke's responsibility. To assist them in this duty, they received a list of temporary laws, most of which simply repeated the provisions of the Western Charter concerning the protection of property and the conduct of the fishery. One new restraint, however, was now imposed upon the settlers: they were forbidden to build or keep their livestock in areas where fish was stored or dried.[56]

A further step towards the central control of the island was taken in 1653 when John Treworgie, who appears to have been in Newfoundland continuously since 1651, was appointed sole commissioner.[57] For the first time a commissioner's authority was to extend over both planters and fishermen, and in case of emergency Treworgie was to command all ships in defence of the island. He was also to consider how the island's harbours might best be fortified. Treworgie thus received powers which had been carefully denied to Sir David Kirke in 1637. It would appear that, whatever the attitude of the fishing merchants, the Interregnum government was prepared not only to allow settlement but to set it on a more formal and better regulated basis than ever before.

It was not, however, a popular policy either with the Kirkes or with the fishermen. In Newfoundland itself the position of the commissioners was complicated by the hostility of the Kirke family and its supporters. In 1652 James Kirke went so far as to arrest the civilian commissioners in retaliation to the seizure of his brother's estates; the following year he again confined Treworgie for a time.[58] When David Kirke was allowed to return to the island in the autumn of 1653 he himself seems to have made no trouble for those who had superseded him. He died at Ferryland shortly thereafter. His widow and other members of his family stayed on and, when Baltimore reactivated his suit after the Restoration, they unsuccessfully continued the fight for control of the island.[59]

At home the agitation against settlement continued, inspired presumably by the fishing merchants. In 1656 the Council of State appointed a special committee to consider a paper which advised that the plantation of Newfoundland be discontinued.[60] What recommendations this committee made we do not know, but they were evidently favourable to the settlers, for the temporary rules drawn up in 1652 and 1653 continued in force until the Restoration. John Treworgie remained in Newfoundland until about 1659, when he petitioned for a new commission to confirm his authority.[61] His request was forwarded to Thomas Povey, the secretary for foreign plantations, in April 1660. Treworgie then claimed to have reported on conditions at the island every year since 1653, despite the fact that his salary had not been paid. He asked for ships to help him collect the imposition on aliens, to

56 PRO, SP 25/29, 11-14, 15-18.
57 PRO, SP 25/69, 160, 197, 204-7, 207-10.
58 PRO, CO 1/12, nos 20, i-vi, 21.
59 See BM, Egerton MS 2395, ff 258-8ᵛ, 263-4, 265, 266; PRO, CO 1/14, nos 8-10.
60 PRO, SP 25/77, 532.
61 BM, Egerton MS 2395, f 262.

surprise Spanish shipping at Newfoundland, and convoy the English fishing fleet.[62] The restoration of Charles II presumably terminated his suit. It is not clear how far Treworgie had been able to enforce his authority, but the presence of naval vessels at the island virtually every year since 1651 may have given him a stronger position than any private individual had ever enjoyed.

By comparison with the twenties and thirties, the fishermen had been extraordinarily subdued during the Interregnum period. They had helped to bring about the downfall of their old enemy Sir David Kirke, but they had acquiesced in the appointment of a series of commissioners without any very strong protest. Apparently the fishing merchants could no longer find such influential support in the capital as they had enjoyed earlier in the century. Then too the problems of simply getting their ships to Newfoundland were so great between 1650 and 1660 as to engross most of their attention. Almost every year embargoes were placed upon ships leaving England and seamen were impressed. Although exceptions were frequently made for the fishing fleet, the dangers to those that did sail were legion. In 1653 the comparatively small port of Barnstaple complained that, whereas it used to send 50 to 60 ships each year to Newfoundland and New England, so many had been lost that only 10 or 12 small vessels now made the voyage.[63] Prince Rupert's ships, pirates and privateers, the Dutch and the Spaniards had all taken their toll of English merchant shipping. So much so that, with a complete change of attitude, the fishermen from a number of west-country ports actually petitioned for a convoy in 1652; the following year the Dartmouth merchants repeated the petition as in 1655 did those of Plymouth.[64] The government, ever mindful of the national importance of the fishing fleet, did try to provide some protection each year. But the demand for men-of-war was so great that usually no more than two ships could be allotted to the Newfoundlanders – hardly an adequate guard for a fleet headed for so many different destinations. Only in one year, 1654, was the government able to provide six ships which were to leave the island in pairs as guardians of three separate fleets. But in that year it had originally been recommended that the Newfoundland ships be forbidden to sail at all, because of the danger from the Dutch.[65] A similar recommendation had been made two years earlier when the government had found itself simply unable to spare any ships at all to convoy the fishermen.[66]

During the Interregnum years the government undoubtedly benefited from the fact that these were the most chaotic years yet experienced by the Newfoundland fishermen. For this reason, perhaps, the fishing merchants accepted the navigation laws and the commissioners with relatively little protest. Indirectly they even encouraged government interference by their repeated requests for convoys. The convoy captains and the civilian commissioners were Newfoundland's first direct links with the central administration, a sign of the realization in London that something had to be done, not only to protect the island from foreign attack, but to end

---

62 PRO, CO 1/33, no 73. Robert Street, one of the commissioners in 1652, also complained of non-payment, see PRO, SP 25/76, 599-600; CO 1/21, no 55.
63 *CSP Dom.*, *1651-52*, p. 277; *ibid.*, *1653-54*, p. 126; *ibid.*, *1655-56*, p. 187; *CSP Col.*, *1574-1660*, p. 443.
64 PRO, SP 25/76, 118; SP 25/132, 2; *CSP Dom.*, *1652-53*, p. 107.
65 *CSP Dom.*, *1653-54*, p. 561; *ibid.*, *1654*, pp. 200-1.
66 PRO, SP 25/132, 2.

the violence and the barren disputes between fishermen and planters which threatened to wreck the industry from within. On the question of whether settlement should be permitted to continue, no firm decision had as yet been reached. But by 1660 a pattern of government interest and involvement in the problems of Newfoundland had been established.

VIII

Conclusion

THE STORY of English activity in Newfoundland throws light on the grand theme of the expansion of England, of how a small island became the world's greatest sea power, founded colonies in four continents, built them into three empires, and then presided over their evolution into a unique commonwealth. Not the least amazing part of that story is the fact that, until the nineteenth century at least, this vast expansion was carried out with inadequate resources.

Not until the Tudors brought a measure of order and stability could permanent expansion begin within the British Isles, a necessary prerequisite for continuous expansion without. A developing economy forced the English, as their old markets declined, to seek fresh outlets in Europe and in the larger world then being unveiled. To develop these new markets companies were founded from the mid-sixteenth century onwards, and within but a short span of time the English became engaged in most of the regions that would comprise their first empire. Into the newly formed companies poured the money of hundreds of private investors: nobility, gentry, above all merchants. Upon the shoulders of these individuals was borne the task of building an empire.

Of this pattern of individual effort Newfoundland was a part. It was the small merchants of the west of England, together with Bretons, Normans, French and Spanish Basques, and Portuguese, who developed the fishery and who, at first, contrived to forget national rivalries in the immediate business of making a profit. But, as the industry grew in value and as international tension mounted in the late sixteenth century, so it became essential that the island be preserved from foreign domination. The maintenance of a supply of fish for the armed forces, the protection of the fishing ships and their crews became national concerns. In time of crisis, then, the government was prepared to do what it had to do for the national safety, but it had no intention of becoming permanently involved in overseas enterprises which were, after all, still regarded as private matters.

The industry, however, did not long remain strictly private, for a trade of such size and value invites monopoly. In the economic climate of seventeenth-century England, the formation of a company to manage the Newfoundland trade was only to be expected. Because it was controlled largely by outsiders – Londoners – rather than by west-countrymen, the destructive rivalries that followed could also have been expected. In fact the Newfoundland Company, with its always inadequate capital, its one small colony, and its four or five fishing ships a year, never posed an effective threat to the freedom of the fishery. But the fishermen could not or would not accept that. They saw a group of men, far wealthier than they, backed by a royal charter, trying to invade the industry which they had built. To them it was yet another move on the part of the giant, London, to gobble up the country's trade.

When the Newfoundland Company and its offshoots failed, the island passed back to the fishermen. As they now contributed even more to the national prosperity, and as they had once again proved their worth to the national defence during the wars of the 1620s, the fishermen had now an even stronger claim to the government's consideration. As a result they drew the government ever deeper into the affairs of Newfoundland. Through the Western Charter of 1634, the government legislated directly for the island for the first time. Through the negotiations between the fishing merchants and the Kirke faction, the government tried to establish some balance between fishermen and planters. During the Interregnum, as in all times of stress, the tendency towards official intervention quickened with the employment of convoys and commissioners. A point had been reached when the government in England, not a group of private individuals, had to decide upon the course of Newfoundland's future development – whether it should become a normal fortified colony with a civil governor, or continue simply as a fishing base.

Like the rest of England's empire then, Newfoundland was developed by private individuals who, for gain or for power, chose to expend their energy and their money on overseas adventure. In the multitude of small west-country merchants, in the compulsive speculation of Sir Percival Willoughby, in the romanticism of Sir William Vaughan, in the hard-headed practicality of David Kirke, can be seen the characteristics of generations of empire-builders. But in some ways, the island's history was unique for the seventeenth century at least. For Newfoundland was the only area of English interest in America that was of continuous strategic importance, partly because cod was a strategic commodity, but mainly because of the fishery's role as a nursery for seamen. It was also the only area in which colonization implied the taking over of an old-established trade by a group of interlopers, and where the original practitioners of that trade formed an influential lobby comparable to that of the West Indian planters in the eighteenth century. Trade, strategy, and political pressure all dragged a reluctant government into the problems of Newfoundland. And there it stayed.

APPENDICES

A

Tables

TABLE I

THE AVERAGE TONNAGE OF NEWFOUNDLAND SHIPS, 1580-1650[1]

HOME PORT	1580s	1590s	1600s	1610s	1620s	1630s	1640s
Barnstaple	45	45	50	45	45	50	—
Bristol	—	55	60	60	50	90	—
Dartmouth	60	55	50	60	75	85	70
Exeter	40	40	40	60	50	80	—
Plymouth	—	45	—	55	65	85	80
Poole	—	—	40	45	50	65	—
Southampton	—	80	—	60	—	105	225
Weymouth	—	—	45	50	—	—	—

1 Figures to the nearest 5 tons. Compiled from port book entries describing ships returning directly from Newfoundland to England (PRO, E 190). No figures can be given for the 1650s as very few port books have survived.

TABLE II

AVERAGE CARGOES OF FISH BROUGHT FROM NEWFOUNDLAND[1]

TONNAGE	AVERAGE IMPORT	MAXIMUM IMPORT	TONNAGE	AVERAGE IMPORT	MAXIMUM IMPORT
30- 39	514	800	120-129	516	1500
40- 49	454	900	130-139	740	980
50- 59	643	1200	140-149	743	1440
60- 69	780	1250	150-159	907	1600
70- 79	569	1200	160-169	1114	2600
80- 89	434	2000	170-179[a]	170	170
90- 99	——	——	180-189	——	——
100-109	571	1530	190-199	——	——
110-119	——	——	200-210	1340	2320

1 Import figures in quintals. Compiled from the port books for Plymouth, Dartmouth, Exeter, Barnstaple, Southampton, Bristol, Weymouth, and Poole, 1580-1650 (PRO, E 190).

a Details for one ship only which was obviously not fully loaded.

TABLE III

EXAMPLES OF THE MONTHLY WAGES PAID TO THE CREWS OF SACK SHIPS[1]

YEAR	1631[2]	1648[3]	1648[4]	1651[5]	1654[6]	1655[7]	LATE C17
Master's mate	30s.	60s.		66s.			60-80s.
Bosun	33s.	30s.	48s.				35-40s.
Bosun's mate						35s.	
Carpenter				35s.		56s.	60s.
Gunner							30-45s.
Gunner's mate					40s.		
Chirugeon	80s.[a]						50-60s.
Chirugeon's mate							
Cook	24s						
Mariner	17-24s			26-7s.			

1 All figures relate to triangular voyages made by Newfoundland sack ships, except those in the last column which are taken from averages of the wages earned by seamen in the later part of the seventeenth century (Davis, "Organization of the English Shipping Industry," p. 264), and which are provided for the purposes of comparison.

2 PRO, HCA 13/50: 7 June 1632, John Hosier. Voyage: Newfoundland, Leghorn, and other Mediterranean ports.

3 PRO, HCA 13/63: 17 May 1650, William Westlake. Voyage: Newfoundland, Mediterranean.

4 PRO, HCA 13/66: 15 Feb. 1652/53, Peter Tombles. Voyage: Newfoundland, Mediterranean, London.

5 SRO, Book of Examinations, 1648-63, ff 76ᵛ-7. Voyage: Brittany (for salt), Newfoundland, Genoa.

6 PRO, HCA 13/70: 24 Jan. 1654/55, James Salmon; HCA 14/111, no 258. Voyage: Newfoundland, Naples, Lepro.

7 PRO, HCA 13/74: 15 April 1662, Henry Buckler. Voyage: Newfoundland, Cadiz, Genoa, Leghorn, Smyrna, Constantinople, Smyrna, Leghorn, Alexandria, Leghorn, Marseilles, Genoa, Lisbon, Madeira, Angola, Brazil.

a Sum paid jointly to the chirugeon and his mate.

TABLE IV

SHIPS RETURNING DIRECTLY FROM NEWFOUNDLAND TO ENGLAND, 1577-1604[1]

YEAR	PLYMOUTH	DARTMOUTH	EXETER	BRISTOL	S'HAMPTON	BARNSTAPLE
1577					1*	0*
1578					4+	0
1579					0*	0+
1580					0	0*
1581			2*		0+	0
1582		6*	1			0+
1583		1+	6+			
1584		3+	3*			
1585			1+		3*	
1586		0*	0*		0	0*
1587		6+	4		2	1+
1588		0*	2		0	3*
1589		14+	10		3	3+
1590			1	0+		
1591	3+	3*	4+	2*		
1592			4*	1+		
1593	1*		7+		0	0
1594	6+		2*	6*	0+	2+
1595			8	4+		6*
1596			6*		0*	4+
1597			6		0	
1598			5	5*	0	
1599		26*	15	7	0+	3*
1600		18+	6+	4	0*	2*
1601			6	10	0	
1602		13*	5	2+	0+	
1603		9*	5+			4+
1604						2+

1 Compiled from the port books (PRO, E 190) and, in the case of Exeter only, from the Exeter Customs Rolls (Exeter City Record Office). Before 1604 customs records were kept from Michaelmas to Michaelmas; therefore it is not possible to obtain a figure for the complete year unless two consecutive books have survived. Incomplete annual figures have been included in this table: + indicates ships returning before Michaelmas, * those returning after Michaelmas.

TABLE V

DARTMOUTH'S EXPORTS OF NEWFOUNDLAND FISH, 1577-1604[1]

YEAR	SHIPS	FISH	VALUE £	DESTINATION
Michaelmas 1582 to Michaelmas 1583	1	22	11	France
1 Jan.-25 March,	9	698	408	France
29 Sept.-25 Dec. 1591	3	3290	1645	Italy
1 Jan.-25 March, 1592	1	30	15	France
29 Sept.-31 Dec. 1599	36	5280	2739	France
	4	5600	2800	Italy
	2	303	153	Channel Is.
1 Jan.-29 Sept. 1600	10	1610	840	France
29 Sept.-25 Dec. 1602	18	5065	2332½	France
	2	900	450	Italy
	1	50	25	Channel Is.
29 Sept.-31 Dec. 1603	7	748	548	France
	2	900	450	Spain
	2	500	250	Portugal
	1	460	230	Majorca
	3	120	75	Channel Is.
1 Jan.-Easter 1604	2	300	150	France
	1	312	162	Portugal

1 Compiled from the port books (PRO, E 190). Fish exports are given in quintals (ie 120 fish), and their value has been reckoned at a standard rate of 10s. a quintal for small dry fish, £1 a quintal for medium-sized dry fish and for corfish, and 30s. a quintal for large fish.

TABLE VI

PLYMOUTH'S EXPORTS OF NEWFOUNDLAND FISH, 1577-1604[1]

YEAR	SHIPS	FISH	VALUE £	DESTINATION
Midsummer to Xmas 1591	13	751	503½	France
	2	60	30	Italy
	5	158	148	Channel Is.
Michaelmas 1593	6	1020	510	France
to Michaelmas 1594	13	1210	605	Italy

1 See footnote to Table v.

TABLE VII

EXETER'S EXPORTS OF NEWFOUNDLAND FISH, 1577-1604[1]

YEAR	SHIPS	FISH	VALUE £	DESTINATION
1 Jan.-Easter 1590				
Michaelmas 1592 to Michaelmas 1593		No Newfoundland fish exported		
Michaelmas 1595 to Easter 1596	1	135	67½	France
Michaelmas 1599 to Michaelmas 1600	8	752	387	France
	1	30	15	Portugal
	1	40	20	Netherlands

1 See footnote to Table v.

TABLE VIII

BRISTOL'S EXPORTS OF NEWFOUNDLAND FISH, 1577-1604[1]

YEAR	SHIPS	FISH	VALUE £	DESTINATION
Easter-29 Sept. 1591	1	14	14	France
1594	1	20	10	France
	1	200	100	Italy
1595	1	30	15	France
	2	180	90	Italy
1596	1	23	11½	France
1 Jan.-29 Sept. 1597	1	3	1½	France
29 Sept.-31 Dec. 1598	2	120	60	France
	1	10	5	Italy
1 Jan.-29 Sept. 1599	2	190	95	France
29 Sept.-31 Dec. 1600	6	405	202½	France
	1	60	30	Italy
	1	100	50	Ireland
1601	3	100	50	France
1 Jan.-29 Sept. 1602	2	115	57½	France
	1	40	20	Italy
	1	180	90	Ireland

1 See footnote to Table v.

TABLE IX

SOUTHAMPTON'S EXPORTS OF NEWFOUNDLAND FISH, 1577-1604[1]

YEAR	SHIPS	FISH	VALUE £	DESTINATION
Michaelmas 1590 to Michaelmas 1591	No Newfoundland fish exported			
Michaelmas 1593 to Michaelmas 1594	2	65	35	France
Michaelmas 1596 to Michaelmas 1597	2	145	90	France
Michaelmas 1597 to Michaelmas 1598	1	80	40	France
Michaelmas 1598 to Michaelmas 1599	3	190	120	France
Michaelmas 1600 to Michaelmas 1601	1	753	383	France
Michaelmas 1601 to Michaelmas 1602	1	40	20	France

1 See footnote to Table v.

TABLE X

BARNSTAPLE'S EXPORTS OF NEWFOUNDLAND FISH, 1577-1604[1]

YEAR	SHIPS	FISH	VALUE £	DESTINATION
1 Jan.-25 March 1591	2	190	145	France
Michaelmas 1593 to Michaelmas 1594	No Newfoundland fish exported			
Michaelmas 1595 to Michaelmas 1596				
Michaelmas 1599 to Michaelmas 1600				
Easter to Michaelmas 1603				
Easter to Michaelmas 1604	1	600	300	Madeira

1 See footnote to Table v.

TABLE XI

SHIPS RETURNING DIRECTLY FROM NEWFOUNDLAND TO ENGLAND, 1605-30[1]

YEAR	PLYMOUTH	DARTMOUTH	BRISTOL	EXETER	SOUTHAMPTON
1605 to 1609	No port books recording overseas trade survive				
1610	32				
1611					
1612			8	13	
1613		13		15	9
1614					4
1615		13	6		
1616					4
1617	24		2		
1618		24			
1619					8
1620	66		11		
1621				10	
1622					
1623				11[b]	
1624		28	4		
1625			10	10[e]	
1626					
1627	21				
1628		18	0		
1629					
1630	13				

YEAR	POOLE	WEYMOUTH	BARNSTAPLE	PORTSMOUTH
1605 to 1609	No port books recording overseas trade survive			
1610				
1611	6	5[a]		
1612		5	18	
1613				
1614				
1615		7	11	
1616	4			
1617			10	
1618			16	
1619	10			
1620	9		18	
1621				2
1622	5			
1623				
1624				
1625	12			
1626		1		
1627				0
1628	0[d]		1	1
1629				0
1630	5			

1 Compiled from the port books (PRO, E 190).

a These five ships probably entered from Newfoundland, but the port book does not supply the port of departure. They have been judged as coming from Newfoundland because they carried cargoes of train oil.

b Minimum total. Many entries in this book are destroyed.

c The total includes one French ship which had come from the Banks.

d Incomplete book.

TABLE XII

PLYMOUTH'S EXPORTS OF NEWFOUNDLAND FISH, 1605-30[1]

YEAR	SHIPS	FISH	VALUE £	DESTINATION
1610	3	220	110	France
	2	800	400	Spain
	2	90	45	Portugal
	1	260	130	Italy
	1	140	70	Netherlands
1617	17	3451	1701	France
	12	7140	3570	Spain
	3	4350	3275	Portugal
	3	2430	1215	Italy
	1	100	50	Madeira
	1	140	70	Channel Is.

1 See footnote to Table v.

TABLE XIII

DARTMOUTH'S EXPORTS OF NEWFOUNDLAND FISH, 1605-30[1]

YEAR	SHIPS	FISH	VALUE £	DESTINATION
1615	29	4281	2142	France
	5	3170	1585	Spain
	14	10615	5365	Portugal
	1	20	10	Netherlands
1618	28	4120	2080	France
	10	9620	4810	Spain
	7	3330	1940	Portugal
	1	200	100	Canaries
	1	15	7½	Netherlands
	1	90	45	Channel Is.
1624	17	3275	1675	France
	10	14340	7175	Spain
	9	10530	5540	Portugal
	2	600	320	Italy
	1	4200	2100	Straights
	1	150	135	Channel Is.
1628	6	11780	5890	Italy
	3	60	30	Channel Is.

1 See footnote to Table v.

TABLE XIV

EXETER'S EXPORTS OF NEWFOUNDLAND FISH, 1605-30[1]

YEAR	SHIPS	FISH	VALUE £	DESTINATION
1612	6	1355	1290	France
	2	740	620	Canaries
1615	5	680	340	France
	9	2890	1445	Spain
	1	600	300	Portugal
	2	650	325	Canaries
	2	90	45	Azores
1617	6	1020	510	France
	3	790	395	Spain
	2	390	195	Portugal
	1	300	150	Canaries
	1	40	20	Azores
1624	2	360	180	Spain
1628	1	670	505	France
	2[a]	55	55	Netherlands
	1	200	100	Barbary

1 See footnote to Table v.
a The entries relating to these two ships have been damaged and therefore figures given for the fish export and its value are incomplete.

TABLE XV

BRISTOL'S EXPORTS OF NEWFOUNDLAND FISH, 1605-30[1]

YEAR	SHIPS	FISH	VALUE £	DESTINATION
1612	1	120	60	France
1616	2	260	130	France
1619 —— 1621		No Newfoundland fish exported		

1 See footnote to Table v.

TABLE XVI

SOUTHAMPTON'S EXPORTS OF NEWFOUNDLAND FISH, 1605-30[1]

YEAR	SHIPS	FISH	VALUE £	DESTINATION
1613	2	32	20½	France
1614	2	15	21	France
1616	3	70	57½	France
1619	4	70	38½	France

1 See footnote to Table v.

INDEX

Index

Alexander, Sir William 75, 85, 113; and
  Newfoundland Company 73, 95; and
  Nova Scotia 78, 95
Alexandria 9
Alicante 13, 17
Angola 9
Anticosti 50
Aquaforte 89, 92
Aston, Sir Arthur (2nd governor of
  Ferryland) 93
Avalon, province of 91, 93, 114; *see also*
  Calvert, Sir George
Avalon peninsula 36, 56, 83, 89; con-
  trolled by English 5, 48, 52; granted to
  Newfoundland Company 60
Azores Table xiv

Baccalieu Island 66, 69
Bacon, Sir Francis (member of New-
  foundland Company) 57
Balin, George 11
Baltimore *see* Calvert, Sir George
Barbary Table xiv; pirates 105, 107, 118,
  120
Barker, John 87, 88
Barlow, Roger 34
Barnstaple 102, Table I; Newfoundland
  ships at 5, 25, Tables IV, XI, XX; coastal
  trade in fish 27, 100n; pattern of trade
  28; loses Newfoundland ships 124; ex-
  ports Newfoundland fish Tables X, XIX,
  XXVII
Basque fishing industry: in St. Lawrence
  5, 48-9, 52; in Placentia Bay 24, 48n;

decline of 24-5, 48; attacked by English
  25, 50, 51; at Magdalen Islands 49, 50-1;
  size of 117; taxed by David Kirke 117
Bay Bulls 19; settlers at 122
Bayonne 29
Bell Island 69, 70; iron deposits at 59, 63,
  72; Sir Percival Willoughby wants 66,
  72
Belle Isle, Strait of 48
Beothuck Indians 68, 69, 70, 114
Berkeley, William 113
Bilbao: Newfoundland ships going to
  10, 21; Newfoundland fish exported to
  104
Bocall, Steven de 49-50
Bordeaux: Newfoundland ships going to
  11; Newfoundland fish exported to 28,
  32, 103
Bottomry loans 10-11, 14
Brazil 9, 35
Breton, Richard 17
Briefe Discovrse of the New-found-land
  see Mason, Captain John
Brigus 69
Bristol 26, 49, 61, 118, Table I; and discovery of Newfoundland 3, 34; Newfoundland ships at 5, 25, Tables IV, XI,
  XX; coastal trade in fish 27, 100n; exports Newfoundland fish 28-30 *passim*,
  101, Tables VIII, XV, Figures I, II; pattern
  of trade 28-30 *passim*, 101-2; trades
  with Spain 98, 101
– merchants: join Newfoundland Company 52-3, 60, *see also* Guy, John;

establish settlement at Harbour Grace 71, 79, 81, 87-8

Bristol's Hope *see* Harbour Grace

Brittany: trade with forbidden 28; ships from, in St. Lawrence 48-50 *passim*, 52; west-country trade with 103

Browne, John (member of Newfoundland Company) 73

Brownists 50

Brydges, Cassandra (née Willoughby), Duchess of Chandos 65

Buckingham *see* Villiers, George

Bull Arm 68, 69

Burghley *see* Cecil, Sir William

Cabot, John 3, 5

Cabot, Sebastian 36

Cadiz: Newfoundland ships going to 6, 9, 17, 21, 31

Calvert, Cecil, 2nd Baron Baltimore 94, 95; upholds claim to Newfoundland 95, 114, 115; claim disregarded 115; sues David Kirke 121, 122

Calvert, Sir George, 1st Baron Baltimore 78, 85, 86, 89, 115, 121; acquires land in Newfoundland 73, 84, 92, 93; early career 92; his objectives 92; his colony at Ferryland 92-5; charter of Avalon 93; protects fishery 94; leaves Newfoundland 94-5; and Maryland 94, 95; on freedom of fisheries 99, 100

Cambrensium Caroleia see Vaughan, Sir William

Canada 49-51 *passim*; conquest of 113

Canaries: Newfoundland ships going to 10; Newfoundland fish exported to Tables XIII, XIV, XXI, XXII, XXIV, Figures V, VI

Candeler, Richard 12

Cape Bonavista 60, 116

Cape Breton 43, 44

Cape Broyle 5n

Cape Race 4, 5, 83, 116

Cape Ray 49

Cape St. Francis 69

Caplin Bay 83, 92

Carbonear 66, 69, 77, 87; settlers at 79, 122

Carrying trade: alien merchants in 30-1, 103-4, 109-11 *passim*, Appendix B; dispute over management of 56-7, 108-12 *passim*; legislation concerning 104, 109, 120; London ships in 105, 110, 111, Appendix B

Cartagena: Newfoundland ships going to 17, 20, 105

Cartier, Jacques 34-6 *passim*

Cartography of Newfoundland 36-8

Cary, Henry, Viscount Falkland 85-92; acquires land in Newfoundland 73, 84, 89; early career 88; dealings with Whitbourne 89, 91

– his colony: propaganda for 89-90; to benefit Ireland 90; established 91; land in, granted to Salusbury 91; fails 92

Cathay Company 38

Cecil, Sir Robert, 1st Earl of Salisbury 27, 29, 98

Cecil, Sir William, Baron Burghley 26, 48, 100, 107; encourages fisheries 23, 33, 44; and Hayes 44-6 *passim*; and St. Lawrence 49, 50

Chandos, Duchess of *see* Brydges, Cassandra

Channel Islands 27; west-country trade with 30, 101, 102; Newfoundland fish exported to Tables V, VI, XII, XIII, XVII, XXI

Charles I, king of England 88; and Sir George Calvert 94, 95; commercial policy under 108, 112

Charter parties: advantages of 8, 10, 18, 19, 21; content of 8; time charters 8, 9-10; lump-sum charters 8, 9; tonnage charters 8, 9, 18, 19; disadvantages of 10, 19-20, 21; used on Mediterranean voyages 19-20

Catchmaid, William (colonist at Cupids Cove) 62

Chester 26, 27, 45, 101n

Civil war 117; disturbs fishing industry 118-19

Civitavecchia 104

Clements, John (Plymouth alderman)
  118
Coastal trade in fish 26-7, 100, 101n
Coke, Sir John 112
Colonists
- at Cupids Cove: numbers of 61, 65, 70;
  government of 62; activities of 63,
  64, 66, 68-9; health of 64, 69-70; short-
  comings of 64, 66; criticize Newfoundland 66; criticize John Guy 70; see also
  under names of individual colonists
- at Renewse 84; at Harbour Grace 87
- at Ferryland: governors of 92, 93, 95,
  116; activities of 92; numbers of 92-5
  passim; health of 92, 95; clergymen
  among 94; and David Kirke 116, 117,
  121-2
- restrictions on 115-16, 123
Colston, William (deputy governor at
  Cupids Cove, 1611) 65
Commissioners 121, 122-3, 124, 127
Commons, House of: supports free trade
  79, 98, 99-100; attitude of, towards
  David Kirke 119
Companies: versus free trade 53, 56-7, 79,
  97-100, 108; investment in 53, 126; see
  also names of individual companies
Conception Bay 63, 64, 68, 76, 89, 93; land
  grants on 66, 87
Constantinople 9
Convoy system: in 1590s 25; during
  Interregnum 120, 121, 124, 127
Conway, Sir Edward 78
Cope, Sir Walter (member of New-
  foundland Company) 57
Copper: in Newfoundland 42, 50, 59
Cornellis, Richard 9
Cortereal, Gaspar 36
Cortereal, Miguel 36
Cottington, Sir Francis 94
Cottington, George 93
Cowper, Thomas (member of New-
  foundland Company) 61n, 73
Craston, William 50, 51
Crewkerne, John 118
Crews see fishing ships
Crout, Henry (colonist at Cupids Cove)

67, 72; joins Newfoundland Company
  61n; as Percival Willoughby's agent
  65, 66; criticizes apprentices 66;
  explores Trinity Bay 68, 70; keeps
  journal(1612-13) 69; leaves Newfoundland (1613) 70; criticizes company 70-1; breaks with Willoughby
  76
Cruse, Thomas 122
Cupers Cove see Cupids Cove
Cupids Cove 66-9 passim, 72, 73, 76, 77,
  79, 84; size of colony at 61, 65, 69, 70;
  as site for colony 63; 1st winter at
  (1610-11) 64; 2nd winter at (1611-12)
  65; apprentices at 65-6; 3rd winter at
  (1612-13) 69-70; expenses of colony at
  70, 79, 81; see also colonists

Daniel, Christopher 14
Dartmouth 19, 102, 125, Table I; Newfoundland ships at 5, 22, 25, Tables IV,
  XI, XX; importance of Newfoundland
  trade to 22, 101, 118; coastal trade in
  fish 27, 100n; exports Newfoundland
  fish 28-30 passim, 101, 103-4, 110, 111,
  Tables V, XIII, XXII, Figures I, II, IV, VIII;
  and dispute over free trade 99, 101;
  pattern of trade 101, 106-7; alien ship-
  ping at 103, 104, 111, Figures I, II, IV,
  VIII; and civil war 119
de la Barre, John 19
Dee, John 37, 39n, 41
Dennes, Anthony 10
Denia 13
Desliens, Nicholas (cartographer) 36
Dewey, James 19
Dildo Arm 68
Discovrse and Discovery of Newfound-
  land, A see Whitbourne, Captain
  Richard
Discovrse Containing a Loving Invitation,
  A see Whitbourne, Captain Richard
Dodridge, Sir John (member of New-
  foundland Company) 57
Dottin, Luke 13
Doughty, John (member of Newfound-
  land Company) 88

Drake, Sir Bernard 44; attacks Portuguese at Newfoundland 24, 31, 47-8, 51
Drake, Sir Francis 38, 39, 47, 48n
Drake, George 49, 50
Dudley, Robert, Earl of Leicester 38
Dutch see Netherlands
Dyer, Edward 39n

Easton, Peter: attacks Newfoundland fishery 67, 105; and Cupids Cove colony 67, 68
Eburne, Richard 85
Eden, Richard 35
Eliot, Thomas 15-16
Elizabeth I, queen of England 43, 44, 47; and Humphrey Gilbert 38, 39
English fishing industry
– before 1604: growth of 3, 22, 23-4, 25, 33; protected by government 23-5 passim, 33
– 1604-30: growth of 53, 75, 100; and debate on free trade 97-100 passim; threatened by pirates 105-6, 107; protected by government 106, 107
– 1630-60: growth of 110, 118; protected by government 108, 120, 121, 124, 126, 127; threatened by pirates 118; damaged by civil war 118-19; states of (1650s) 124
Exeter Table I; Newfoundland ships at 5, 22, 25, Tables IV, XI, XX; importance of Newfoundland trade to 22, 102; coastal trade in fish 27, 100n; exports Newfoundland fish 28, 102, 106, Tables VII, XIV, XXIII, Figures I, IV, IX; trades with France 25, 98, 101-2, 106; trades with Spain 102, 106; alien merchants at 102, Figures I, V, IX; during civil war 119

Factors 10, 19, 20
Falkland see Cary, Henry
Fécamp 28
Fermeuse 19, 69, 83, 84, 90-2 passim
Fernandez, Simon 37
Ferryland 83, 86, 89; fishing ships at 25,

70; colony at 92-6, see also Calvert, Sir George; colonists; David Kirke at 116, 117, 121-2, 123
Fish
– Newfoundland cod: sold in Europe xi, 9-10, 12, 13, 15, 18-21 passim, 32, 98, 105, 118; European demand for 3, 23, 100; sold in west-country 5, 6, 28, 118; as victualls 5, 26, 27, 101; price of 16, 18, 19, 20, 32, 149, 152; sold at Newfoundland 19, 20, 105, 152; English demand for 26, 100; coastal trade in 26-7, 100-1; exported from west-country 27-31 passim, 101-5 passim, 106-7, 110-14, 118, Tables IV-XXVII, Figures I-X
– stockfish 3, 23, 27, 32; pilchards 98, 101, 103, 109, 111; herrings 101, 103, 109, 111
Fishbourne, Richard (member of Newfoundland Company) 60
Fisheries see Iceland; Ireland; Newfoundland; Shetland; Scotland
Fishing industries see Basque; English; France; Netherlands; Portugal; Spain
Fishing merchants see west-country merchants
Fishing ships
– cost of 3, 7, 149; size of 3, 7, Table I, size of catch 3-4, Table II; ownership of 7; chartering of 8-10; insuring of 11-14; cost of equipping 14, 149, 150-2
– crews: size of 3, 149; payment of 9; payment by shares 14, 15-17 passim; payment by wages 16, 17, Table III; payment by lump-sum 17; right of portage 17-18
Fletcher, John 20
France
– market for fish 3, 28, 30, 102-3, 105, 118, Tables V-X, XII-XIX, XXI, XXII, XXIV-XXVII, Figures I, III-VIII, X; freedom of trade with 98
– trade with: damaged by war 22, 28, 29, 106, 107, 120; from Bristol 28-30 passim; from Southampton 29, 30, 102; from Exeter 29, 98, 101-2, 106; from

Plymouth 101; from Dartmouth 101, 106
– French fishing industry: in St. Lawrence 5, 45, 48-52 passim; payment in 16; size of 40, 117; attacked by English 50-1, 94; at "French shore" 52
– French merchants: in west-country 30, 104, 110, 111, Figures I-x; compete with English 45, 107, 112
French Company 98
Freeman, Ralph (member of Newfoundland Company) 54-5, 60
Freeman, William (member of Newfoundland Company) 54, 55
Frobisher, Martin 38, 43

Garton, Edward (colonist at Cupids Cove) 66, 70
Gellet, Richard 11, 14
Genoa 9; Newfoundland fish sold at 20, 98, 104
Gifford, Philip (member of Newfoundland Company) 58
Gilbert, Sir Humphrey 23, 26, 32, 43, 60; 1st voyage (1578) 35, 41; 2nd voyage 4, 35-6, 41-2, 44, 46, see also Hayes; maps connected with 37; Discourse 38-9, 47; propaganda for 39-40, 42; patent (1578) 39, 41, 43; disposes of land 41
Gilbert, Sir John 43, 44, 46
Glanvyle, John (MP for Plymouth) 100, 101
Golden Fleece, The see Vaughan, Sir William
Goodman, William 11
Gorges, Sir Ferdinando 80, 99, 100
Gourney, Thomas 19
Green Bay 69
Gualle, Francisco (cartographer) 37
Guy, John (1st governor at Cupids Cove) 66, 70, 76, 86, 115; promotes colony 54; on financing Newfoundland Company 57; establishes colony (1610) 61-4 passim; company's instructions to 61-2, 63; authority as governor

62; Guy's laws 64-5, 112; goes on leave (1611) 64-5; returns (1612) 65; and Easton 67; explores Trinity Bay 68-9; leaves colony (1613) 70; criticized 70; breaks with company 71, 87; later career 71, 99-100, 101; advises Salusbury 91
Guy, Philip (brother of John; deputy governor at Cupids, 1611) 62, 65, 88
Guy, Nicholas 69, 78-9, 91

Haddock, Captain William 121
Hakluyt, Richard (the younger): as propagandist 35-8 passim, 49, 50; "Discourse of the Western Planting" 42-3
Hakluyt, Richard (the elder) 39, 40
Hamburg Tables XXII, XXIV
Hamilton, James, marquis of 114
Hannam, William (colonist at Cupids Cove) 76
Harbour Grace (Bristol's Hope) 67, 70, 95; Bristol colony at 77, 79, 81, 87-8
Harembilett, Stephen de 51n
Hariot, Thomas 36
Harwick, Abraham von 50
Harwick, Stephen von 50
Hatton, William (colonist at Cupids Cove) 70
Hawkings, Samuel 13
Hawkins, Sir John 35, 48n
Hayes, Edward 28, 40, 47, 59; proposes Newfoundland company 26, 43-6; on Spanish trade 31-2; describes Humphrey Gilbert's 2nd voyage 35, 41-2, 43; relations with William Cecil 44, 46; treatise on New England 46
Hayman, Robert (governor of Harbour Grace) 77, 91; on Vaughan's colony 85, 86; Qvodlibets Lately Come Over from New Britaniola 85, 88; at Harbour Grace 87-8; dies in Guiana 88
Hearts Content 66, 76
Herbert, William, earl of Pembroke 114
Herle, William 48
Hill, Charles 116
Hill, Peter 31, 49, 50

Hill, Captain William 95

Hiring of ships see Charter parties

Hitchcock, Robert: on fishing ships 3-4, 7; describes bottomry loans 10, 11; on marine insurance 12, 13

Holland, Earl see Rich, Henry

Holworthy, Richard 55n

Homem, Lopo (cartographer) 37

Hondius, Jodocus (cartographer) 37, 38

Howard, Henry, earl of Northampton (member of Newfoundland Company) 57, 68

Iceland: fishery 3, 6, 31, 40; decline of 23

Insurance 7; history of 11-12; and Newfoundland trade 12-13; cost of 12, 13-14

Ireland 3, 4, 23, 27; fish exported to Tables VIII, XVII-XIX, XXII, XXVII

Iron: in Newfoundland 40, 42, 66, 70, 78; on Bell Island 59, 63, 72; to be smelted in Newfoundland 63, 77, 79

Italy 20, 105, 118; west-country trade with 29, 98, 104; Bristol's trade with 30; Southampton's trade with 30, 102; Dartmouth's trade with 101, 107, 111; Newfoundland fish exported to Tables V, VI, VIII, XII, XIII, XVII, XXI, XXII, XXIV, Figures I, III, IV, VII

James, Thomas (mayor of Bristol) 49

Jávea 13

Jeffrey, John 11

Jones, Thomas (member of Newfoundland Company) 60

Jones, Captain, Thomas 121

Jones, William (member of Newfoundland Company) 60

Juxon, Thomas (member of Newfoundland Company) 60

Kirke, Sir David 69, 112, 120, 127; taxes fishery 44, 114-17 passim; and Cecil Calvert 95, 114, 115; early career 113; objectives in Newfoundland 114; compromises with fishermen 115; terms of patent (1637) 115-16; behaviour in Newfoundland 116-17, 121-2, 123; criticized by fishermen 117, 119, 124; government inquiry into 121-3; hostility of settlers to 121-2; death of 123

Kirke, Gervase (father of David) 113

Kirke, James (brother of David) 123

Kirke, Lewis (brother of David) 117

Kirke, Lady Sara (wife of David) 123

Kirkham, Robert (member of Newfoundland Company) 57-8

La Rochelle: Newfoundland ships going to 10, 11; Newfoundland fish exported to 28, 103, 106

Lane Richard 19

Langton, John (member of Newfoundland Company) 55n

Langton, Thomas (member of Newfoundland Company) 55n

Lasso, Bartholomew (cartographer) 37

Laud, William, archbishop of Canterbury 16

Le Havre 29

Leghorn 9; Newfoundland fish sold at 20, 98; west-country trade with 29, 98, 104

Leicester see Dudley, Robert

Leigh, Charles 50-1

Levant Company 24, 98, 104

Ley, Philip 13

Lisbon 9; Newfoundland fish sold at 15, 19

Littlebury, John 121

Lok, Michael 37

London 5-6; fish imports 6, 26, 100

- merchants: join Newfoundland Company 54-5; prefer regulated trade 97-9 passim; export fish 103-4, Appendix B; and carrying trade 104-5, 109-12 passim

London and Bristol Company see Newfoundland Company

Lords, House of 100

Lyde, George 11

Lynne, John 105

Madeira 9, Tables XII, XVIII

Magdalen Islands (Ramea), French at 49, 50-1; walrus fishery at 49; English voyages to 49-51
Mainwaring, Henry 105
Majorca Table v
Malaga: Newfoundland ships going to 9, 32, 105; Newfoundland fish sold at 77
Marseilles 10, 14, 104; Newfoundland ships going to 9, 12, 13, 32, 103; price of fish at 20, 32, 152; fish exported to 28, 103; west-country trade with 29; popularity of 103
Marston, William 21
Martyr, Peter 35, 37
Mason, Anne (wife of John) 77
Mason, Captain John (2nd governor of Cupids Cove) 85, 115; as governor 73-5 *passim*; his maps 73, 83, 84, 85, 87; *Briefe Discovrse* 75-6; leaves Newfoundland 77
Master, ship's; payment of 14, 15, 16; duties of 15-16; restrictions upon 18-19, 20
Mercator, Gerard (cartographer) 36, 37
Mollineux, Emmeric (cartographer) 37-8

Nantes 13
Naples 13, 104
Navigation acts 120, 124
Netherlands 23, 27, 97; west-country trade with 30, 101, 102; fish exported to Tables VII, XII-XIV, XVII
- Dutch fishing industry 102, 105, 110, 117
- Dutch merchants: in Baltic 23, 102; in carrying trade 30-1, 103-4, 109, 110-11, Appendix B
New England 45, 53, 77, 101, 119, 120, 124; control of fishery at 79, 99-100
New England Company 79, 99-100
Newfoundland
- discovery of 3, 34; voyage to 4; voyage from 5; management of voyages to 6-21
- in early literature 34-5; limited knowledge of, before 1580 35-6; cartography

of 36-8; strategic importance of 34, 39, 40, 51, 126, 127; advantages of, for colonization 39-40, 43, 44-6, 53, 56; resources of 40, 42, 56, 59, 63, 76, 78; climate of 40, 43, 64, 69, 92, 94-5; problems of colonizing 46, 70, 74, 79-80, 81, 94-5; exploration of west coast 49-50, 74
- pirates at 67-8, 74, 75, 105, 118; problem of order at 64-5, 74-5, 112-13, 116, 120, 123-4, 127; and navigation acts 120, 124; commissioners appointed for 121, 122-3, 124, 127
- fishery: beginning of ix, 3; season 4, 5; methods 4-5; London interest in 5-7; mentioned in legislation (1540s) 22; value of 44, 75, 86, 100, 110; freedom of 56-7, 74, 79, 99-100, 101, 108; *see also* English fishing industry
Newfoundland Company (London and Bristol Company) ix, 45, 117, 126-7 formation of 53, 55-6; aims of 53-4, 55, 56-7, 60, 67; membership of 53-5, 57-8, 61n, 72; charter of (1610) 56, 60; grants land to subscribers 56, 66, 72-3, *see also* Willoughby, Sir Percival; financing of 57, 60-1, 62; council of 60
- orders journal kept 59-60, 62; instructions to governor 61-2; conflicts with fishermen 62, 64-5, 74-5, 77, 79, 81, 108, 126-7; compared with Virginia Company 62, 63, 81; finances fishing voyages 64, 67, 70, 71; postpones 2nd colony at Renewse 67; and independent proprietors 67, 71, 73, 79, 81, 87, 88-9, 92, *see also* Alexander, Sir William; Bristol; Calvert, Sir George; Cary, Henry; Vaughan, Sir William
- achievements of 70, 79-80; reduced activity after 1613 71, 77, 79, 100; reservation of minerals to 72; plans to smelt iron 77; and charter of Avalon 93
Newhaven 27
Newlanders Cvre, The see Vaughan, Sir William
Noel, Jacques 38, 49
Normandy: Newfoundland fish exported

to 28, 103; west-country trade with
29, 30, 103
Nova Scotia 78, 85, 95, *see also*
Alexander, Sir William
Nyell, William (MP for Dartmouth) 99,
101

Oglander, Sir John 57
Old Perlican 9
Ortelius, Abraham (cartographer) 36
Oughtred, Henry 24, 48, 51

Palmer, Edmond 49, 50
Parker, Clement 13
Parkhurst, Anthony 41, 42, 45; on size of
Newfoundland fleet 22, 40; and Hum-
phrey Gilbert 39; and William Cecil
39; letters on Newfoundland 39-40
Parliament: debates on free trade 98, 99-
100, 101; and David Kirke 119; *see also*
Commons, House of; Lords, House of
Parmenius, Stephen 42-3
Payne, William (member of Newfound-
land Company) 72, 78
Pearson, Bartholomew (colonist at
Cupids Cove) 66
Peckham, Sir George 42
Penguin Island 89
Perrot, Sir John 24
Pescod, Nicholas 15
Petty Harbour 93
Philip II, King of Spain 38, 47, 48
Philpott, Robert 19
Piracy: at Newfoundland 67-8, 75, 105;
and Newfoundland Company 68, 73,
75; endanger Newfoundland trade
105-6, 107, 117-18, 120, 124; *see also*
Barbary; Easton, Peter; Mainwaring,
Henry
Placentia Bay 24, 48n, 68, 74, 83, 89, 91,
93, 95
Plaine Path-way to Plantations, A see
Eburne, Richard
Plancius, Petrus (cartographer) 37, 38
Plymouth 102, 124, Table I
– Newfoundland ships at 5, 25, 100,

Tables IV, XI, XX; importance of Newfoundland trade to 22, 25-6, 101, 118;
coastal trade in fish 27, 100n; exports
Newfoundland fish 30, 101, 103, Tables
VI, XII, XXI; aliens at 30, 101, 104, 110-11,
Figures I, II, III, VII; pattern of trade
101, 111
– merchants: and free trade 99-101 *passim*; and carrying trade 110; and
David Kirke 119
Pont-Gravé, François 38
Poole 26, Table I; Newfoundland ships
at 5, Tables XI, XX; coastal trade in fish
27, 100n; importance of Newfoundland trade to 102, 107; exports Newfoundland fish 107, Tables XVII, XXV;
shipping losses 107
Portugal
– English trade with 23, 98, 118; west-
country trade with 28, 101, 102, 106;
fish exported to 30, 105, Tables V, VII,
XII-XIV, XVII-XIX, XXI, XXII, XXIV, XXV,
Figures III-VIII, X
– Portuguese fishing industry: decline of
24, 48; harassed by English 24, 47-8;
size of (1578) 40
Powell, Captain Daniel 92
Privy Council: dealings with Newfoundland Company: charter 56, 60; commissions against piracy 68, 75; and
disputes with fishermen 74-5, 99, 106;
receives complaint against George
Calvert 94; and free trade 99; provides
convoy 107; and carrying trade 109-
11; and Western Charter 112, 116; and
David Kirke 117
Prowse, Daniel W. (historian) 83, 91
Purchas, Samuel 60n, 65
Putt, William 11
Pyle, Captain William 122

Quebec 113, 117
*Qvodlibets Lately Come Over from
New Britaniola see* Hayman, Robert

Raleigh, Carew 47n

Raleigh, Sir Walter 35, 43, 45, 46, 84, 85; on importance of Newfoundland trade x, 25

Ramea *see* Magdalen Islands

Rastell, John 22, 38

Redwood, Captain Nicholas 122

Renewse 66, 89, 90; settlement at postponed 67; Vaughan's colony at 74, 83, 84, 96

Rich, Henry, Earl Holland 114

Roanoke Island 36, 46, 47

Roche, Marquis de la 45, 51, 56n

Rossell, Robert (colonist at Cupids Cove) 70

Rowley, Thomas (colonist at Cupids Cove) 74, 76-7

Rye 27

Sack ships: used in Newfoundland trade 6, 9, 19, 20; ownership of 7; cost of hiring 9-10

St. John's 63; fishing ships at 9, 19, 23, 70; Humphrey Gilbert at 19, 41-2; Easton at 67; grant of, made by Newfoundland Company 73, 78, 93

St. Lawrence 36, 39; French in 5, 45, 49-52 *passim*; Anglo-French rivalry in 41, 49-51, 94, 113

St. Lucar: Newfoundland ships at 10, 15, 21, 118

St. Mary's Bay 60, 74

St. Sebastian: Newfoundland fish sold at 18; Newfoundland fish exported to 28, 104

Salt: used in drying fish 4, 5; English shortage of 5; cost of 14, Appendix c, Appendix d

Salisbury *see* Cecil, Sir Robert

Salusbury, Sir Henry 86, 91

Sandys, Sir Edwin 96n, 99, 101

Savage Harbour *see* Dildo Arm

Scottish fishing industry 102

Scurvy 64, 69, 70, 86, 95

Seville 21

Sherwill, Thomas (MP for Plymouth) 101

Shetland: fisheries 23

Shipping industry: character of 6-7; and charter parties 8, 18-19, 20; and insurance 11-12, 14

Ships:
  Adventure 10
  Alethia of London 7, 15
  Barbara 5
  Blessing of Southampton 14, 17
  Bonaventure of St. Malo 49
  Charity of Southampton 7
  Clemence of Cherbourg 9
  Comfort of Topsham 13
  Delight 35, 43
  Diamond of London 7
  Elizabeth Constant of Dartmouth 119
  Evangelist of Gosport 15, 16
  Exchange of Southampton 14, 20
  Fisher of Southampton 5n
  Frances and Thomas of London 20
  Friends Adventure 9
  George of Southampton 11
  Golden Hind 41
  Grace of Dartmouth 13
  Handmaid of Torbay 119
  Hector 20
  Hopeful Luke 11
  Hopegood 16, 17
  Hopewell 50
  Hopewell of London 12, 13, 32
  John of London 18
  John and Ambrose 19
  Jonas 15
  Judith 9
  Little Lewis of London 9, 17
  Marigold 49
  Mary and John of London 9
  Mary Barking of Guildford 5
  Matthew and John 10
  Naples Adventure 13
  Olive of Dartmouth 13
  Owners Adventure 9
  Peter of Milbrook 13
  Pleasure of Dartmouth 13
  Providence of Barnstaple 7
  St. Mary St. Vincent of Ciboure 51n

Seth of Poole 13
Solomon of London 32
Speedwell of Barnstaple 10
Sunne of London 31, 32
Sweet Rose of Salcombe 11
Syon of London 19, 20
Thomas of Southampton 15, 17
White Hinde of London 31, 32
William and John of London 19
Sikes, Walter 121, 122
Silver: in Newfoundland 42, 59, 78
Slany, Humphrey (member of New-
foundland Company) 54, 55n, 58, 60,
77
Slany, John (treasurer of Newfoundland
Company) 68, 79, 81, 87; commercial
interests 54; will of 55n; and Percival
Willoughby 58, 67, 72, 73, 77-8; on
company council 60; quarrels with
John Guy 71; optimism of 73, 78;
death of 78
Smith, Sir Samuel (company treasurer
for Cary) 90
Smyrna 9
Southampton 3, 6, 9, 11, 100, Table I;
Newfoundland ships at 5, Tables IV,
XI, XX; importance of fishery to 26;
and triangular trade 26, 31, 32; coastal
trade in fish 27, 100n; exports Newfoundland fish 28, 30, 102, 103, Tables
IX, XVI, XXIV, Figures I, VI, X; general
trade of 29, 30, 102; decline of, 102
Spain, 25, 35, 41, 101
– as market for fish 3, 22-4 *passim*, 97,
120; fish exported to 28-32 *passim*, 110,
111, 118, 121, Tables V, XII-XIV, XVII-XIX,
XXI-XXIII, XXVI, XXVII, Figures III-IX;
west-country trade with 28, 29, 101-7
passim; English relations with 47, 48,
106, 120; price of fish in Appendix C
– Spanish fishing industry: in St. Lawrence 5, 48, 52; decline of 24-5, 33,
48; English plans to destroy 39, 47, 51;
size of (1578) 40; harassed by English
48, 51
Spanish Company 24, 98

Spencer, Humphrey (member of New-
foundland Company) 55n
Stanley, William 13
Stockley, John (member of New-
foundland Company) 60
Stone, Simon (member of Newfound-
land Company) 57-8
Stourton, Erasmus 94
Street, Robert 122
Suckling, Sir John 107
Supracargo *see* Factors

Tanfield, Sir Francis (governor of Cary's
colony) 90, 91, 92
Tanfield, Sir Lawrence (member of
Newfoundland Company) 57, 91n
Therrye, Peter 13
Thevet, André 35
Thoroughgood, Captain Thomas 121
Tilliard, Captain Henry 116
Torbay 69
Toulon 12, 13
Trepassey Bay 83, 84, 94
Treworgie, John 121, 123-4
Triangular trade 103; problems of deal-
ing with x-xi, 32; pioneered by
Londoners 5-6; examples of 9-20
passim, 31, 32; size of, before 1604 31;
reasons for popularity of 32; foreign
competition in 105; size of (1604-30)
105, 106; size of (1630-60) 118, 121
Trinity Bay 5, 19, 69, 72-3; Willough-
by's land on 66, 72, 76, 77; Indians on
68-9, 70; Cary's Land on 89-91 *passim*;
Lewis Kirke in 117
Trinity House: and Newfoundland
Company 56, 60n; and carrying trade
109; opposes David Kirke 114-15
Turner, William (member of Newfoundland Company) 58, 60

Vaughan, Anne (wife of Sir William)
86
Vaughan, Sir William 87, 89, 91, 127
– acquires land in Newfoundland 67, 73,
83; establishes colony 74, 83; motives

83; location of colony 83-5 *passim*; disposes of land 84, 89, 92, 93 interests after 1620 84-5, 86
– author of: *The Golden Fleece* 83, 85-6; *Cambrensium Caroleia, The Newlanders Cvre* 85, 91
Venice 17; west-country trade with 29, 30
Viddomas, Gabriel 122
Villiers, George, duke of Buckingham 88, 91, 93
Virginia 56, 117, 118, 119
Virginia Company 58, 62, 63, 81, 99, 114
Vries, David de 105

Walrus 49, 50
Walsingham, Sir Francis 24, 38; plans raid on Spanish fishery 39, 47, 48
Weld, John of Middlesex (member of Newfoundland Company) 58, 60
Weld, John of Shropshire (member of Newfoundland Company) 58, 60
Welstead, Lionel (agent to Cary) 90
West-country
– merchants: develop fishery x, 3; importance of fishery to x, 21, 25; rivalry with London 6, 21, 45, 97-8, 99, 126; dominate fishery 6, 108, 126-7; antagonism towards Newfoundland Company 62, 74-5, 79, 99-101, 108, 126-7; and convoy system 107, 108, 121, 124; and debate on carrying trade 109-10, 111-12; oppose Kirke 114-17 *passim*, 119; protest Navigation Act (1651) 120
– trade: with Spain 28-9, 30, 106; with France 106; during civil war 118-19; in 1650s 124; *see also* Barnstaple; Bristol; Dartmouth; Exeter; Plymouth; Poole; Southampton; Weymouth; France; Italy; Portugal; Spain
Western Charter 116, 123; terms of 112-13; significance of 112, 127; effectiveness of 113, 114; David Kirke ordered to respect 117
Weymouth 26, Table I; Newfoundland

ships at 5, Tables XI, XX; coastal trade in fish 27, 100n; importance of Newfoundland trade to 102, 105-6; exports Newfoundland fish 107, Tables XVIII, XXVI
Whitbourne, Captain Richard 85, 86, 108; on management of fishing voyages 3, 7, 14, 16, 20, 31, Appendix D; on size of industry 100; as governor of Vaughan's colony 83-4; and Cary 84n, 89, 91; *Discovrse and Discovery of Newfoundland* 84; *Discovrse Containing a Loving Invitation* 89
White, John 36
Wilkins, William 15-16
Willan, Thomas S. (historian) 27
Willoughby, Lady Bridget (wife of Sir Percival) 58
Willoughby, Edward (son of Sir Percival) 73
Willoughby, Sir Francis (father-in-law of Sir Percival) 58, 59
Willoughby, Sir Percival (member of Newfoundland Company) 63, 68, 81; his papers ix-x, 61, 76, 79; joins Newfoundland Company 58, 60; financial problems 58-9, 76; expects iron in Newfoundland 59, 66, 72, 79-80; character 59, 77, 79, 80, 127; investment in Newfoundland 61, 67, 78; sends colonists to Newfoundland 65-6; land in Newfoundland 66-7, 72, 73, 76, 78-9, 87; dissatisfied with company 71-2; death of 79
Willoughby, Thomas (son of Sir Percival) 66, 69; sent to Newfoundland (1612) 65; goes home (1613) 70; returns (1616) 76
Windebank, Sir Edward 17, 112
Winne, Captain Edward 92, 93, *see also* Calvert, Sir George
Wright, Edward (cartographer) 38
Wyet, Sylvester 50

Young, James 4n

Zante 17

This book
was designed by
WILLIAM RUETER
under the direction of
ALLAN FLEMING
and was printed by
University of
Toronto
Press